Tourism Impacts, Planning and Management

Tourism Impacts, Planning and Management is a unique text, which links these three crucial areas of tourism – impacts, planning and management.

Tourism impacts are multi-faceted and therefore are difficult to plan for and manage. This title looks at all the key players involved – be they tourists, host communities or industry members – and considers a number of approaches and techniques for managing tourism impacts successfully.

Now in a third edition, this bestselling text has been fully revised to include:

- New material on: terrorism, sustainability, climate change, sex tourism, heritage tourism, theories of tourism planning and GIS.
- A new chapter on destination planning and management.
- Updated tourism data and statistics.
- Case studies on urban tourism, pro-poor tourism, cruise ship tourism, coral reef tourism, historic monuments, eco-labels, codes of conduct and sustainable tourism from both developed and developing regions, including Australia, Iceland, Spain, the UK, Namibia, the Arctic and Antarctica.
- A companion website including PPTs, video and web links.

The text is written in an accessible style and includes a plethora of features that engage and aid understanding. This accessible yet academically rigorous introduction to tourism impacts, planning and management is essential reading for all tourism students.

Peter Mason has a fractional position as Professor of Tourism Management at Bedfordshire University, is a Visiting Professor of Tourism at London South Bank University and has a fractional position at London Metropolitan University. He has taught for over 40 years, 25 of them in higher education institutions (HEIs). This book is based largely on his own research and teaching at HEIs in the UK, New Zealand, Australia, France and the Middle East.

Tourism Impacts, Planning and Management

Third edition

Peter Mason

Routledge
Taylor & Francis Group

LONDON AND NEW YORK

Third edition published 2016
by Routledge
2 Park Square, Milton Park, Abingdon, Oxon OX14 4RN

and by Routledge
711 Third Avenue, New York, NY 10017

Routledge is an imprint of the Taylor & Francis Group, an informa business

British Library Cataloguing in Publication Data
A catalogue record for this book is available from the British Library

First edition published by Butterworth-Heinemann 2003
Second edition published by Routledge 2008

Library of Congress Cataloging in Publication Data
Mason, Peter, 1951-
Tourism impacts, planning and management / Peter Mason. – 3rd edition.
    pages cm
Includes bibliographical references and index.
1. Tourism–Management. 2. Tourism–Planning. I. Title.
G155.A1M344 2015   2015012738
910.68–dc23

ISBN: 978-1-138-01630-9 (hbk)
ISBN: 978-1-138-01629-3 (pbk)
ISBN: 978-1-315-78106-8 (ebk)

Typeset in Frutiger
by Sunrise Setting Ltd, Paignton, UK

Contents

Contents

Contents

Illustrations

Figures

Photographs

Tables

Case studies

Case studies

Preface to the third edition

I am very pleased that a third edition of this book has been published. It started life in 2003 with Butterworth-Heinemann, who were later taken over by Elsevier, and I am happy that it is now with Routledge! For this Third Edition, I have taken the opportunity to make a number of significant changes, although keeping largely to the original structure used in the First Edition. One important addition is a completely new chapter on destination management – colleagues commented to me, and at least one reviewer argued, that a key focus of the book was on destinations, but there was no separate section/chapter on this topic. So I have responded with what I hope is a suitable chapter! Most of the original case studies have been retained and have been updated where appropriate. The 'Stonehenge' case study has been augmented by a table comparing its tourism management issues with nearby Avebury. The 'Bali bombings' study is now supported by reference to primary research data, the New Zealand 'Pohangina' study has new observations via personal communication, whilst the 'Great Barrier Reef' study and 'Namibian tourism development' study have been updated from secondary sources. More theoretical perspectives on tourism planning are discussed and there is an extended section on the topic of sex tourism. Tourism data and statistics have been updated. The new case studies and related material are on the following themes (with specific geographical locations, where appropriate, in brackets): urban tourism destinations (Birmingham, Barcelona); coastal resorts (Brighton, Scarborough); community-based, pro-poor tourism (Namibia); cruise ship tourism waste disposal; cruise ship codes of conduct (the Arctic); eco-labels (the Blue Flag award in Europe); tourists as ambassadors for the environment (Antarctica); GIS and fragile landscape zoning (Iceland); and issues with achieving sustainable tourism.

Acknowledgements: third edition

In addition to those I thanked for their help with the first and second editions, I would like to indicate my gratitude to the anonymous reviewers of the proposal for this third edition. I would like to thank, in particular the following academics: Professor Andrew Holden, Professor Robert Maitland, Dr I-Ling Kuo, Dr Duncan Tyler and Professor Richard Sharpley, for their continued advice and support.

I would also like to thank Master's students at Bedfordshire University, UK, London Metropolitan University, UK, South Bank University, UK, the Ecole de Management de Normandie, Deauville, France and the Ecole Supérieure d'Hôtellerie, Paris, with whom, over the past seven years, I have trialled new material for this edition.

The team at Taylor and Francis deserve a special mention, particularly my commissioning editor, Emma Travis, and Pippa Mullins, who patiently and professionally advised and supported me in the practicalities of the book production. Also, in terms of production I would like to thank Jessica Stock and Marion Moffatt at Sunrise Setting Ltd, Paignton.

I would like to give special thanks to my wife, Patsy, and my children Jess and Will for their continued support.

Peter Mason, Norfolk, March, 2015

Abbreviations

AFTA	Australian Federation of Travel Agents
DEH	Department of Environment and Heritage
DMO	destination management organization
DMS	destination management systems
DOC	Department of Conservation
EH	English Heritage
EIA	Environmental Impact Assessment
FENATA	Federation of Namibian Tourism Associations
GIS	geographical information system
ISO	International Standards Organization
IT	information technology
LAC	limits of acceptable change technique
MRWBT	Manawatu Riverside Walkway and Bridle Track
NGO	non-governmental organization
NSW	New South Wales
NT	National Trust
ODI	Overseas Development Institute
PNCC	Palmerston North City Council
PPT	pro-poor tourism
RMA	Resource Management Act
SWOT	Strengths, Weaknesses, Opportunities and Threats
THL	Tourism Holdings Ltd
UAE	United Arab Emirates
VFR	visiting friends and relatives
WCED	World Conference on Environment and Development
WHS	World Heritage Site
WTO	World Tourism Organization
WTTC	World Travel and Tourism Council
WWF	World Wide Fund for Nature

Introduction

Part I

The first six chapters of the book discuss the growth, development and impacts of tourism. It is assumed that all readers will have some understanding of the concepts of tourism. However, a brief discussion on the emergence and development of tourism is provided in Chapter 1. The reasons behind the development are also provided in this first chapter. The chapter attempts to establish the global significance of tourism, but it also points out some data limitations. Chapter 2 provides a discussion of key theories that are important within the context of tourism planning and management. Chapter 3 indicates that much tourism planning and management takes place in relation to tourism impacts. This chapter also considers factors that influence tourism impacts. The three chapters following Chapter 3 consider, in turn, economic impacts, socio-cultural impacts and environmental impacts. Case studies are provided in each chapter to exemplify these different impacts. These studies are also employed to provide stimulus material for students and at the end of each chapter a number of student activities are suggested.

Part II

Chapters 7–14 discuss concepts of, issues concerning and the players involved in tourism planning and management. Chapter 7 focuses on key concepts in tourism planning and management. It investigates the general relationship between planning and management before a discussion of tourism planning and management. This chapter also focuses on policy issues and introduces ideas in sustainability in tourism. Chapter 8 considers the major players in tourism planning and management and discusses visitors, host communities, the tourism industry and government. This chapter also discusses the role of the media and non-governmental organizations in tourism planning and management. Chapters 9–13 provide more detailed discussion of visitors, host communities and the tourism industry, as well as focusing on the environment as a key resource in tourism and the role of partnerships and collaboration in tourism planning and management. Chapter 14 focuses on destination management. As with the first part of the book, this second part uses a number of case studies. Here they are used to illustrate major concepts, themes and issues and once again a number of student activities are linked to the case studies in each chapter.

Part III

This section is concerned with particular techniques used in tourism planning and management. It focuses on education and the role of interpretation (Chapter 15), self-regulation in tourism planning and management, and, in particular, codes of conduct (Chapter 16) and the use of information technology as a tool in tourism planning and management (Chapter 17). As with previous sections, case studies are an important feature of these chapters and as before they are included to provide stimulus material for students.

Part IV

The final part of the book is concerned with sustainability issues and tourism planning and management. A number of theoretical perspectives are discussed and case studies, with accompanying student activities, are presented to investigate some of these perspectives. A short concluding chapter is also provided and in addition this has ideas on the future of tourism. This final part of the book also uses case studies with related questions for students.

PART I

Tourism growth, development and impacts

Chapter 1

Social change and the growth of tourism

Learning objectives

At the end of this chapter you should:

- be aware of a variety of definitions of tourism;
- be aware of a number of dimensions and components of tourism, viz. the components of the tourism industry, motivations for tourism, tourism systems, data limitations in tourism;
- understand major social and economic changes that have contributed to the growth of tourism.

Introduction

Tourism is now a global industry involving hundreds of millions of people in international as well as domestic travel each year. The World Tourism Organization (WTO, 2014) indicated that there were for the first time more than one billion international travellers in 2012. By 2013 this figure had reached 1.087 billion international travellers, which amounts to almost 14 per cent of the world's population (WTO, 2014). Although some of this activity may comprise the same travellers involved in more than one journey per year and hence the precise scale of tourism as an industry is in some doubt (Leiper, 1999), tens of millions of people globally work directly in the industry and many more are employed indirectly. Hundreds of millions of people are on the receiving end of tourism activity as they live in what are termed destination areas, in supposed 'host' populations. Millions of dollars are spent each year on advertising and promoting holidays and tourism products.

For much of recorded history, travel was difficult, uncomfortable, expensive and frequently dangerous (Williams, 1998). Yet journeys were undertaken and this implies some strong motivating factors. However, it is only in the last 150 years, as travel has become more affordable and less difficult, that some of those who travelled were prepared to openly admit that pleasure was one of the motivations for their journeys.

As recently as the 1960s, tourism was an activity in which relatively few participated regularly, and was primarily confined to Europe, North America and a small number of locations in other parts of the world. International travel, prior to the 1960s, was still largely the preserve of a wealthy minority who had the time as well as money to afford long distance sea or air travel. Major changes in the second half of the twentieth century led to the rapid and massive growth of the phenomenon known as modern tourism. For example, these changes contributed to the Pacific Region/East Asia becoming the fastest growing area for international tourism in the period from 1985 to 2005. In 1975, East Asia and the Pacific Region accounted for only 4 per cent of international tourist arrivals, but by 1995 the share of world arrivals had increased to almost 15 per cent (Pearce, 1995) and by 2006 to 20 per cent (WTO, 2007) and this figure was almost 23 per cent in 2013 (WTO, 2014). It should be noted that this change has occurred at a time when tourist numbers were growing globally. The increase in the share of international tourist arrivals in the Pacific Region therefore indicates a very significant increase in actual tourists between 1975 and 2013. There were approximately 78 million visitor arrivals in the Pacific Region/East Asia in 1995 (Pearce, 1995). This compares with approximately 100 million in the combined area of North and South America and 305 million in Europe in 1995 (Pearce, 1995).

With approximately 52 per cent of international arrivals in 2013 Europe remained, in the early part of twenty-first century, the single most important region for international travel arrivals (WTO, 2014) although this percentage has fallen from 55 per cent in 2006 (WTO, 2007). In fact in 2013, Europe had five countries in the top ten tourism destinations – France, Spain, Italy, the United Kingdom and Germany, with France (first in the top ten) and Spain (third in the top ten) having combined totals accounting for 13 per cent of total international arrivals (WTO, 2014).

This introductory chapter considers what has made this growth possible. It involves discussion of a number of economic and social factors. This chapter also explores changing attitudes to travel, as well as presenting a discussion of how opportunities for travel have increased.

Key perspectives

Definitions of tourism and tourists

This book is an introductory text to tourism planning and management at undergraduate level. However, some understanding of the nature of tourism is assumed. Nevertheless, as there is no full agreement on the meaning of the term tourism, nor is there complete agreement on what a tourist is, this section contains a brief discussion of these concepts as they are clearly important in relation to the planning and management of tourism.

In the early 1980s, Matthieson and Wall (1982: 1) indicated that tourism comprised:

> The temporary movement of people to destinations outside their normal places of work and residence, the activities undertaken during the stay in those destinations, and the facilities created to cater for their needs.

In 1991, the WTO created a definition, primarily to assist those whose responsibility it was to compile statistics in tourism. This definition reads as follows (WTO, 1991):

> The activities of a person travelling outside his or her usual environment for less than a specified period of time whose main purpose of travel is other than for exercise of an activity remunerated from the place visited.

Neither of these two definitions makes reference to the impacts of tourism. Impacts are key factors in any discussion of the planning and management of tourism. However, Jafari (1981) did include reference to impacts in his definition. Jafari (1981: 3) stated:

> Tourism is a study of man [sic] away from his usual habitat, of the industry which responds to his needs and the impacts that both he and the industry have for the host socio-cultural, economic and physical environments.

Most definitions of the term tourist are based on the concept of tourism. Usually, such definitions make reference to the need for the tourist to spend at least one night in a destination to which he or she has travelled. Tourists can be distinguished from excursionists in such definitions, as an excursionist is someone who visits and leaves without staying a night in a destination (Prosser, 1998). However, as Prosser suggested, it is relatively common for the two terms to be combined. The term visitor is often used in preference to either tourist or excursionist. Theobold (1994), for example, used the concept of 'visitor' to combine elements of tourists and excursionists.

When discussing the impacts of tourism, a classification involving terms such as excursionist or tourist is not particularly helpful. For example, in relation to the environmental impacts of the feet of a walker on a natural or semi-natural landscape, it matters little whether the person involved is classified as a tourist or an excursionist; the feet will have the same effect! As the actions of day visitors (excursionists) and those of longer stayers may be almost indistinguishable, the view that a definition of tourism does not need reference to an overnight stay has been become far more acceptable (Williams, 1998).

The distance travelled is often seen as important in definitions of both tourism and tourists. However, there is no commonly accepted international distance used in connection with definitions of tourism. As with the need of at least some definitions to include reference to an overnight stay, there is a good deal of debate and unresolved confusion about distance travelled and tourism definitions. For example, in the latter part of the twentieth century, the United States Travel Data Center reported on all trips with a one-way distance of 100 miles, the Canadian Travel Survey used a lower one-way limit of 50 miles, and the Australian Bureau of Industry Economics employed a one-way distance of 25 miles (Prosser, 1998).

One of the continuing problems caused by a lack of a clear definition of tourism is that tourism studies are often poles apart in philosophical approach, methodological orientation or intent of the investigation (Fennell, 1999). Nevertheless, if there is no complete agreement on the definition of tourism, it is still important to understand the key aspects of the processes of tourism and the reality of being a tourist. Prosser (1998: 374) indicated that the central components of any definition of either tourists or tourism are as follows:

> movement, non-permanent stay, activities and experiences during the travel and stay, resources and facilities required and impacts resulting from the travel and stay.

Tourism is multi-dimensional and can be compartmentalized in a number of ways. According to Prosser (1998), there are two major variables. These are the origin–destination relationship and the motivation for travel. It is possible to create the following categories using Prosser's origin–destination relationship:

● international tourism
● internal tourism
● domestic tourism
● national tourism.

Prosser indicated that international tourism involves overseas visitors to a destination, while domestic tourism relates to nationals of one country visiting that same country. Internal tourism can relate to a region within a country, while national tourism considers all forms of tourism within one particular nation or country.

Motivations for travel

In any tourism trip, there are likely to be a number of reasons which, when combined, can be considered as the motivational factors for the journey. These can be characterized as 'push' and 'pull' factors. The 'push' factors are a number of perceived negative factors about the context in which the potential tourist currently finds himself or herself. The 'pull' factors are perceived positive factors of a potential or real destination. The nature, extent and significance of particular 'push' and 'pull' factors will vary according to the particular tourism context.

The classification of motivations into 'push' and 'pull' is linked closely with the psychological model of tourism motivation developed by Iso-Aloha (1980). The two dimensions in the model can be summarized as 'seeking' motives and 'escaping' motives (Pearce, 1993). In Iso-Aloha's model, individuals seek personal and interpersonal rewards and at the same time wish to escape personal and interpersonal environments. The main criticism of Iso-Aloha's model is that, with only two dimensions, it is limited by its level of aggregation (Raybould *et al.*, 1999). Hence, the use of the concepts 'push' and 'pull' may oversimplify a complex process. Nevertheless, investigating motivations in an attempt to understand the behaviour of tourists has become an important area of tourism research (Ryan, 1997). This can help with the categorization of tourists as well as provide a better understanding of their impacts. Tourist behaviour can be influenced by a number of factors including cultural conditioning, social influences, perception and education, but as Crompton and McKay (1997) indicated, motives are the starting point of the decision-making process that leads to particular types of behaviour. It is particularly in the related fields of psychology and sociology that researchers (including Iso-Aloha, 1980) have developed significant theories on motivation. In the field of cognitive psychology, motives are seen as largely a function of the expected consequences of future human behaviour (Dunn-Ross and Iso-Aloha, 1991). In this sense, motives can be considered as internal factors that have initially aroused a person and then direct his or her behaviour (Iso-Aloha, 1980). The main components of a general psychological model of motivation are needs and motives, behaviour or activity, goals or satisfactions and feedback (Harrill and Potts, 2002). Mannell and Kleiber (1997: 190) provide an example to indicate the links between the main concepts in this psychological model:

> People who have a strong need or desire to be with others (motive) may attempt to engage in leisure activities, such as going to bars and drinking that allow them to increase their interactions with other people (behaviour) in hopes of developing more friendships (goal and satisfaction).

This is an iterative model, in that the feedback component leads back into the initial needs and motivations (Harrill and Potts, 2002). In other words, during an activity, an individual interacts with the environment in which the activity takes place and possibly with others involved in the activity and this results in more, or perhaps, different motivation.

Several sociological theories have been put forward in the tourist literature in an attempt to explain motivation. One of the earliest was that of Cohen (1972) who sub-divided tourists into four types, based on motivation. Cohen asserted that the main variables forming the basis of his theory and hence leading to the four-fold classification were 'strangeness' versus 'familiarity'. Hence, at one end of his continuum was the 'organized mass tourist' seeking some degree of familiarity in holiday surroundings, while at the other end, the 'drifter' is willing to accept far more 'strangeness'.

Cohen developed his theory to investigate how various types of tourist might interact with host communities. This approach also influenced Plog (1973) who developed a continuum, using two concepts: allo-centric and psycho-centric. Plog suggested that psycho-centric individuals are concerned primarily with the self, are inhibited and relatively non-adventurous. In terms of tourist behaviour, psycho-centrics want the familiar and are unlikely to travel great distances to explore new tourism destinations. Conversely, Plog asserted allo-centrics are confident, naturally inquisitive and seek out the unfamiliar when travelling. Both Cohen's (1972) and Plog's (1973) theories have been tested, but with varied success and they have not met with universal acceptance. Nevertheless, they remain as key theories in tourism motivation, although both are largely descriptive rather than explanatory (Harrill and Potts, 2002). Cohen's (1972) and Plog's (1973) theories are discussed in more detail in Chapter 2, which investigates important theories in tourism planning and management.

A number of sociological and psychological theories tend to imply that motivation is a fairly static concept. However, Pearce (1988), using the concept of a 'travel ladder' when investigating motivation for tourism, suggested that motivations are multivariate and dynamic, changing particularly as a result of ageing and life-cycle stage, as well as being influenced by other people. Pearce acknowledged that he was influenced by the work of the psychologist Maslow (1954), who created a hierarchical range of needs from low level, primarily physical needs, to high level intellectual needs. Maslow termed these needs, in ascending sequence, as 'physiological', 'safety', 'social', 'self-esteem' and 'self-development'. Pearce, using Maslow's (1954) ideas, proposed the following tourism motivation categories: 'relaxation', 'excitement and thrills', 'social interaction', 'self-esteem and development' and 'fulfilment'.

In attempting to summarize the major motivations of tourists, Ryan (1991) drew on the work of Cohen (1972), Crompton (1979) and Matthieson and Wall (1982) and presented 11 major reasons for tourist travel. These are as follows:

1 Escape
2 Relaxation
3 Play
4 Strengthening family bonds
5 Prestige
6 Social interaction
7 Sexual opportunity
8 Educational opportunity
9 Self-fulfilment
10 Wish fulfilment
11 Shopping.

This list of 11 motivations for tourist journeys can also be seen to be linked to the concept of 'push' and 'pull' factors with, for example, 'escape' clearly a 'push' factor and 'prestige' clearly a 'pull' factor. Ryan (1991) indicated that often, holiday choices are based on a combination of motivations that are seen as a set of priorities by the potential tourist at the time. These priorities may change over time and realizing some travel needs may be deliberately delayed (Ryan, 1991, 1997).

Chadwick (1987) provided a more simplified categorization of the reasons for tourist-related journeys when he summarized the motivations for, and purpose of travel, under three main headings. These are as follows:

● Pleasure: leisure, culture, active sports, visiting friends and relatives (usually abbreviated to VFR).
● Professional: meetings, missions, business, etc.
● Other purposes: study, health, transit.

At the end of the twentieth century, the Annual International Passenger Survey carried out by the British Tourist Authority distinguished five types of tourism-related visit (cited in Prosser, 1998):

● Holiday independent
● Holiday inclusive
● Business
● VFR
● Miscellaneous.

As Prosser (1998) indicated, the VFR segment is important in the United Kingdom and Europe and particularly significant within Australia, New Zealand and Canada with as many as 20 per cent of visitors to Australia being in the VFR category. Partly in relation to this high figure, Prosser (1998) suggested a three-fold categorization of visitor motivation, as follows: (i) pleasure, (ii) business and (iii) VFR.

Despite being originally produced over twenty years ago, and the emergence of new forms of tourism in this period, for example ecotourism, volunteer tourism and pro-poor tourism, the theoretical perspectives on motivations discussed in this section can still be seen to apply. Using volunteer tourism as the particular example of a new form of tourism – one which may at first glance appear to have very different motivational factors than more traditional forms

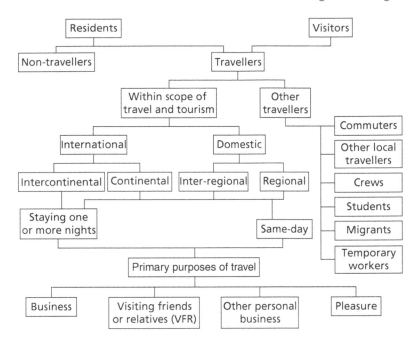

Figure 1.1 A classification of travellers and tourists
Source: Adapted from Brent, Ritchie and Goeldner (1994).

of tourism – it is still possible for this type of tourism to fit with Chadwick's (1987) classification under the heading 'Other purposes' and Prosser's (1998) tourist trip grouping 'Miscellaneous', and using Ryan's (1991) categories, self–fulfilment and education would seem to be at least two of the major motivational factors.

With reference to attempts to classify tourist motivation, it should not be forgotten that many trips have multiple purposes and are likely to involve different forms of transport and accommodation types. Hence, this tends to limit the usefulness of any classification. Despite these limitations, Figure 1.1 is an attempt to classify tourists.

The tourism industry

An important issue in this book is the relationship between different sectors of the tourism industry. The book also investigates the relationships between tourists, tourism stakeholders and governments and industry representatives. A summary of different sectors of the tourism industry, referring to a travel sector, accommodation sector, leisure and entertainment sector and a sector concerned with tourism organizations, is shown in Figure 1.2. A slightly different summary of the tourism industry is shown in Figure 1.3. In this summary, based on Middleton (1994), there are five sectors and although these are similar to Lavery's sectors (Lavery, 1987), there is more emphasis on tourism organizations and the attractions for tourists.

Tourism systems

The location of tourism activity is a major component of tourism (Mason, 1990). Leiper (1990) attempted to link the tourism destination with the tourism generating region and his model is shown in Figure 1.4. Leiper's model is an attempt to view tourism as a form of system, in

(i) Travel
Including travel agents, tour operators, airlines, cruise companies, coach companies, railways, taxis, tourist guides, couriers, reservations and sales staff.

(ii) Accommodation, catering and related services to tourists
Hotels with all their staff from receptionist to chambermaids, chefs and cooks, waiters, waitresses, bar staff, porters, caravan/camping site staff, self-catering enterprises, restaurants and cafés.

(iii) Leisure facilities and entertainment
These will include theatres, museums, art galleries, theme parks, zoos, willdlife parks, sports centres, gardens, historic houses, country parks and cinemas.

(iv) Tourism organizations
Whose aim is to market and monitor the quality and development of the tourist region. These will range from national and regional tourist organizations to staff at local tourist information centres.

Figure 1.2 A summary of sectors of the tourism industry
Source: Adapted from Lavery (1987).

Accommodation sector
- Hotels/motels
- Guest houses/bed and breakfast
- Farmhouses
- Apartments/villas/flats/cottages/gîtes
- Condominiums/time share resorts
- Vacation villages/holiday centres
- Conference/exhibition centres
- Static and touring caravan/camping sites
- Marinas

Attraction sector
- Theme parks
- Museums and galleries
- National parks
- Wildlife parks
- Gardens
- Heritage sites and centres
- Sports/activity centres

Transport sector
- Airlines
- Shipping lines/ferries
- Railways
- Bus/coach operators
- Car rental operators

Travel organizers' sector
- Tour operators
- Tour wholesalers/brokers
- Retail travel agents
- Conference organizers
- Booking agencies (i.e. accommodation)
- Incentive travel organizers

Destination organization sector
- National tourist offices (NTOs)
- Regional/state tourist offices
- Local tourist offices
- Tourist associations

Figure 1.3 The main sectors of the tourism industry
Source: Adapted from Middleton (1994).

which there is an operational structure built up of interacting components. In the model there are three interactive components: (i) the tourism generating region, (ii) the destination region and (iii) transit routes which link the two regions. However, Leiper's model has been criticized for being simplistic (Prosser, 1998). Prosser provided a more detailed model that, he claimed, represents more effectively the inner complexities of the tourism environment. Prosser's model is shown in Figure 1.5.

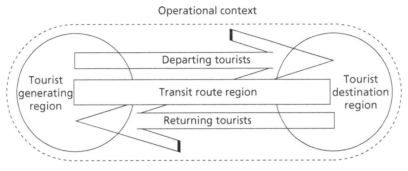

Figure 1.4 The tourism system: a spatial construct
Source: Adapted from Leiper (1990).

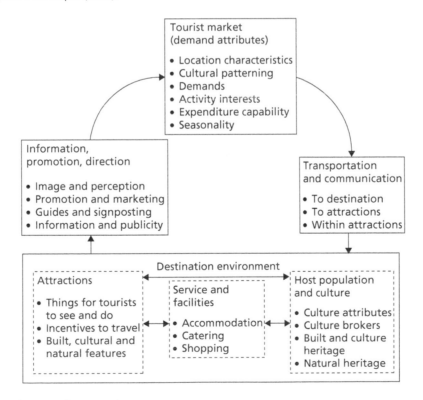

Figure 1.5 The tourism environment
Source: Adapted from Prosser (1998).

Much of the discussion in this book focuses on the location that tourists visit, that is, the tourism destination. It is in the destination (at the receiving end of tourism) that most impacts tend to be noted and may be felt particularly strongly by resident populations. Hence, there is a major need for planning and managing at the tourism destination.

The growth of tourism

Modern tourism developed largely as a result of urbanization in Western Europe. Prior to this, societal divisions, responsibilities and allegiances led to the great majority of people in Western Europe being born in small communities and living and dying in these same tightly focused, relatively small communities. These people worked the land and were tied to this by seasonal demands for labour input and social relationships that required service to a land-owner and quite possibly the established church. Such people had little leisure time and what they had was often linked to family responsibilities. Recreation was largely a spiritual activity that took place through the church, although festivals and religious holidays provided a few opportunities for leisure pursuits. However, the great majority of people lacked the ability or desire to travel away from their birthplace (Mason, 1990). Frequent travel was confined to the small elite, the ruling class made up of large landowners, church leaders and monarchs and their entourage. For the majority of the masses, the only possibility of long-distance travel was likely to be linked to a pilgrimage, a religious crusade or time spent as a mercenary.

When urban settlements expanded from about 1750 in Europe, the old bond to land and landowners was broken. Large numbers of people left their place of birth and moved to these rapidly growing settlements. Here, by 1800, employment opportunities were in factories, where for the first time workers received wages and, despite long hours of work, had both time and money to engage in leisure activities. Gradually, with the change in living environment and working relationships came new attitudes to life. Recreation was increasingly viewed as an important part of life and this could involve physical as well as mental activity.

Although an increasing number of people resident in Europe were able to travel, from the Middle Ages onwards up to the eighteenth century, it was still the preserve of a small, wealthy elite. It was not until the era of the Industrial Revolution, and particularly after 1800, that travel became far more accessible to a significantly high percentage of the population. Greater access to travel was accompanied by certain other developments in society, and this contributed to the growth in demand for and provision of tourism experiences.

A variety of important factors contributed to the development of tourism during the nineteenth and early part of the twentieth century. Mason (1990) suggested five major reasons for the growth of tourism. These are as follows:

1   A rise in industrial output associated with the Industrial Revolution that in turn led to an increase in the standard of living.
2   Improvements in transport technology, which led to cheaper and more accessible travel. Railways and ocean liners appeared in the nineteenth century and cars and aircraft in the first half of the twentieth century.
3   The introduction of annual holidays towards the end of the nineteenth century.
4   Changing perceptions of the environment. Locations that were once viewed as hostile, were now seen as attractive.

5   An increasing desire to travel. This was related partly to improvements in education and also to greater overseas travel, which was mainly the result of war. This created interest in foreign locations and also overseas business travel.

A number of the social and economic changes that had been occurring before the second half of the century continued and accelerated after the Second World War. Salaries and wages steadily increased and this meant more disposable income to spend on leisure pursuits. The amount of leisure time also went up as the working week decreased in terms of number of hours required at work, and the length of the annual holiday increased. This greater access to recreation activities was accompanied by a rapid rise in car ownership, particularly in North America in the 1950s and Western Europe during the late 1950s and early 1960s. Roads and motorway systems in Europe and North America were greatly improved during this period. For the first time, large numbers of potential tourists could plan their own trips without having to rely on either publicly or privately owned transport organizations. Aircraft also became more comfortable and sophisticated and an increasing number and range of passengers were flying. In this period, flying to a distant overseas destination became a real alternative in financial terms to a journey by ship. During this time, public transport, in particular trains and coaches, improved in terms of comfort and comparative costs, hence allowing a wider range of users.

In the last quarter of the twentieth century and early part of the twenty-first century, the relationship between demand and supply in tourism was based largely on the dynamics of people's perception, expectations, attitudes and values (Prosser, 1994). As Prosser argued, tourism had become very much a fashion industry, in which there were very close links between tourism demand and the concepts of status and image. This ensures that as societies that generate tourists frequently change their motivations, expectations and demands, tourism is a notoriously fickle industry. Therefore reasons for travel can change rapidly, although they may appear at any one time to be unchanging. For example, throughout much of the period from the late 1950s to the late 1980s getting a suntan was central to a large number of people's expectation of a holiday. This 'getting bronzed' mentality appeared endemic and eternal at the time. However, this desire only dated back to the lifestyle of leisured classes on the Côte d'Azur, France, in the 1920s (Prosser, 1994). Prior to this, most Europeans kept out of the sun. This was especially so for women for whom a pale complexion was seen as more attractive. In the early twenty-first century, pale skin became once again fashionable, but this time the reason was more health related, with growing concerns about skin cancer caused by too much exposure to the sun.

Not only have people's motivations and expectations of holidays changed, but geography plays a major part as well. Where tourism experiences can be obtained is itself subject to variations in demand and, hence, supply. For instance, in the 1970s it was not sufficient just to get a suntan, but where one got it was vital (Prosser, 1994). In the early 1960s, in Britain getting a suntan in Brighton or Blackpool was sufficient; by the early 1970s to achieve the desired status the tan had to be brought back to Britain from Benidorm, and by the 1980s it had to have been obtained in Belize! In Australia, Bondi Beach would have been good enough for most sun-seekers in the 1970s, but, by the 1980s, to really enhance one's status it was necessary to get the tan in Bali! However, reference to Bali emphasizes the unpredictability of tourism. Until October 2002, Bali was a major destination for sun-seeking tourists from many locations in the developed world. The terrorist attack at two night clubs in Kuta, a resort in Bali, on 19 October 2002, in which almost 200 young people from Australia, New Zealand, the United States, Canada, Britain and other European countries died, resulted in a collapse of tourism numbers. Although the numbers had recovered to some extent by late 2003, another major setback to tourism occurred in 2005 when there was a second bombing incident in the same area of Bali and there has been relatively slow improvement since.

In the last 15 years or so of the twentieth century, changing attitudes also contributed to a re-evaluation of the nature of the tourist experience. Accompanying the growing realization that tourism takes place in finite geographical space, was the notion that it consumes environmental resources (McKercher, 1993). Increasingly, tourists became concerned about the effects their activities were having on the environment (Fennell, 1999). This led to the growth of what some consider as more environment friendly forms of tourism, such as ecotourism (Wearing and Neil, 1999). Additionally, some tourists sought experiences that would give them more contact with the population in the destination region and potentially contribute more to the local economy. In this way, these tourists demonstrated that they were concerned about the ethics of the tourist–host relationship and were seeking a more just and equitable form of tourism than was achievable in more conventional types of the activity (see Mason and Mowforth, 1996; Malloy and Fennell, 1998; Fennell and Malloy, 2007).

Data limitations

One of the key problems in assessing the scale, importance and hence impacts of tourism is the inconsistency and incomparability of figures collected. Leiper (1999) indicated that the WTO is frequently cited as a source of data on international tourism. Leiper quoted figures from 1996 that suggested there were almost 600 million international tourists, representing more than 10 per cent of the Earth's population at that time. Leiper stated that this figure was not truly tourists but 'arrivals'. He argued that WTO statistical data ignore patterns of trip frequency and multi-destination itineraries and that a large proportion of these arrivals are by the same travellers, not separate individuals. Therefore, Leiper suggested, nearer to 200 million individuals travelled internationally in 1996, which is only one-third of the WTO figure. Although WTO figures show a continuing increase in international tourist numbers during the early twenty-first century, there is no reason to believe that the great majority of international tourism data is able to distinguish tourists who make only one international journey per year, from others who make many repeat trips.

Data problems can be found at all scales: international, national and internal (Prosser, 1998). As Theobold (1994) indicated, this can even be a problem within one country. For example, in the context of the United States, a tourist in Florida is 'an out-of-state resident who stays at least one night in the state for reasons other than the necessary layover for transportation connections or for strictly business transactions'. However, in Alaska a tourist is defined as 'a non-resident travelling to Alaska for pleasure or culture and for no other purpose' (Theobold, 1994).

Middleton (1994: 7) has indicated that despite efforts to create a degree of comparability of tourism statistics, achieving precision is very complex and 'despite various guidelines, no uniformity yet exists in the measurement methods used around the world'. This point was made over twenty years ago, but despite some changes in how data are collected and processed, it is still the case that achieving complete accuracy in relation to tourism numbers continues to be very difficult.

The case study below provides information on the growth of tourism in one particular country – Australia. The case study also considers the factors that have contributed to this growth.

Case study: tourism growth in Australia

Early European travellers to Australia were usually reluctant visitors. The commander of the First Fleet dispatched from Plymouth, England in 1787, to establish the colony of New South Wales described the 736 convicts on board as 'unwilling tourists'. For much of the nineteenth century European visitors to Australia were either convicts or business people. At this time, Australia suffered from the 'tyranny of distance' in terms of its links with Europe – it took several months to get to Australia by ship. The commentaries on Australian life which were published in Britain from the early nineteenth century, in order to attract settlers, were extremely important to the commencement of tourism. Australia was often pictured to the rural audience as an Arcadia where the fruits of the soil could be easily won. Such romanti-cized imagery was important in attracting both tourists and immigrants to Australia.

The Australian experience of Victorian attitudes towards leisure and recreation runs directly parallel to British developments. The North Shore Steamboat Ferry Service that linked Sydney City with the then rural North Shore, and the ferries to take customers to Botany Bay Zoo may be regarded as the antipodean equivalent to the ferrying of city-weary Londoners to the coastal resorts of Margate and Southend. On land, however, perhaps the most significant event for making travel accessible to all social classes was the coming of the railway, and with it came the development of mass tourism. The onset of rail led to a revolution in tourism and recreation activities. Prior to this, recreational travel was restricted to immediate areas surrounding population centres. The railways helped open up the hinterland for domestic travellers.

Mass tourism is usually acknowledged to have begun in 1841 when Thomas Cook, the world's first noted tour operator, conducted an excursion train from Leicester, England. Later Cook used a combination of rail and ship to organize and run tours to Europe, the Middle East and North Africa. By 1872, Cook offered a world cruise on steamboats that included glimpses of both Australia and New Zealand. The inclusion of Sydney and Melbourne in the itinerary marked the beginning of packaged international travel to Australia. Cook's significant role in relation to international tourism can also be noted in relation to his company's publishing of advice and a guidebook for travellers to Australia and New Zealand in 1889.

Accompanying the economic development of Australia was a number of social devel-opments. Unlike British working practices, in Australia most urban trade unions adopted the principle of 8-hour labour, 8-hour recreation and 8-hour rest. This ensured leisure was viewed in a positive way. The railways assisted in the pursuit of leisure as they made new destinations accessible and helped make travel a permanent part of Australian cul-ture. The first railway lines were important in the establishment of Australia's national parks. These were initially set up as areas for recreational activity of city dwellers, rather than being for the protection of flora and fauna.

By the end of the nineteenth century, tourism and leisure were not just the regime of the wealthy. The railways, in particular, had made travel possible for the majority of the population. The railways helped open up the interior for domestic tourism, while the steamship brought Australia closer in terms of travelling time to Europe. Urban attractions such as museums, art galleries and parks, still important today, were already significant visitor attractions at the end of the nineteenth century.

(continued)

Case study: tourism growth in Australia (continued)

The first true coastal resorts were also established by the end of the nineteenth century, in such places as Sandgate and Cleveland in Queensland, Glenelg in South Australia and Brighton and Sorrento in Victoria. However, at none of these places did swimming become legal until the early part of the twentieth century, as the original role of the coastal resorts was as places to take the sea air and seawater as a cure for a variety of ailments. The railways helped boost inland tourism destinations in Australia that developed as health spas. After the building of the Sydney to Blue Mountains railway, the Blue Mountains became an area visited for the supposed health-giving properties of the mountain air, as well as the spectacular scenery.

Photo 1.1 Uluru (Ayers Rock): a symbol of modern Australia?

In the 1920s and 1930s, the expansion of mass transport enabled once remote beaches and attractions to come within easier reach. During this period a bush walking movement also developed in Australia. Several clubs were established, such as the Sydney Bushwalkers, set up by prominent walkers and conservationists Paddy Wallin and Myles Dunphy.

Regular airline services between Australia and overseas only began in the 1930s. The first airmail service from Britain to Australia was set up in 1934 and this provided the stimulus for the establishment of Qantas Empire Airways, the forerunner of the current Qantas Airlines.

After the Second World War, most people had greater disposable income as well as more leisure time, particularly as three-week holidays became standard. Car ownership increased. This led to important changes in the accommodation sector as hotels and boarding houses declined in popularity and motels became more prominent. In the postwar period of the 1950s, Qantas became the major Australian airline, and in 1958 it introduced its first round-the-world service.

During the more recent period, particularly since the late 1970s, tourism activities became more closely linked with Australia's heritage. There was a recognition by the Australian public that tourists want to see Australia's past, and government and operators have also noted that heritage pays. Tourism has also assisted Australians in their search for social meaning in their environment, and helped them better appreciate their national identity. As Horn (1994: 3) indicated, 'As the Swiss found national identity in the Alps, Australians have found identity in the red granite [*sic*] of Ayer's Rock' (see Photo 1.1).[1]

(Adapted from Hall, 1995.)

Summary

This chapter has considered the problems of trying to define tourism and tourists. It has briefly outlined the motivations for tourism, considered the nature of tourism as an industry and discussed tourism as a system. This chapter has also explored changing attitudes to travel, as well as presenting a discussion of how opportunities for travel have increased. The problems with and limitations of tourism data have been presented. The main focus has been an investigation of a number of important economic and social factors that have contributed to the growth of tourism in the past two centuries. Discussion has centred on changes in Europe since 1750 or so, but a case study of socio-economic change in Australia since Western colonization has indicated both similarities with and differences from the European experience.

Student activities

1   What are the key social and economic changes suggested by the information in Figure 1.6?

- The first steam railway, carrying passengers between Manchester and Liverpool, opened in 1830.
- On 5 July 1841, Thomas Cook chartered a train from Leicester to Loughborough and took 570 passengers at a round trip fare of 1 shilling (5p). In 1851, Cook organized rail trips from many parts of England to the Great Exhibition at the Crystal Palace, in London. In 1869 he organized the first trip to Egypt and the Holy Land.
- In 1911, there were 22,000 miles of railway in the United Kingdom.
- The first August Bank Holiday was on 7 August 1871. This was introduced by an Act of Parliament to make life more bearable for the working class.
- Seaside resorts expanded rapidly in the nineteenth century mainly due to the impact of the railways. In 1841, Blackpool's population was 2,000, by 1901 this had risen to 47,000 and in 1921 had reached 96,000.
- The first holiday camp was established by Butlins at Skegness in 1939.
- In 1895 the National Trust was set up with the main aim of looking after 'places of historic interest and natural beauty'.
- In 1938, there were 2 million private cars in the United Kingdom, in 1949, 2.5 million, by 1969, 11 million, and by 1983 this had risen to 16 million.
- In 1982, more than 50 per cent of British people had taken a holiday abroad.
- In 1983, 6.8 million 'inclusive', or package tours, were taken by British tourists. This represents 55 per cent of all overseas holidays taken by British tourists.

Figure 1.6 Some important dates in the growth of tourism in the United Kingdom
Source: Adapted from Mason (1990).

2 Sub-divide the information shown in Figure 1.6, under the following headings:

- transport changes
- leisure time changes
- tourist destination changes
- recreation/tourism activity changes.

3 Study the information contained in both the case study of tourism growth in Australia and Figure 1.6. To what extent were the social and economic changes occurring in the United Kingdom: (a) similar to and (b) different from those operating in Australia?

4 Consider a holiday that you have taken recently and attempt to classify your motivations for the holiday under the headings of 'push' and 'pull'. What are the limitations of this approach?

Endnote

1 Uluru is composed not of granite but of arkose, a coarse-grained sandstone rich in the mineral feldspar.

Chapter 2

Theoretical perspectives on tourism development

Learning objectives

At the end of this chapter you should be:

- aware of historical and geographical factors that have contributed to the growth of tourism and particularly the emergence of tourist resorts and areas;
- aware of important theories informing discussion about tourism planning and management, in particular those of Christaller, Plog, Cohen and Doxey;
- able to demonstrate awareness of factors influencing the development of Butler's life-cycle model of tourism destinations;
- able to demonstrate an understanding of Butler's life-cycle model of tourist destinations;
- aware of applications of Butler's model;
- aware of critiques of Butler's model.

Introduction

As travel for pleasure became a significant activity, so tourist destinations emerged. New forms of transport (such as rail in the nineteenth century, road in the mid-twentieth century and air from the 1960s) linked the tourist generating regions with tourist resorts. Over time, due to factors such as geographical proximity to generating regions and climatic advantage, particular destinations and resort areas emerged and became popular with visitors. This popularity was maintained by return visits by tourists, as well as marketing of the resort attractions. A number of changes, some outlined in the previous chapter, such as those related to visitor motivations, transport and disposable income, and in addition negative consequences of tourism at the destination led, over a longer period, to some resorts declining as tourist attractions.

A major geographical focus of tourism planning and management is tourism destinations and later in the book, Chapter 14 focuses on destination management. It is in destinations that tourists encounter and interact with the local community and the local environment. This interaction leads to impacts on the local population, the environment and also on the tourists themselves. As will be discussed in later chapters, these impacts can be beneficial in relation to, for example, the local economy. However, the encounter between tourists and the destination they are visiting can also lead to, for example, damage to the local environment. It is in relation to these impacts that much tourism planning and management is targeted. Subsequent chapters investigate these impacts. However, it is first necessary to understand how tourism destinations have emerged.

Hence, this chapter focuses on the development of tourism destinations and in particular is concerned with major theories in tourism that assist with our understanding of how destinations have emerged, grown and in some cases declined.

Key perspectives

The development of tourism destinations: important theoretical perspectives

One of the earliest writers to consider the development of tourism destinations was Christaller, who was a German geographer and planner. As Christaller worked as a planner during the Nazi era in Germany, his work was not well known in the English-speaking world until after the Second World War. In 1963, an article by Christaller was published in which he suggested that there was a process of continual development of recreation/tourist areas. He used the example of late nineteenth century Paris and discussed how a specific area within the city developed from one where, in his example, a group of painters visit. In a step-by-step process this becomes an artists' colony. Later, poets, musicians and gourmets seek out this place. The place becomes fashionable and it is marketed. Members of the local community move into accommodation and food provision. Meanwhile the 'real' painters/artists move on and only those with commercial interests to sell to increasing numbers of tourists remain. Christaller (1963) suggested that elsewhere the cycle is beginning again. As Christaller (1963: 3) put it:

> The typical course of development has the following pattern. Painters search out untouched and unusual places to paint. Step by step the place develops as a so-called artist colony. Soon a cluster of poets follows, kindred to the painters: then cinema people, gourmets . . . The place becomes fashionable and the entrepreneur takes note. The fisherman's cottage,

the shelter-huts become converted into boarding houses and hotels come on the scene. Meanwhile the painters have fled . . . only painters with commercial inclination remain; they capitalize on the good name of the former painters . . . and on the gullibility of tourists. More and more townspeople choose this place which is now advertised in the newspapers . . . At last the tourist agencies come with their package rate traveling parties. At the same time in other places the same cycle occurs again.

Christaller's ideas were particularly influential on some later theorists of tourism planning and management. His ideas on how tourist areas develop over time can be summarized as follows:

- Destinations develop and change over time.
- The tourist experience (the product) changes.
- There are different types of visitors at different times, over time.
- The impacts on the destination change over time.
- The involvement of locals in tourism destinations changes over time.
- New cycles involving new tourist destinations will occur.

The American researcher Plog developed ideas on the psychology of tourists and these were published in 1973. His theory was based on a study of the attitudes to travel of New York residents. Plog's (1973) important contribution was the notion of allo-centric and pyscho-centric types of tourist. He argued that there are particular psychological types who do not like unfamiliar environments or cultures, so when they select a holiday they will seek the familiar (these he termed psycho-centric). Plog argued that there are other groups in society who will be prepared to risk a visit to a far more uncertain holiday destination, and they actively seek out the strange or unfamiliar and these he termed allo-centric. Plog indicated that those whom he termed psycho-centric would not travel far from the local environment/region to take a holiday, while those he termed allo-centric would travel long distances to unfamiliar locations. Plog suggested that the majority of tourists were neither fully psycho-centric nor fully allo-centric in relation to their holiday destination choices. In terms of his theory, the great majority of tourists were located close to a mid-point between the extremes of psycho-centric and allo-centric. Nevertheless, Plog suggested in relation to their selected holiday destination, the majority of tourists seek the familiar and prefer not to travel great distances to get there.

A major implication of Plog's theory for destination development is that tourist areas are attractive to different types of tourists as the areas evolve. The theory also indicates that the majority of tourists will prefer to travel short distances to take holidays. Hence, the theory suggests that destinations, particularly in developed countries, close to major population areas are likely to be established and grow more quickly than those more distant, remote areas. Therefore, this will contribute to the growth of resorts/destinations close to the generating regions. However, Plog's theory was developed from relatively limited empirical research.

If Plog's theory was closely linked to the psychological make-up of tourists, then Cohen's ideas related to the behaviour of tourists. Cohen (1972) developed a typology of tourists in which there was a four-fold classification. This classification is summarized as follows:

1   *Organized mass tourists*: These tourists travel together in groups. According to Cohen, they take a packaged holiday (travel, accommodation and food are also arranged in advance of the trip, usually by a travel agent and/or tour operator).
2   *Individual mass tourists*: This group uses the same facilities as the organized mass tourists, but makes more individually based decisions about their tourist activity.

3 *Explorers*: Such tourists arrange their own visit/trip. They go 'off the beaten track'. They wish to meet locals. However, they still tend to use the facilities of the mass tourist.
4 *Drifters*: The drifter shuns contact with other tourists and 'goes native' by staying with locals. He/she stays longer than most tourists and does not regard himself/herself as a tourist.

It is possible to combine the key ideas of Cohen with those of Plog. In this way, it can be suggested that the majority of Cohen's 'mass tourists' and 'independent mass tourists' are likely to conform to Plog's category of psycho-centric tourists. At the time when both Plog and Cohen were writing, the early 1970s, this tended to suggest that significant tourism destinations, in developed countries, would be developed in relative close proximity to the tourism generating regions. As most tourists prefer the familiar when choosing their holiday destination, the theories of both Plog and Cohen also suggested that relatively few tourists would come into contact with more distant and 'different' cultures.

During the mid-1970s, there was a growing concern about both the potential, and real, negative impacts of tourism on destination regions. At this time, Doxey proposed what was termed an Irritation Index, or, in its shortened form, what was known as an Irridex. Doxey's (1975) Irridex considered the relationship between tourists and locals. The main idea in Doxey's Irridex was that, over time, as the number of tourists increased, a greater hostility from locals towards tourists would emerge. The process by which this occurs is summarized in Figure 2.1.

Doxey's theory is built upon the premise that destinations will develop and grow over a period of time. However, an important implication of his theory is that destinations may not have the ability to grow without check. Doxey's Irridex suggests that, over time, as locals become more hostile to visitors, visitor numbers will not continue to grow at the same rate as previously and may actually decline. Although regarded at the time as important, and still seen as adding to our understanding of tourist–host interactions, Doxey's Irridex was not based on any detailed empirical research, but mainly on conjecture at a time when researchers and commentators were considering the negative consequences as well as the benefits of tourism.

Butler's theory

The geographer Butler built on the ideas of Christaller, Plog, Cohen and Doxey to create his theory, or model. Butler's model appeared in 1980 and he not only acknowledged that his ideas were linked to earlier theories, but he also indicated that they were based on the business/

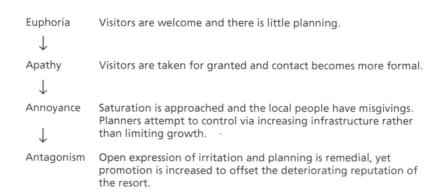

Figure 2.1 Doxey's Irritation Index

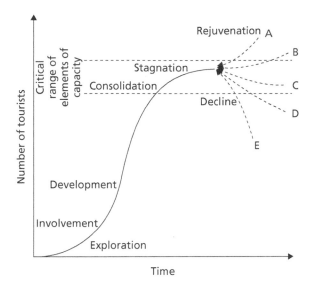

Figure 2.2 The resort cycle of evolution
Source: adapted from Butler (1980).

marketing concept of the 'product life cycle'. In summary, the product life cycle is a theory in which sales of a new product are seen initially to grow slowly and then to experience a period of rapid growth, before stabilizing and subsequently declining. When applied to tourism destinations, the model suggests that resorts develop and change over time and there are a number of linked stages: exploration, involvement, development and consolidation (shown in graphical form in Figure 2.2). During these stages a tourism industry develops and the destination has an increasing number of tourists.

Figure 2.3 shows more detail on the processes occurring during each stage of Butler's model. After the consolidation stage there are a number of possibilities. The resort/destination could 'stagnate', without any increase or decrease in numbers; it could 'decline'; or it could 'rejuvenate'.

In the 35 years since its creation, a number of attempts have been made to apply Butler's theory. Such an attempt is presented in the following case study, in which Agarwhal applies Butler's theory to the development of tourism in the Torbay area of southwest England.

In 1998, Butler reconsidered his model and indicated that, despite criticism, after almost 20 years there was also much support for his original model. In the paper, Butler indicated that the main criticisms of his theory were:

● doubts on there being a single model of development;
● limitations on the capacity issue;
● conceptual limitations of the life-cycle model;
● lack of empirical support for the model;
● limited practical use of the model.

In this same paper, he indicated a number of key points that he suggested confirmed the validity of his original theory. These were as follows:

● The key concept is *dynamism*. Hence resorts do change over time.
● There is a common *process* of development of tourist destinations.

- There are *limits to growth*. If the demand for visits exceeds the capacity of the destination, then the visitor experience will be diminished and visitors will subsequently decline.
- There are *triggers*. Factors that bring about change in a destination.
- *Management* is a key factor. Management may be necessary, in particular, to avoid the 'decline' stage of the model.
- *Long-term viewpoint*. There is the need for a long-term view. Resorts need to look ahead for 50 years, not 5 years, to avoid some of the pitfalls suggested by the model.
- *Spatial component*. There is likely to be a spatial shift of tourism activity as the destination declines (i.e. tourists go elsewhere).
- *Universal applicability*. The model applies to all destinations.

In the 35 years since Butler first developed his model, there have been many attempts to apply the theory including that by Zhong *et al.* (2007) in the relatively unusual setting of a national park in China. In this context there was almost no tourism before the late 1950s, but Zhong *et al.* (2007) indicated that they believed that the area had passed through the first four stages of Butler's theory, reaching the consolidation stage by 2000, and they provided a significant amount of evidence to support this. Bernerman and Petit (2007) applied Butler's theory to the

Stage	Characteristic
Exploration	• Few adventurous tourists, visiting sites with no public facilities • Visitors attracted to the resort by a natural physical feature • Specific visitor type of a select nature
Involvement	• Limited interaction between local residents and the developing tourism industry leads to the provision of basic services • Increased advertising induces a definable pattern of seasonal variation • Definite market area begins to emerge
Development	• Development of additional tourist facilities and increased promotional efforts • Greater control of the tourist trade by outsiders • Number of tourists at peak periods far outweighs the size of the resident population, inducing rising antagonism by the latter towards the former
Consolidation	• Tourism has become a maojor part of the local economy, but growth rates have begun to level off • A well-delineated business district has taken shape • Some of the older deteriorating facilities are perceived as second rate • Local efforts are made to extend the tourist season
Stagnation	• Peak numbers of tourists and capacity levels are reached • The resort has a well-established image, but it is not longer in fashion • The accommodation stock is gradually eroded and property turnover rates are high
Post-stagnation	• Five possibilities, reflecting a range of options that may be followed, depending partly on the success of local management decisions. At either extreme are rejuvenation and decline

Figure 2.3 Stages of resort development and associated features

Case study: an application of Butler's theory – Agarwhal's (1997) study of Torbay, England

Torbay has been and continues to be an important tourist destination in the southwest region of England. At the time Agarwal was researching, the southwest of England was the most important region of England for domestic British tourists.

In 1995, there were approximately 4.5 million visitors, of which 3.5 million were domestic visitors. Agarwhal attempted to apply Butler's model to Torbay. In summary form she indicated the following:

- Exploration stage (1760–1920): There were particular types of tourists and these were linked to the health/medicinal virtues of seawater.
- Involvement stage (1831–1950): In this period, the local provision of facilities/tourism infrastructure developed. This was in the form of hotels/boarding houses.
- Development stage (1910–1975): New tourist facilities and also tourist attractions were created in this period.
- Consolidation stage (1950–1975): A period of general take-off of trade. Visitor numbers exceeded the local population in this period and the economy was closely tied to tourism. However, antagonism began to grow between the local population and the tourists. The major causes of this were increased traffic problems and high local council rates.
- Stagnation stage (1975–1986): Numbers peaked in the mid-1970s. Immediately following this there was a great reduction in tourist numbers. Holidaymakers who had previously taken holidays in the southwest were increasingly going elsewhere, particularly Spain and France.
- Post-stagnation stage (1986 onwards): There is some evidence of aspects of Butler's 'rejuvenation' phase. Attempts were made to regenerate tourism with new (indoor) facilities, for example, the Riviera Leisure Centre, an indoor shopping centre (the Pavilion) and the Hollywood Bowl, a ten-pin bowling alley.

Major differences between Agarwhal's study of Torbay and the Butler model are as follows:

- The stages of development in Torbay were not discrete – there is an overlap in dates/periods.
- In Torbay, unlike Butler's model, there was very early involvement of locals in tourism to try to provide tourist infrastructure.
- In one part of the Torbay area (Paignton), the visitor type did not change over time, but stayed the same until very recently.
- The decline of this resort area is not necessarily irreversible. Post-stagnation planning and management have attempted to overcome the downturn.

(Adapted from Agarwhal, 1997.)

development of festivals and events in the Rhone-Alpes area of France and they indicated that the theory was not only useful to indicate the stage a particular festival in the area was at, but it was also potentially useful to predict what might happen in the short and long term.

Not only have there been attempts to apply the theory, but also new theories based on Butler's original ideas have been developed. Of particular significance are Weaver's (2000) ideas. Weaver argues that Butler's model is just one interpretation of resort development and given the point in time that it was developed, does not take into consideration attempts at alternatives to mass tourism and the development of sustainable tourism that have occurred since 1980.

Weaver (2000) proposed an alternative model to Butler's theory with four types of tourism:

- circumstantial alternative tourism
- deliberate alternative tourism
- sustainable mass tourism
- unsustainable mass tourism.

Weaver suggests that the four types of tourism result in seven possible scenarios (Figure 2.4). As Figure 2.4 shows, it is possible for tourism that has developed without careful planning ('circumstantial' in the figure) to become sustainable, but also that even when tourism is planned, there is no guarantee that it will remain sustainable. There is a detailed discussion of sustainable tourism in Chapter 18.

Prideaux (2000) was also critical of Butler and developed a somewhat more geo-political model of resort development. He suggested that initially a destination would have a local

Circumstantial alternative tourism – unregulated, small scale tourism	Transforms to	Unsustainable mass tourism – outcome of continued unregulated development
Circumstantial alternative tourism		Deliberate alternative tourism – outcome of planned and regulated tourism – small scale
Circumstantial alternative tourism		Sustainable mass tourism – high intensity large scale tourism development maintained with carrying capacity
Deliberate alternative tourism – small scale regulated tourism		Sustainable mass tourism – large scale regulated tourism
Deliberate alternative tourism		Unsustainable mass tourism – existing regulatory framework removed, or not adhered to
Sustainable mass tourism		Unsustainable mass tourism, carrying capacity limits not adhered to
Unsustainable mass tourism		Sustainable mass tourism – reversal of environmental damage adoption of regulatory framework

Figure 2.4 Weaver's seven scenarios

significance and could grow to have regional and even international importance. The stages of Prideaux's model are as follows:

- Phase 1 – Local tourism
- Phase 2 – Regional tourism
- Phase 3 – National tourism
- Phase 4 – International tourism
- Phase 5 – Decline/stagnation/rejuvenation.

However, Prideaux suggested his model was not to be viewed as unidimensional, linear or that what is proposed in the model will automatically occur. Prideaux indicated that although market forces are very important in his model, these can change. He also argued that innovation can impact upon the internal dynamics of the resort and the way it reacts to market forces and that resorts can also be susceptible to forces external to the tourism industry.

Summary

There are a number of important theories relevant to tourism planning and management and a selection of these has been discussed in this chapter. The German geographer Christaller suggested a process in which tourism enclaves can develop. The American writer Plog investigated the psychological make-up of tourists and the effects on their destination choices and travel patterns, while Cohen created a typology of tourists. Doxey considered the likely reaction of host populations to increases in tourism numbers over time.

Probably the single most important theory in tourism contributing to planning and management and certainly the best known is that of Butler. He suggested a model in which a tourism destination develops over time. He claimed that there were a number of processes that contribute to this. He also argued that resorts develop in particular stages over time. Butler claimed that the processes and stages of growth are applicable to all tourism destinations. However, applications of his model have not always found appropriate supporting evidence and new theories based on Butler's model have been developed more recently. Nevertheless, a key aspect of Butler's model for tourism planning is that he suggests that resorts are likely to go into decline unless remedial action is taken.

Student activities

1 Construct a table to indicate the major ideas contained within the theories discussed by Christaller, Plog, Cohen and Doxey.
2 Use this chapter to show how the ideas of Christaller, Plog, Cohen and Doxey are linked.
3 What are the key stages of Butler's theory?
4 What factors contribute to the changes noted in Butler's model?
5 Why does Butler suggest that destinations need to look 50 years ahead, not just 5 years?
6 With reference to Butler's model, what factors could lead to the rejuvenation of a destination?
7 How well does Butler's model fit the case study by Agarwhal?
8 What does Butler consider to be the main criticisms of his model?

9 To what extent does Butler consider his model to be applicable almost 20 years after it was first published?

10 How is Weaver's model similar to Butler's model and how is it different from it?

11 How applicable do you think Butler's model is to resort development in other developed countries such as Australia and New Zealand?

Chapter 3

An introduction to tourism impacts

Learning objectives

At the end of this chapter you should:

- have a basic understanding of the various impacts of tourism;
- be aware of a number of influences on tourism impacts;
- be aware of why tourism has the particular impacts that it has;
- be aware that tourism impacts can be considered as positive or negative;
- be aware of a range of perspectives on tourism impacts.

Introduction

Tourism takes place in the environment, which is made up of both human and natural features. The human environment comprises economic, social and cultural factors and processes. The natural environment is made up of plants and animals in their habitat. It is possible to make a distinction between the human environment and the natural environment and this is particularly useful when discussing the impacts of tourism. However, it is important to note that, in a real setting, the human environment and the natural environment are interwoven and human activity is both affected by and has effects on the natural environment.

Tourism, as a significant form of human activity, can have major impacts. These impacts are very visible in the destination region, where tourists interact with the local environment, economy, culture and society. Hence, it is conventional to consider tourism under the headings of socio-cultural, economic and environmental impacts. This convention is followed in the three chapters that follow this introduction to tourism impacts. In the real world, tourism issues are generally multi-faceted, often having a combination of economic, social and environmental dimensions. Therefore when considering each of the types of impact in turn, it should be remembered that the impacts are multi-faceted, often problematic and not as easily compartmentalized as is often portrayed. In other words, tourism impacts cannot easily be categorized as solely social, environmental or economic, but tend to have several inter-related dimensions. It should also be noted that much tourism planning and management is in relation to tourism impacts in destinations and resorts.

Key perspectives

The impacts of tourism can be positive or beneficial, but also negative or detrimental. Whether impacts are perceived as positive or negative depends on the value position and judgement of the observer of the impacts. This can be illustrated through the use of the following example. In this case, only economic impacts are considered and the example relates to the building of a hotel in an area with currently little tourism activity. It is possible for one observer to express a view that the building of the hotel will create more jobs, both in the building and running of the hotel, and the observer would consider this to be a positive impact. Conversely, another observer may claim that, although jobs will be created, they will only be part-time, semi-skilled, poorly paid and lacking a career structure, as well as taking people away from traditional forms of employment. This observer would view the building of the hotel as having a negative impact on the local economy.

Another example, in this case relating to environmental effects, may help with an understanding of the importance of attitudes and value positions in relating to tourism impacts. One observer may suggest that the creation of a footpath through a national park to cater for tourists can be viewed as a way of routeing tourists and therefore limiting damage – a positive impact. Another observer may claim that this footpath routeing will promote an increase in tourist numbers and hence the likelihood of more damage to the environment – a negative impact. Therefore, any discussion of tourism impacts needs to consider the value positions of observers and commentators and should be set within considerations of the wider context of tourism.

However, it is conventional for researchers and policy makers to note a number of both positive and negative effects of tourism. Positive economic benefits usually include contributions to the local economy, increases in tax revenue and job creation. Positive social impacts of tourism can include the revival of traditional art or handicraft activity as a result of tourist demand. Positive environmental effects of tourism may include revenue generated from visits to sites of natural attraction being used to restore and maintain the attraction, as well as enhanced interest from visitors in the importance of the natural environment and therefore a greater willingness to support measures to protect the environment.

Negative economic effects of tourism may include increases in the price of land, houses and even food prices in tourist destinations, which become particularly evident during the tourist season. Negative socio-cultural impacts may include the loss of cultural identity, particularly when tourists are from the developed world and the hosts are located in a developing country. This may be part of what is usually referred to as the demonstration effect. This occurs when inhabitants of a developing country imitate the activities of the visitors, who are from developed countries. This may start off as what may be considered relatively innocuous behaviour, such as the desire to wear brand-name jeans and consume branded fast food and drink, but can take the form of far more undesirable activities such as drug taking and prostitution. Negative environmental consequences include pollution from vehicles, litter dropped by visitors, disturbance to habitats and damage to landscape features.

Much research work on tourism impacts in the period since the late 1970s has tended to suggest that negative impacts outweigh positive impacts (Jafari, 1990; Wall, 1997). However, large numbers of residents of destination areas have continued to want tourists to come and often want them very much (Wall, 1997). Jobs, higher incomes, increases in tax revenues and better opportunities for children are frequently stated reasons for wanting more tourists (Wall, 1997). Residents may be prepared to put up with some negative impacts in return for what they regard as desirable positive impacts. This introduces the concept of trade-offs, which are frequently involved in relation to tourism impacts.

The discussion so far has been concerned with different types of impact and whether they should be classified as positive or negative. However, this discussion has assumed, through the use of the term impact, that tourism has some form of effect on society, the environment or the economy. So the term impact really is a way of indicating that there has been a change in something over time as a result of tourism visitation (see Hall and Page, 2014). In fact, it would probably be better to use a term such as 'tourism-related change' rather than impact (Hall and Lew, 2009).

There is another problem with the term impact as it implies a one-way process; in other words, 'A has an effect on B', or using a specific example, 'tourism has an effect on the environment'. Therefore, using the word impact may obscure the fact that 'B also has an effect on A', or referring again to the example above, 'the environment has an effect on tourism'. Hence, using the term impact may imply solely a one-way process – a form of cause and effect relationship in which only 'A has an effect on B'. In reality, it is very likely that 'A and B' have effects on each other – so it is a two-way process. It is even more likely that not only do 'A and B' have effects on each other, but they are set within a wider context in which there are other factors that affect both 'A and B', and 'A and B' also have effects on certain aspects of this wider context. So the term impact is really a short-hand way of presenting tourism-related change (Hall and Lew 2009). Hence, the term impact is strictly speaking limited and not completely accurate, but it is the word that is in common use, so as Hall and Page argue (2014: 140) 'we are stuck with it!'

As has been stated above, it is often easy to see impacts in a unidimensional manner, when in reality they should be viewed within a wider context of not just tourism factors but also wider societal considerations. As Wall (1997: 2) stated:

> The situation is extremely complex . . . but impacts are often desired, are extremely difficult to assess, may require the acceptance of trade-offs and in a policy context, may involve the development of strategies to mitigate undesirable impacts.

As noted in Chapter 2, tourism impacts are likely to change over time as a destination area develops (Butler, 1980). According to Wall (1997), key factors contributing to the nature of the impacts are the type of tourism activities engaged in, the characteristics of the host community in the destination region and the nature of the interaction between the visitors and residents. Davison (1996) suggested a range of similar influences and also included the importance of time and location in relation to tourism impacts.

In stressing the importance of the 'where' and the 'when', Davison (1996) claimed these influences set tourism's impacts apart from those of other industrial sectors. In relation to tourism being concentrated in space, Davison indicated that tourism production and consumption, unlike many other industrial activities, take place in the same location. This means that the tourist consumes the product in the tourist destination. Therefore tourism impacts are largely spatially concentrated in the tourism destination.

In relation to tourism impacts being concentrated in time, Davison (1996) suggested that it is the seasonal nature of much tourism activity that makes time important. The seasonality of tourism is largely due to two major factors: climate and holiday periods (Burton, 1992; Davison, 1996). Climate is a significant factor in that it controls important resources for tourism, such as hours of sunshine or amount of snow cover occurring at particular times of the year. Tourists' ability to visit a destination at a particular time of the year, for example, during school holidays, tends also to make it a seasonal activity.

In the case of Australia and New Zealand, the seasonal nature of tourism is closely related to climate. The summer period coincides with the traditional break at Christmas. In New Zealand, until relatively recently, the majority of businesses were closed during the last few days of December until late January. Although changing social circumstances mean that more people now work over the Christmas and New Year break, as well as in January, the period from late December until late January is still the main school holiday time. In France, it has been traditionally the case that many businesses are closed throughout the whole of August which is both part of summer and the period when many French people take their annual holiday.

Some of tourism's impacts also occur beyond the destination. For example, transport from the tourist's home to the destination – the transit zone as shown in Leiper's tourism system (Figure 1.4) – has an effect on the transit zone itself. Also, a package tour purchased in the tourist's home region is likely to benefit the travel and tour operator based there, rather than one in the destination.

Tourism also has an impact on tourists themselves. These effects may be noted in their behaviour in destinations. The impacts may also become apparent when the tourist has returned from a visit. For example, the tourists' experiences may affect their decision on a future visit to the destination. In this case, some of the experiences gained would be in the actual destination, although the reflection on that experience and its effects on future tourism choices could take place elsewhere.

Major factors influencing tourism impacts have been synthesized and summarized below. These factors are based at least in part on the work of Davison (1996) and Wall (1997) and are set out in the form of questions, with some comment following the questions as examples or to provide explanation.

Major influences on tourism impacts

- Where is tourism taking place? (For example, is it in a rural/urban location, a coastal/inland location, a developed/developing country?)
- What is the scale of tourism? (For example, how many tourists are involved?)
- Who are the tourists? (For example, what is their origin? Are they domestic or international visitors? Are they from a developed or developing country?)

- In what type of activities do tourists engage? (For example, are these passive/active? Are these consumptive of resources? Is there a high/low level of interaction with the host population?)
- What infrastructure exists for tourism? (For example, roads, sewage system, electricity supply.)
- For how long has tourism been established? (See particularly Butler's (1980) theory of the destination life cycle.)
- When is the tourist season? (What is the time of year and the importance of rainy/dry seasons?)

McKercher (1993) argued that although the impacts of tourism are well documented, little research has been conducted into why impacts appear to be inevitable. He claimed that there is a number of what he referred to as structural realities – he used the term 'fundamental truths' – which explain why the various effects, particularly adverse effects of tourism, are felt, regardless of the type of tourism activity. McKercher's 'fundamental truths' can be considered as major influences on tourism impacts and hence are presented in the case study below (with comments added under the headings McKercher employed), and there are a number of questions about these in the student activities that follow on from the case study.

Case study: some fundamental truths about tourism

- *Tourism consumes resources and creates waste*: Tourism is essentially a resource-based industry. These resources are natural, man-made or cultural resources. Tourism is a voracious consumer of resources. The resources are typically part of the public domain (e.g. woodlands, coasts, mountain regions), and hence tourism can be very invasive. Tourism is an industrial activity that creates waste with sewage, rubbish and car exhaust fumes common by-products.
- *Tourism has the ability to over-consume resources*: The natural, man-made and cultural resources that tourism relies upon are liable to be over-consumed. If threshold limits have been reached, adverse effects over large areas can occur. This can be in relation to the natural, man-made or cultural resources.
- *Tourism competes with other resource users and needs to do this to survive*: To survive it may be necessary for tourism to gain supremacy over competitors. Tourism and other, non-tourism, but leisure related activities often share the same resources. Hence, two people may be doing precisely the same activity (e.g. mountain biking) with one being classified as a tourist (because they are non-resident), the other (a 'local') as being only involved in recreation. Tourism may also compete with other non-leisure activities such as agriculture and forestry in rural locations.
- *Tourism is private sector dominated*: As much tourism is private sector dominated, the profit motive is the key one. Investment is far more likely in profit centres (e.g. a swimming pool/leisure complex) than a cost centre (a sewage system). Governments have had a key role in promoting and developing tourism, but have been little involved in controlling it. Voluntary compliance of the industry with environmental protection is almost impossible.
- *Tourism is multi-faceted and is therefore almost impossible to control*: Tourism is a very diverse industry including suppliers, producers, government agencies as well as a

(continued)

Case study: some fundamental truths about tourism (continued)

very large number of consumers. In Australia, for example, there were approximately 45,000 tourism businesses in the early 1990s. The great majority of these were small independently owned family businesses. Unity only comes through trade associations, which are usually voluntary organizations. This makes controlling tourism extremely difficult. It is, however, the most difficult challenge facing industry and government agencies. In a free market system, it will be very difficult to control, and to restrict expansion of, a diverse and highly unregulated industry such as tourism.

- *Tourists are consumers, not anthropologists*: Most tourists are consumers who want to enjoy tourism experiences. Tourists are pleasure seekers and except for a minority they are not anthropologists. Tourists are trying to escape their everyday life and hence tend to want to over-consume and are generally not interested in modifying their actions in relation to the host community or environment.
- *Tourism is entertainment*: Most tourism products have to be manipulated and packaged to satisfy the needs of tourists to be entertained. This can lead to the commoditization of local cultures and traditional activities. Existing products such as dances, festivals or even religious activities may need to be altered to satisfy the tourist demand. Questions of authenticity are likely to be raised as a result.
- *Unlike other industrial activities, tourism imports the clients rather than exports a product*: Tourism does not export products, but brings clients to consume the product in situ. This means tourism cannot exist in isolation from the host community. Tourism consumption usually takes place in concentrated geographical spaces. When planning for tourism, local regional and national governments should be aware of the stresses on the physical and social environment that an influx of visitors causes. Host communities also need to be aware that tourism is likely to cause a wide range of impacts.

(Adapted from McKercher, 1993.)

Summary

This chapter has provided an introduction to the study of tourism impacts. It has indicated that although tourism impacts tend to be multi-faceted, it is conventional to sub-divide them under the following headings: economic, socio-cultural and environmental. It is also conventional to present tourism impacts as either positive or negative. This chapter has indicated that such categorization depends upon the value position of the observer, and has also suggested that the term 'impact' is, in reality, a short-hand version of the concept of 'tourism-related change'. As impacts tend to be multi-faceted, often having a combination of economic, social and environmental dimensions, it may not be that straightforward to classify impacts at one particular tourism destination under the heading of either solely 'positive' or solely 'negative'. It is quite likely that there is a combination of impacts of tourism in relation to a destination and some of these impacts may be viewed as positive, while others are seen as negative.

The nature of particular tourism impacts is related to a variety of factors, including what type of tourism is under discussion, where it is happening, when it is happening, as well as the infrastructure for tourism. Ideas put forward by McKercher (1993) on the commercial and entertainment aspects of tourism have also been introduced and these have been considered in relation to tourism impacts. This chapter has also suggested that it is important to note that much tourism planning and management occurs in relation to impacts at tourism destinations.

Student activities

1   How do McKercher's 'fundamental truths' affect your views on tourism impacts?
2   To what extent do you agree with McKercher's 'fundamental truths'?
3   What are the major influences on tourism's impacts?
4   Consider a tourism activity/business in your local area and the impacts of this activity:

- Make a list of the impacts under the headings 'positive' and 'negative'.
- When complete, consider which of the two types of impacts are more important in relation to your example. Note: This does not necessarily correspond to the longer list of the two.
- Look again at the list and consider your own value position and indicate which of the impacts could be regarded in a different way, from your own assessment by another commentator, and how these impacts could be viewed.
- How important do you believe the nature of tourist activities is in relation to the impacts of tourism?

Chapter 4

The economic impacts of tourism

Learning objectives

At the end of this chapter you should be able to:

- describe in your own words the major economic impacts of tourism;
- demonstrate an awareness of a range of both 'positive' and 'negative' economic impacts of tourism;
- compare the economic impacts of tourism in developed and developing countries;
- discuss the implications of the economic impacts of tourism for the management of the tourism industry

Introduction

Historically, the impacts of tourism have been the most researched area of tourism, and economic impacts have been more researched than any other type of impact. As Pearce (1989: 2) indicated:

> Studies of the impact of tourist development on a destination or destinations have been the largest single element of tourism research . . . much of this is predominantly the work of economists and has concentrated on the effects of income and employment.

Despite this quotation coming from a quarter of a century ago, and the development of many different research areas in tourism, it is still the case that economic impact studies are a key focus in tourism research. Although, as has been stated in Chapter 3, economic impacts of tourism are linked to, and cannot easily be separated from, other types of impact, largely in an attempt to assist with understanding, economic impacts are discussed in this chapter separately from other tourism impacts.

Key perspectives

Chapter 3 provided a general indication of the key influences on the impacts of tourism, but of particular importance in relation to economic impacts are the following: scale of tourism activities, when tourism occurs (particularly whether tourism is a seasonal activity) and the historical development of tourism (with a particular emphasis on infrastructure for tourism). It is also worth considering again Butler's (1980) model and criticisms of it (see Chapter 2) in relation to the economic impacts of tourism.

As was discussed in Chapter 3, impacts can be considered under the headings of positive and negative. In relation to economic impacts the following are usually considered to be positive effects (Lickorish, 1994):

- contribution to foreign exchange earnings;
- contribution to government revenues;
- generation of employment;
- contribution to regional development.

Such benefits can usually be measured either at a national level or at the local or regional scale.
Negative consequences of tourism include the following (Pearce, 1989; Mason, 1995):

- inflation
- opportunity costs
- over-dependence on tourism.

Inflation relates to the increases in prices of land, houses and food that can occur as a result of tourism. Prices for these commodities can increase when tourists place extra demands on local services at a tourism destination. The term opportunity costs refers to the cost of engaging in tourism rather than another form of economic activity. For example, in a coastal area, with a predominantly rural hinterland, opportunity costs refers to investing in tourism instead of in arable farming, market gardening or fishing. Over-dependence on tourism can occur in, for example, small states where tourism is seen by the government as the best method of development. Over time, the emphasis on tourism becomes such that there is virtually no other approach to development. As a result, the country becomes dependent on tourism revenue to the extent that any change in demand is likely to lead to a major economic crisis.

One significant factor when discussing economic impacts of tourism is scale. Although similar processes may be operating, effects can be different as a result of them operating at different scales. The global economic importance of tourism has been briefly referred to above with discussion of employment and contribution to balance of payments and global gross domestic product. In addition to these data is the projection that jobs in tourism are likely to increase steadily during the early part of the twenty-first century, unlike jobs in other economic sectors. These macro-level figures, however, hide the unbalanced nature of global tourism. One continent alone, Europe, was the single most important tourist destination with over half of all international visitor arrivals in the early part of the twenty-first century and most international arrivals of tourists in Europe were visits from other European countries.

The United States and Canada are also both important destination areas and tourism generating regions. Asia is an important destination for tourists from Europe, North America and Australasia, but is also becoming increasingly important as a source of tourists. These tourists, from Japan, Korea and Taiwan in particular, are visiting other parts of Asia and the Pacific Rim but are also making visits to Europe and North America. Two continents, in particular, reveal the uneven balance of international tourism. South America is a growing destination for tourists, but produces few visitors, relatively speaking, to other parts of the world. Africa shows this to an even greater extent with increasing numbers visiting the continent, with the game reserves of East Africa, parts of the Mediterranean coast and South Africa becoming significant tourist attractions, but the percentage of world tourists originating in Africa is still very low.

Economic impacts of tourism can be particularly marked in developing countries. The Indonesian island of Bali provides a good example of both the gains and problems that can arise from tourism development in a destination located in a developing country. Since tourism began to grow in importance in the 1960s, a significant number of jobs have been created. These have been in the relatively obvious categories of hotel workers and bar staff, but also in perhaps less obvious areas such as boat hire, cycle hire and repair, car and motorcycle hire, food and drink selling and souvenir making and selling. Tourism is also said to have revived the arts and crafts activities of painting and wood carving, as well as the introduction of new arts activities, including batik making (Mason, 1995).

Residents have tried to benefit from tourism, through direct involvement in tourism in hotel, restaurant and guide service jobs, as well as through the manufacture and sale of craft products, the undertaking of cultural performances and food production to feed tourists (Wall, 1997). Particular examples of ways in which Balinese have benefited from tourism include the provision of home-stays and the increase in those providing informal services to tourists (Wall, 1997). Home-stays are the Balinese equivalent of the Western bed and breakfast. The great majority of home-stays are run by local residents, rather than outsiders, and hence almost all of the economic gain from the activity goes directly to the local population (Cukier and Wall, 1994).

A large number of young males (aged 15–25) have traditionally worked as street and beach vendors in Bali. They mostly lack formal education, but have substantial language skills. In the mid-1990s, although they worked long hours, and believed they had few alternative job opportunities, most of these vendors were relatively happy with their lifestyle and were well remunerated by Indonesian standards (Cukier and Wall, 1994). Tourism grew so rapidly in Bali in the period after 1970 that by 1995, if the associated craft industries were included, then tourism contributed over 30 per cent of the gross provincial product (Wall, 1997).

On the negative side, however, Bali provides evidence of tourism promoting inflation. Before 1968 (roughly the beginning of the growth of tourism) land prices had been steady for about 20 years. However, during the following 25 years land prices rose by nearly 100 per cent on average, but by over 150 per cent in the tourist areas (Mason, 1995). Although it is difficult to calculate opportunity costs, there is some evidence from the large-scale tourism development at Nusa Dua, on the southern coast of Bali (which was supported by the World Bank), that the money might well have been better spent on a smaller scale, less intrusive hotel complex. Something smaller would have been more in keeping with local values and might have contributed more to the local economy. It has been argued that the money would have been better spent on agriculture or forestry or locally based retailing rather than tourism that is primarily aimed at an up-market, international segment (Mason, 1995).

The future of tourism in Bali was far from clear after the terrorist bombings at Kuta in October 2002 and the second bombings in almost the same area in October 2005. Over time, Bali has become heavily dependent on tourism and what happens, in the longer term, following these events may indicate whether the island has become economically over-dependent on tourism. There is further discussion of tourism issues in Bali in the final chapter of the book where the nature and impacts of the bombings of 2002 and 2005 are presented as well as findings from research conducted after the second bombings.

Similar issues to those of Bali in its early stages of tourism development can be found in the Himalayan country, Nepal. As in Bali, tourism was relatively unimportant until the second half of the twentieth century, but more recently has come to be very significant to the economy. Nepal, the fourth poorest country in the world at the end of the twentieth century, is a landlocked Himalayan kingdom relying on access to imports via India. Throughout the period of European global exploration, dating from about 1400 until as recently as the 1950s, Nepal was almost inaccessible to outsiders and hence it holds attractions for significant numbers of potential tourists. Tourism began in the early 1960s but took off in the 1970s and by 1999, there were approximately 500,000 tourists annually. Although this total had fallen to approximately 350,000 in 2005, due partly to the political instability in the country (IRIN, 2007), it had risen again to over 800,000 by 2012 according to the Nepalese ministry responsible for tourism (MOTCCA, 2013).

However, particularly rapid growth took place in the 1980s. Between 1977 and 1988 there was a 60 per cent increase in tourist numbers and foreign earnings from tourism went up by 75 per cent. In the capital city Kathmandu, there were 2,800 people employed in the accommodation sector in 1977 and 14,500 rooms for tourists, but by 1988 there were 4,100 employers and 23,700 tourist rooms (Department of Tourism, 1990).

Nepal also shares some similarities with Bali, in that violence there has had an adverse effect on tourist numbers and hence the economic contribution of tourism to the economy. Although not usually direct targets, tourists have been put off visiting by Maoist rebels who have become particularly active since the mid-1990s as well as the legacy of the, still not fully explained, killing of almost all members of the Nepalese royal family in June 2001. In early 2005 a state of emergency was declared in Nepal after an intensification of the Maoist insurgency which did little to entice tourists to the country in the numbers that were visiting in the late 1990s (IRIN, 2007). However, if government figures are to be relied upon, since the latter part of the first decade of the 2000s, tourist numbers have been rising steadily again.

As in Bali, jobs in Nepal's tourism industry are often outside the formal sector and hence difficult to measure but include part-time guide work (often undertaken by students/teachers and lecturers as this pays as much as US$20 a day, compared with a typical monthly wage averaging less than US$50). Souvenir producing and selling is also important in terms of job creation. Hand massage is a speciality of Nepal and there is a charge of about US$2 a time. Those involved can make more than US$20 a day.

The negative effects of the rapid expansion of tourism in Nepal, and the desire of local people to derive economic benefit, can be seen at important Buddhist and Hindu temples. These temples are not just tourist attractions but are used for religious activities. Those who wish to use the temples for religious activities have to deal not only with the crowds of tourists who are causing physical damage to buildings but also with those who are becoming economically dependent on tourism. These include service providers such as the souvenir sellers, the drink hawkers and even beggars of all ages and both sexes who are there because of the reliance on tourist handouts (Mason, 1991). The major earthquake of April 2015 in Nepal, which killed nearly 9,000 people and injured over 23,000, also had a significant impact on the tourism infrastructure of this poor, landlocked country. This is likely to have serious consequences for the tourism industry in Nepal in general, and specifically for the areas directly affected, particularly Kathmandu and to the north of the capital, at least in the short term, if not for several years.

Some parts of Europe are not completely unlike developing countries, in terms of being resource frontiers for tourism development. In the far north of Europe is the unlikely setting for the 'Santa Claus Industry'. This industry, a focal point for domestic and international tourism, is located in Finnish Lapland and is centred on the Santa Claus Village. The village opened in 1986, focusing on the concept of it being the home of Santa Claus. An account of its foundation and economic impacts is provided in the following case study.

Case study: tourism in Lapland, the Santa Claus industry

Lapland is the northern-most province of Finland and is the least populated region of the country. Traditionally, the region has attracted two major types of tourists. Lapland provides wilderness and solitude sought by those escaping from routine who wish to find solace in the forest. Many of this type of tourist come from within Finland. The other main type of tourist is interested in the indigenous culture of the Sami (Lapp) people.

The economy of Lapland has become increasingly dependent on tourism, with in excess of 6,000 people in the industry in the early 1990s. The Finnish Tourist Board expected the number employed to rise to between 9,500 and 10,000 by the early part of the twenty-first century. The Board was particularly keen to encourage more foreign tourists. Despite the success of encouraging more domestic tourism in the 1980s, when the volume of overseas tourists also appeared to be rising, numbers of both types of tourist then fell in the 1990s. However, overseas tourists still made up about 20 per cent of all tourists in Lapland in the early 1990s. The main overseas generating countries were Germany, the Netherlands, Switzerland, Italy and France. Most tourists from these countries visited in summer. Many of them were in transit to the North Cape, the most northerly point of mainland Europe. Tourists from Britain and Japan came in winter to take part in winter sports, experience a 'white winter' or see reindeer.

In the late 1970s and early 1980s, the Board declared that the natural and cultural attractions of Lapland were not sufficient to attract tourists in the desired numbers and decided that a new attraction had to be created. The idea of promoting Santa Claus as an attraction was viewed as appealing.

The Santa Claus industry

In 1985, the Governor of Lapland declared the entire state 'Santa Claus Land'. However, there were also a number of rival claims for the home of Santa Claus at this time, in Alaska, Norway, Sweden and Greenland. In 1989, the Santa Claus Land Association was founded by 16 Finnish companies and this was connected to the Finnish Tourism

Board. This association had as its sole role the marketing of the Santa Claus idea. The Association operated the Santa Claus Postal Service, coordinated Santa Claus visits overseas and promoted Santa Claus at various international gatherings.

The Santa Claus Village

The showpiece of Santa Claus Land is the Santa Claus Village. This is located exactly on the Arctic Circle a few kilometres north of the town of Rovaniemi, the capital of Lapland (see Photo 4.1). The site was chosen because prior to the establishment, tourists had stopped at the Arctic Circle sign to have their photograph taken. The village site is on the main north–south route through Lapland. The village was opened in 1985 and contains Santa's workshop, where he may be visited at all times of the year, Santa's Post Office, a reindeer enclosure, several restaurants and many gift and souvenir shops. The Santa Claus Village property is owned by a company based in Rovaniemi and individual businesses within the village are privately owned.

Of particular significance within the village is the Santa Claus Postal Service. In the 1950s, letters written to Santa Claus by European schoolchildren were received in Helsinki. In 1976, the Santa Claus Postal Service was moved to Lapland when some 18,765 letters were received. The number of letters steadily grew. Visitors to the Santa Claus Village were encouraged to sign their names in Santa's guest book and in 1990 over 550,000 letters were sent out at Christmas, each containing a free gift. By the early 1990s, letters were dispatched to 160 countries.

Nearby, Rovaniemi has an international airport and can handle international jet aircraft. The most famous international flights were the regular flights by British Airways Concorde at Christmas between 1986 and 1992.

Photo 4.1 The Santa Claus Village, Rovaniemi, Finland, which has been specifically located on the Arctic Circle. (Courtesy: Petteri Lampi. Copyright © Rovaniemi Region.)

(continued)

Case study: tourism in Lapland, the Santa Claus industry (continued)

Economic impacts

In 1985, 225,000 visitors came to the village and the number of visitors increased rapidly from then until the late 1980s, reaching 277,000 in 1989. In the early 1990s, owing to the general global depression, visitor numbers fell. However, in the second part of the 1990s visitor numbers once again increased and reached over 300,000 in 1995. In 1996, there were 1.6 million international and domestic visitors to Lapland and 325,000 visited the village. In excess of 300,000 tourists visited the village each year in the period between 1995 and 2005, with 317,000 visitors in 2002 and 321,000 in 2004 (Finnish Tourist Board, 2007). In 2012 the number of international visitors to the village exceeded 500,000 (Santa Claus Village, 2014) and this accounted for one third of the total of 1.5 million overseas visitors to Lapland in 2012 (VisitFinland, 2014).

The contribution of the village to revenue and employment can be seen in the following information. Visitors to Lapland increased by 22 per cent between 1986 and 1994 and foreign earnings were up by 29 per cent and this was attributed mainly to the Santa Claus Village. The village employed 290 people, which in 1990 was 7 per cent of total tourism employment in Lapland.

Although this development is a totally artificial creation, it is an attempt to bring tourists to an area perceived as lacking many natural attractions. The village has been heralded as a great success in bringing tourists to a relatively remote and inhospitable location, and there has been little recorded environmental or social damage there.

(Adapted from Pretes, 1995.)

Other relatively peripheral areas in terms of the global reach of tourism have also gained tourists in the past 25 years or so. Hence, although New Zealand received only 0.2 per cent of international travellers in 1996, this percentage increased in the last decade of the twentieth century and the economic impacts were highly significant. (Figures presented below are based on New Zealand Tourist Board data from 1996, 2000, 2001 and 2002.) From 1993 to 1996, the number of visitors increased by an average of 6.5 per cent per year. The average spend per trip in 1993 was NZ$2,041, but in March 1996 this had increased to NZ$2,776. By 2000, the average visitor spend per trip had risen to NZ$3,222. Spend continued to rise in the early 2000s and the 2006 figure was up by 4 per cent on that for 2005, so that international visitors spent $NZ 6.4 billion in 2006 (New Zealand Tourist Board, 2007).

In terms of the main groups of tourists, Australia, United Kingdom, Japan and the United States were the major origin areas. New markets were Taiwan and South Korea and in March 1996 these two areas made up 15 per cent of total visitors, which was an increase over 1995 of 3 per cent. Japanese, Taiwanese and South Koreans were the biggest spenders, averaging over NZ$200 per day. The importance of this expanding market can be seen in the following figures: there were 216,162 visitors from these three countries in 1996 with an estimated spend per head of NZ$234 per day. By 2000, the average spend per head had increased to NZ$330 for Japanese visitors (the largest daily spend of any visitor group) and NZ$221 for Koreans. Only

American visitors (averaging NZ$ 248 per day) in 2000 spent more than Koreans (Hall and Kearsley, 2001).

However, the economic crisis in Asia that occurred in late 1997/early 1998 affected the projected continued growth in this Asian market and in 1998–1999 the percentage of visitors from this region fell in relation to total visitors. Nevertheless, in 2000, visitor numbers from Asia recovered and there was a 13 per cent increase on the 1999 figure by the end of December 2000, a further 7 per cent increase during 2001 and an 8 per cent increase in 2002. By the end of 2002, visitors from Asia exceeded 500,000 for the first time, with Korea (104,000 visitors in 2002) and China (71,000 visitors in 2002) growing particularly rapidly in the first years of the new millennium. This trend of increasing visitor numbers from Japan and Korea continued throughout the first decade of the 2000s, although the rise in numbers was not as pronounced after 2008. At the end of 2002, for the first time, New Zealand received more than 2 million visitors in one year. In relation to employment, in 1995 there were 155,000 jobs in New Zealand tourism and by the end of 2001 this had reached 176,000. This upward trend continued during the early years of the twenty-first century, so that visitors to New Zealand reached 2.4 million in 2006 and by then there were 183,000 jobs in tourism (TIANZ, 2007). Despite the global recession of 2008–2012, when there was only slow growth in international tourism, in 2013 visitor numbers exceeded 2.7 million, the number of jobs was approximately 170,000 and total visitor numbers appeared to be continuing to increase in 2014 (TIANZ 2014).

It is not the intention of this book to discuss techniques for assessing economic impacts (or other impacts) of tourism in any detail. However, a very common tool for assessing economic impacts of tourism is the multiplier and this frequently has a prominent place in government and international reports on the impact of tourism on an economy. The multiplier effect takes place when spending is circulated throughout an economy. It is a form of 'knock-on effect'. In tourism it is a useful way of conceptualizing what happens when tourists spend money in a destination. The multiplier concept is used to distinguish between direct and indirect income derived from tourism (Lominé and Edmunds, 2007). Hence, the local (or regional/national) economy can be seen to benefit not only directly from money that tourists spend, but also when staff working in tourism spend their wages on goods and services in the economy. This circulation of income derived from tourists is the secondary or indirect income. Figure 4.1 shows, in relatively

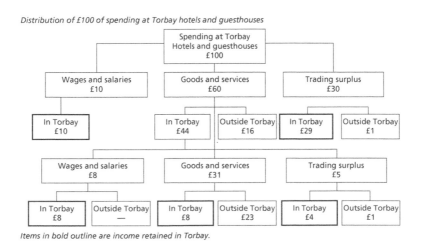

Figure 4.1 The multiplier: effects of tourist spend in a hotel in southwest England
Source: Mason (1995).

simple terms, the direct and indirect effects of tourism spend. In most real settings, multiplier analysis is complex and involves various tools, data sources and statistical analysis. It enables the calculation of, for example, income multipliers, output multipliers and government revenue multipliers. However, there is a lack of agreement about precise values in multiplier calculation. Nevertheless, most commentators agree that although it is not an entirely accurate technique, it can provide a valuable framework for assessing economic impacts of tourism (Lominé and Edmunds, 2007).

Summary

Economic impacts are one of the most researched areas of tourism. They have tended to be far more researched than other forms of impact. Economic impacts can be sub-divided into both positive and negative groupings. Often, countries perceive positive economic benefits as the major type of tourism impact and hence are supportive of tourism development. Evidence suggests that a number of developing countries have selected tourism as part of their approach to development. Such countries desire the positive economic benefits; however, they tend to be less aware that their tourism may also bring some negative economic effects.

Tourism is often one of a range of development options facing both developed and developing countries and regions within countries. Tourism is often viewed as a preferred option, in relation to other possible choices. Hence, either where there are old, dying industries and the area is in need of revitalization, or in relatively unexploited locations seeking new developments, but with few choices, tourism can bring significant economic benefits. Nevertheless, this chapter has raised the issue that to maximize economic benefits and minimize costs, tourism requires careful planning and management.

Student activities

1 From the perspective of a community affected by tourism that you know well, identify the positive and negative economic impacts of tourism.
2 Suggest what type of economic impacts of tourism might occur in small states, such as tropical islands or landlocked states.
3 How might the economic impacts of tourism in these small states differ from those in more developed countries, such as those in Europe, North America or Australasia?
4 What factors could contribute to the impacts being different in these small developing countries?
5 What factors (a) acting internally within a country and (b) acting externally (beyond the country) could affect the economic impacts of tourism, particularly in a negative way?

Chapter 5

The socio-cultural impacts of tourism

Learning objectives

At the end of this chapter you should be:

- able to describe in your own words the nature of socio-cultural impacts of tourism;
- aware of the range of socio-cultural impacts of tourism and aware of the context in which these occur;
- able to discuss the implications that these impacts have for the good management of the tourism industry.

Introduction

Any discussion of socio-cultural impacts of tourism will require reference to and discussion of meanings of the terms society and culture. Sociology is the study of society and is concerned with people in groups, their interaction, their attitudes and their behaviour. Culture is about how people interact as observed through social interaction, social relations and material arte-facts. According to Burns and Holden (1995), culture consists of behavioural patterns, knowl-edge and values which have been acquired and transmitted through generations. Burns and Holden (1995: 113) also indicate that 'culture is the complex whole which includes knowledge, belief, art, moral law, custom and any other capabilities and habits acquired by man as a member of society'.

Key perspectives

This chapter is concerned with the study of the impacts of tourism on people in groups, and this includes both residents of tourism areas (such people are usually referred to as hosts) and tour-ists themselves. It also concerned with impacts on the culture of the host population (and with any effects on the culture of the visitors themselves). The ways in which culture can be used and even packaged to promote tourism, and hence the subsequent effects this has on culture, are also topics investigated.

Cultural attractions in relation to tourism include the following (Ritchie and Zins, 1978):

- handicrafts
- language
- traditions
- gastronomy
- art and music
- history of the area (including visual reminders)
- types of work engaged in by residents
- architecture
- religion (including visible manifestations)
- education systems
- dress
- leisure activities.

Before proceeding with a discussion of socio-cultural impacts, it is worth considering once again the influences on the impacts of tourism which were presented in Chapter 3. All factors discussed there are important in relation to socio-cultural impacts. Clearly, a key influence is 'who is involved', and the 'activities engaged in' will be significant. Of particular importance, in relation to socio-cultural impacts of tourism, is the nature of both visitors and host popu-lations. The interaction of the two groups will be a major issue in affecting the types of impact. As Burns and Holden (1995) argued, when there is a large contrast between the culture of the receiving society and the origin culture, then it is likely that impacts will be greatest.

Some of the more beneficial impacts of tourism on society include the following: the crea-tion of employment; the revitalization of poor or non-industrialized regions; the rebirth of local arts and crafts and traditional cultural activities; the revival of social and cultural life of the local population; the renewal of local architectural traditions; and the promotion of the need to conserve areas of outstanding beauty which have aesthetic and cultural value (Mason, 1995). In developing countries in particular, tourism can encourage greater social mobility through changes in employment from traditional agriculture to service industries and may result in higher wages and better job prospects.

However, tourism has the reputation for major detrimental effects on the society and culture of host areas. Tourism can cause overcrowding in resorts, which can cause stress for both tourists and residents. Where tourism takes over as a major employer, traditional activities such as farming may decline. In extreme cases, regions can become over-dependent on tourism. Residents may find it difficult to co-exist with tourists who have different values and who are involved in leisure activities, while the residents are involved in working. This problem is made worse where tourism is a seasonal activity and residents have to modify their way of life for part of the year. In countries with strong religious codes, altered social values caused by a tourist invasion may be viewed as nationally undesirable.

One of the more significant socio-cultural impacts of tourism is referred to as the 'demonstration' effect. This depends on there being visible differences between tourists and hosts. Such a situation arises in many developing countries. In the demonstration effect, it is theorized that simply observing tourists will lead to behavioural changes in the resident population (Williams, 1998, 2014). Under these conditions, local people will note the superior material possessions of the visitors and aspire to these. This may have positive effects, in that it can encourage residents to adopt more productive patterns of behaviour. However, more frequently it is disruptive in that locals become resentful because they are unable to obtain the goods and lifestyle demonstrated by the visitors (Burns and Holden, 1995). Young people are particularly susceptible to the demonstration effect. Tourism may then be blamed for societal divisions between the young and older members. The demonstration effect may also encourage the more able, younger members of a society to migrate from rural areas in search of the 'demonstrated' lifestyle in urban areas or even overseas.

The demonstration effect is most likely to occur where the contacts between residents and visitors are relatively superficial and short lived (Williams, 1998). Another process, known as acculturation, may occur when the contact is for a longer period and is deeper. As Williams (1998: 153) noted:

> Acculturation theory states that when two cultures come into contact for any length of time, an exchange of ideas and products will take place that, through time, produce varying levels of convergence between the cultures; that is they become similar.

However, this process will not necessarily be balanced, as one culture is likely to be stronger than the other. As with the demonstration effect, it is in developed world/developing world relationships where the process is most likely to occur. As the USA has one of the most powerful cultures, it is usually the American culture that predominates over the one from the developing country in any such meeting of cultures. This particular process of acculturation has been dubbed the 'McDonaldization' or 'Coca-colaization' of global cultures (Mason, 1992; MacCannell, 1995). One of the perceived negative effects of this acculturation process is the reduction in the diversity of global cultures.

At the beginning of the age of mass tourism in the early 1960s, it was possible for a number of researchers and commentators to view the relationship between tourists from the developed world and residents of developing countries as a potentially positive one (see Tomlejnovic and Faulkner, 2000). Such writers considered that tourism could act a positive global force for the promotion of international understanding. An example of such a statement is presented in Figure 5.1.

Approximately a quarter of a century later, views on tourism's potential to contribute to greater global understanding had changed somewhat as is illustrated in Figure 5.2. As the figure indicates, misunderstanding rather than understanding among different people was a more likely outcome of an encounter between visitors from the developed world and residents of the developing world.

Although acculturation became an important process towards the end of the twentieth century, the desire of many tourists to experience a different culture is still a major motivation for tourist visits (Ryan, 1997). The motivation is to see and experience, at first hand, the actual culture and its manifestation, in terms of art, music, dance and handicrafts. This desire has

> Tourism has become the noblest instrument of this century for achieving international understanding. It enables contacts among people from the most distant parts of the globe, people of various languages, race, creed, political beliefs and economic standing. Tourism brings them together, it is instrumental in their dialogue, it leads to personal contact in which people can understand attitudes and beliefs which were incomprehensible to them because they were distant. In this way it helps to bridge gaps and erase differences. Since its focal point is man and not the economy, tourism can be one of the most important means, especially in developing countries, of bringing nations closer together and of maintaining good international relations. This noble task is today more important than ever. It therefore overshadows all other means striving for international friendship.

Figure 5.1 Tourism and international understanding
Source: Adapted from Hunziker (1961).

> [T]ravel in its current form hardly helps to bring people closer together and promote their mutual understanding. The dim glasses of prejudice are never taken off. Although there are studies of the subject, all indications are that travel, especially to countries with a totally different culture, does not diminish prejudice but reinforces it. The other people are poor but happy. Carefree, easy-going, and hospitable, but yes, a bit untidy, not so clean you understand, yes, even dirty and unhygienic, certainly unreliable, lazy too, and well, not so very intelligent. Well, that's exactly what one had expected, it's not surprising, that's what Africa's like – people say. . . . The image we have of other nationalities is as distorted as their image of ourselves. For the native, the tourist's behaviour is typical of his country. In his eyes, for example, tourists are immensely rich and never have to work. . . . Or because they walk around half-naked, they must come from 'cold islands'. 'In the cold parts they cannot go to the beach because snow is falling and certain parts of the beach is frozen.' . . . . Neither the native nor the tourist knows what their respective worlds are really like. In this way travel confirms the clichés of both host and guest.
>
> Misunderstanding instead of understanding among peoples. At times confrontation instead of meeting. In the worst case mutual contempt instead of esteem: tourists despise the 'underdeveloped' natives, and natives in their turn despise the unrestrained foreigners.

Figure 5.2 The glasses of prejudice
Source: Adapted from Krippendorf (1987).

contributed to a revival of traditional crafts as well the development of new activities, in a number of locations, including, for example, Bali (Cukier and Wall, 1994; Mason, 1995). In Bali, this in turn has promoted the growth of a souvenir trade that has made a significant contribution to the local economy.

However, on the negative side, the desire of visitors to experience the 'real' culture has brought into question the authenticity of the tourist experience. In some developing world locations, for example, Bali, the Solomon Islands and developed world locations with indigenous cultures, such as Canada, Arctic Norway and Finland, demand for cultural artefacts and performances has become packaged for convenient consumption by visitors. Such commoditization has led to challenges concerning the authenticity of the tourist experience. The commoditization has led to pseudo-events that share the following characteristics: they are planned rather than spontaneous; they are designed to be performed to order, at times that are convenient for tourists; and they hold at best an ambiguous relationship to real elements on which they are based (Mason, 1995; Williams, 1998). Also, of particular concern, as Williams noted, is that these pseudo-events eventually become the authentic events and replace the original events or practice.

As Mason (1995) reported, the keechak dance, part of a traditional religious ritual, performed originally only on special occasions in Bali's Agama Hindu culture, has been shortened, taken out of its religious context and performed on a daily basis, to paying tourist groups. Tourists observing such an inauthentic pseudo-event may feel cheated, although this assumes that they have the knowledge in the first place to comprehend the local traditions and they may not even be aware that they are watching a pseudo-event. It can be argued that this type of performance may actually relieve pressure upon local communities and even help to protect the performance's real cultural basis from the tourist 'gaze' (see Urry, 1990; Funkyluke2009, 2012). However, there is danger that the local performers may, over time, forget the true meaning and significance of the practice or event now staged mainly for tourists (Mason, 1995). Likewise, traditional objects that are reproduced and marketed as tourist souvenirs may lose their meaning and value.

Much of the preceding discussion has focused on the interaction between tourists and residents of tourist destinations, with an emphasis on the effects on the resident population. However, contact between tourists and residents also will clearly have an impact on the tourists themselves. As is indicated in Figure 5.2, this can contribute to the reinforcing of stereotypes, rather than the broadening of the mind that, according to the aphorism, travel experiences are meant to bring about. Nevertheless, there is increasing evidence to suggest that the impacts of experiences on tourists themselves can not only lead to changes in their thinking and attitudes, but also result in behavioural changes. A growing number of tourists visited the Antarctic continent in the last decade of the twentieth century. However, the continent still remains relatively inaccessible and expensive to visit; for many who travel there it is a once in a lifetime journey. Those who visit often have a profound interest in nature and the wildlife of the continent. It would appear that those who have visited return from the Antarctic with not only increased knowledge, but also a far greater awareness of the need to conserve this unique wilderness environment (Mason and Legg, 1999). Therefore, it is possible to suggest, as the experience of the visit may have had such a marked effect, that these tourists have become significant ambassadors for the continent (Maher, 2011). There is further discussion of this concept of tourists as ambassadors in Chapter 15.

A significant problem in assessing socio-cultural impacts is that it is difficult to differentiate these from other impacts and hence particularly difficult to measure them. This partly explains why these impacts have been regarded in the past as less significant than economic impacts. Much of what has been written about socio-cultural impacts of tourism has been based on research that has required those actually affected by these types of impact to assess the impact on themselves, or on others. This form of research tends to be more qualitative and subjective in comparison with the more quantitative approaches used to assess and measure economic impacts of tourism, such as the multiplier. For some commentators, this qualitative approach is less acceptable than quantitative approaches as it is argued that such an approach is less scientific. A number of criticisms of this quantitative position can also be made as those who support the more qualitative approach would argue, among a number of points, that their techniques are more flexible, achieve a higher response rate and their data are likely to be richer, more detailed and hence more meaningful (see Tribe, 2000).

A number of theories have been put forward regarding the socio-cultural impacts of tourism. One of the best known is Doxey's Irritation Index or Irridex and this was previously discussed in Chapter 2. As a reminder, in this theory, advanced in the mid-1970s, Doxey claimed that the resident population, or hosts in a tourist area, would modify their attitudes to visitors over time. Doxey suggested there are a number of stages in the modification of resident attitudes. When tourists first visit, Doxey argued, they will be greeted with euphoria and then, over time, as the tourist numbers grow, attitudes will move through stages of apathy, annoyance and finally to outright aggression towards the visitors.

Several pieces of research have been conducted to apply theoretical perspectives on socio-cultural impacts of tourism. An important study was conducted by Getz (1978, 1994), who attempted to apply Doxey's theory in the Scottish Highlands. The study is particularly interesting as it is one of the few attempts in tourism to conduct a longitudinal study (or at least an approximation to one, as it was in reality two snapshots taken at different dates). Getz investigated the Spey Valley in the late 1970s and then again in the early 1990s. Such return visits to the same investigation site are unusual in tourism literature and hence the findings are particularly important. The sample size and question content for Getz's studies of 1978 and 1992 were fairly similar, but there were different individuals involved on each occasion. Each used a sample of 130 households. The main findings were as follows:

- In both surveys residents were mainly supportive of tourism.
- Despite mainly positive views, by 1992 there was much more of a negative feeling towards tourism. This was partly related to the fact that by 1992 tourism was not found to be as successful as had been hoped in the 1970s.
- Those directly involved in, and hence dependent on, tourism were more likely to be positive about tourism.
- There was some support for Doxey's idea that, over time, locals become more negative towards tourism. However, the attitudes appeared more linked to a general feeling of economic depression than concerned solely with tourism. Getz suggested that if an economic upturn occurred, then views would probably improve towards tourism. Also, it would appear residents were particularly concerned that there were few viable alternatives to tourism in the area, so despite the lower satisfaction with tourism's impacts it was still felt that it was the best alternative. Hence, the notion of 'trade-offs', discussed earlier in Chapter 3, was important here.
- Over the 14-year period, the attitudes of locals had not greatly changed with the growth and change of the tourist industry. Also, the number of tourists did not appear to have gone beyond a threshold in Speyside. This was not because of the attitudes of the locals, but due to more general concerns with environmental impacts of tourism and restrictions on skiing development, although it would seem residents did not feel particularly concerned about environmental impacts.

In summary, the research by Getz (1978, 1994) suggested that, unlike the theoretical statements of Doxey, the attitudes of residents do not appear to change greatly over time. However, Getz noted some increase in negative attitudes to tourism in this time period, but not to the extent indicated by Doxey (1975). Getz, in fact, discovered that attitudes to tourism by the host population were closely linked to economic fluctuations, both nationally and locally, as well as to an awareness of the small range of other options other than tourism in the local region.

In the mid-1990s, research was conducted into resident attitudes to tourism growth on the Greek island of Samos. The main results from this research are discussed in the following case study as this provides a particularly good example of the attitudes to tourism that can be gained via a survey. In this case the views of local residents revealed a variety of perceived different positive and negative socio-cultural impacts of tourism.

Case study: attitudes to tourism on the Greek island of Samos

The study was concerned particularly with impacts of tourism on the host population in one town (Pythagoreion) on the island of Samos and their attitude to visitors and tourism in general. In this study 20 per cent of households in the town were given a questionnaire. As many as 71 per cent of those questioned were involved in a tourism-related business and 59 per cent had a member of the family involved in tourism. Most of those interviewed were relatively wealthy in comparison with the average Greek wage earner.

The main results were as follows:

- In general, residents favoured tourism (as high as 80 per cent strongly favoured tourism in their area).
- As many as 84 per cent indicated that the image of Pythagoreion had improved since tourism developed.
- Residents were in favour of more tourism, indicating visitor numbers could increase.
- As many as 87 per cent of the residents perceived that tourists were different from them.
- Specific questions were asked about the perceived social impacts. The top three factors seen to improve as a result of tourism were: employment, personal income and standard of living.
- Factors that were seen to worsen as a result of tourism, in order of importance, were as follows: drug addiction, fighting/brawls, vandalism, sexual harassment, prostitution and crime in general.
- A number of tests were conducted to investigate whether those with direct involvement in tourism had different views to those with no direct involvement. The researchers found, perhaps not surprisingly, that those with direct involvement in tourism did have more positive views on it. Even those with no personal involvement indicated that tourism had positive effects, but were generally less keen on the activity than those directly involved and they also had more neutral and negative views in relation to other effects.
- In terms of socio-demographic factors and attitudes, age was important; the young were generally more in favour of tourism. Length of time in the area was also important;

(continued)

Case study: attitudes to tourism on the Greek island of Samos (continued)

the longer people had been resident, the less keen they were on tourism. Bigger family size also led to more positive views on tourism, and this was probably due to perceived job opportunities. More educated residents were more likely to have positive attitudes to tourism. Increasing sexual permissiveness was the only factor seen negatively by all groups, except the young.

(Adapted from Haralambopolous and Pizam, 1996.)

The case study of the Greek island of Samos indicates that socio-cultural effects tend to be unbalanced in relation to different groups in society. In the Samos example, those who were more actively involved in tourism were more likely to be supportive of it. However, there is often a gender dimension to socio-cultural impacts of tourism.

There is now significant evidence to indicate that women are on the receiving end of different effects of tourism, particularly within the context of the developing world. The exploitation of mainly women (but also children – both male and female) through prostitution in the developing countries was a feature of the last three decades of the twentieth century and has continued into the twenty-first century. Prostitution is only one form of sex tourism (massage parlours, sex shops, sex cinemas are other examples), but it is particularly strong in developing countries. Although sex was identified by Ryan (1991) (see Chapter 1 on tourist motivations) as a key tourist motivation amongst several others, sex tourism is the activity of 'travelling with express intent of engaging in sexual activity' (Page and O'Connell, 2009: 647).

In a number of Southeast Asian countries/destinations, prostitution and some form of sex tourism have been in existence for a long period. Such areas include Thailand, the Philippines, Korea, Taiwan and the Indonesian island of Bali. In these countries, traditional attitudes, particularly of males towards females, mean that the use of female prostitutes by males is a relatively common practice. Therefore this activity does not carry the same stigma as it would in a Western society. Hence, prostitution has become institutionalized in countries such as Thailand and the Philippines. However, prostitution is not necessarily legal in countries of Southeast Asia, although laws tend not to be always enforced.

What has been unusual in the past 50 years or so has been the growing scale of sex tourism and that it increasingly involves international tourists. The great majority of these international tourists originate in developed countries (O'Grady, 1980; Hall C. M., 1992). One of the reasons for this has been the cost differential for sexual services in the developing world compared with the developed world (Hall C. M., 1992). Other reasons include the difference in attitudes to women in Southeast Asian societies compared with Western societies, and the actual status of women in Western societies and Southeast Asian societies, respectively (Mason, 1995). Throughout much of the period from the 1970s until the late 1990s, sex tourism in, for example, the Philippines and Thailand was also strongly promoted and marketed to mainly male tourists from Australia, the United States and Europe.

In an attempt to trace its history, Hall, C. M. (1992) suggested that sex tourism in Southeast Asia passed through four stages. The first stage was indigenous prostitution, dating back several centuries, in which women were subjugated within the patriarchal nature of most Southeast Asian societies. The second stage came about as a result of militarization and economic colonialism. An example would be American service personnel satisfying their sexual needs in Thailand during 'rest and relaxation' from the Vietnam War. This was made possible as a result of the infrastructure that existed for indigenous prostitution. During this period, economic development was closely linked to the selling of sexual services. The third stage involved the substitution of international tourists for the military personnel. Hall suggested that the authoritarian nature of many Asian political regimes meant that sex was often considered as an important commodity that could be traded in an attempt to achieve economic growth. As a saleable commodity, little regard was actually given to individuals involved in providing the sexual services. This attracted media condemnation from Western societies, but also is likely to have stimulated increased sex tourism, as potential customers noted that the attitudes of the authorities were not condemnatory of the tourist's activities.

In the early 1990s, Hall suggested that standards of living in Southeast Asia had been improved, meaning less dependency on sex tourism as a means to economic development. However, it was too early to say whether attitudes to sex tourism as a saleable commodity had changed. Nevertheless, in the last decade of the twentieth century, there was growing awareness of the spread of AIDS via prostitutes in developing countries (Mason, 1995). This, coupled with the attempts of some politicians and influential members of Thai society to move the image of the destination away from one where sex tourism is a key activity, may be reducing the dependency on sex tourism in the early part of the twenty-first century.

However, sex tourism is not confined to Southeast Asia and neither is it the case that it is men who are always those seeking sex, and women providing it. For example, in The Gambia in West Africa and Barbados in the West Indies, since at least the early 1990s, beach boys have been performing sexual services for female travellers, most of whom are from Europe and North America, for financial or some other form of reward. During the first years of the twenty-first century it is becoming clear that there are significant numbers of paedophiles, mostly from developed countries, who are seeking to have sex with children. For these people (almost always men) this activity would be a criminal offence in their own country in the developed world, so instead they turn to locations where they believe they will not face punishment and the developing world has been the setting for this, largely because authorities in developing countries, such as Vietnam and Cambodia, have traditionally not prosecuted the foreign tourists involved. However, recently, partly as a result of sectors of the developed world media applying pressure on their own governments and through campaigns run by pressure groups such as Tourism Concern in the UK, as well as closer liaison between the authorities in the origin and destination countries, those involved are being prosecuted – either where the men have committed the offence, or on their return home. Nevertheless, this form of 'cultural imperialism' (Page and O'Connell, 2009: 541) has not yet been eradicated and seems likely to continue until attitudes change and economic conditions in developing countries improve.

Summary

There is a range of both positive and negative socio-cultural impacts of tourism. Much has been written about the supposed negative impacts, including the demonstration effect, cultural damage, authenticity and specific issues such as increases in sex tourism, drug taking and crime in general. The negative consequences have been noted, particularly where there is a major cultural difference between the tourists and the local population.

Assessing and measuring socio-cultural impacts is not straightforward. Most research has relied on the attitudes of a range of respondents, particularly local residents, but also tourists themselves and other players in tourism. As local communities are not homogeneous, socio-cultural impacts are perceived differently by different individuals.

A good deal of research has also been an attempt to apply various theories, such as that of Doxey (1975), to specific contexts. Empirical research tends to suggest that local residents in many locations are willing to consider trade-offs in relation to tourism – they are willing to accept some negative consequences as long as tourism is perceived as bringing some benefits. This is particularly so where tourism is one of a small range of choices.

Student activities

1 In relation to a tourism development/activity in your area, identify the main types of socio-cultural impact. What characteristics do they exhibit? Arrange these impacts under the headings of positive and negative. Look again at the lists you have prepared and consider whether someone else asked to carry out this task would put the impacts under the same headings.

2 Consider an aspect of your culture that could be packaged and commoditized for tourist consumption. What would be the likely reaction of tourists? What would be the likely impacts of this commoditization on the aspect of culture you have selected?

3 Under what conditions would Doxey's theory apply? Can you think of any locations in your region/country where Doxey's theory is applicable?

4 What would you suggest are the main reasons for the responses obtained in the survey conducted on the Greek island of Samos? How well do these findings relate to Doxey's theory?

5 Getz's findings from his research in the Spey Valley, Scotland were not closely related to Doxey's theory? What reasons would you give for this?

6 Why has sex tourism become so important in society in countries such as the Philippines and Thailand? What factors make it difficult to stop sex tourism being a prominent tourism activity in many developing countries?

7 Hold a class/group debate in which the main proposition is as follows: 'As a female citizen of Thailand, I believe it is better to be involved in prostitution than trapped in poverty.'

Chapter 6

Environmental impacts of tourism

Learning objectives

At the end of this chapter you should be able to:

- describe in your own words the main types of environmental impacts of tourism;
- be aware of the various meanings of the term 'carrying capacity' in relation to environmental effects of tourism;
- describe in your own words the key tourism management and planning issues that result from the environmental impacts of tourism;
- discuss the implications that these issues have for the good management of the tourism industry.

Introduction

This chapter is concerned with the impact of tourism on the environment. The environment is made up of both natural and human features. Human settlements set within the countryside may contain a large number of attractions for tourists. Often the natural environment is referred to as the physical environment. The natural or physical environment includes the landscape, particular features such as rivers, rock outcrops, beaches and also plants and animals (or flora and fauna).

Key perspectives

The environment is being increasingly recognized as the major resource for tourism. It has been noted that tourism depends ultimately upon the environment, as it is a major tourism attraction itself, or is the context in which tourism activity takes place (Holden, 2008). However, tourism–environment relationships are complex. There is a mutual dependence between the two, which has been described as symbiotic. Williams (1998) explains this relationship as one in which tourism benefits from being in a good quality environment and this same environment should benefit from measures aimed at protecting and maintaining its value as a tourist resource.

In the post-Second World War period and especially since the beginning of mass tourism in the 1960s, it has become clear that the relationship between tourism and the environment has become unbalanced. Tourism has become a major cause of damage to the environment rather than a force for enhancement and protection in the past 50 years. The term environment is often assumed to mean no more than the physical or natural features of a landscape. However, as Figure 6.1 shows, according to Swarbrooke (1999), there are five aspects of the environment. These are: the natural environment, wildlife, the farmed environment, the built environment and natural resources. Figure 6.1 indicates the components of each of these five. It should also be remembered that these five aspects are not separate entities, but linked. For example, a bird of prey, an example of wildlife, may nest in a mountain area (the natural environment), will certainly consume water – a natural resource – is likely to visit farmland in search of live prey and nest material, and may even go to a town (the built environment) in search of carrion.

Chapter 3 indicated the main factors influencing tourism impacts and it is advisable to reconsider these again. However, in relation to environmental impacts the following are particularly significant:

- The 'where' factor is important. Some environments are more susceptible to tourism impacts than others.
- The type of tourism activity.
- The nature of any tourist infrastructure will also be important.
- When the activity occurs, particularly any seasonal variation.

In relation to the 'where' factor, an urban environment is likely to be affected differently, in comparison with a rural environment. An urban environment, being a largely built one, can usually sustain far higher levels of visitors than most rural environments. This is not just because a city has, for example, roads and paths, which minimize the direct impacts of tourists' movements, but is also the result of the nature of the organizational structure such as the planning process

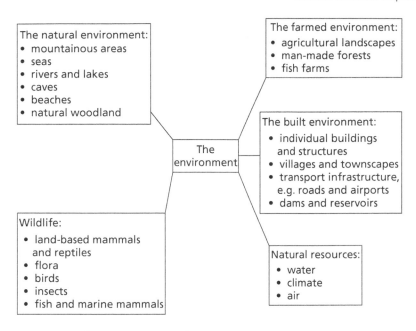

Figure 6.1 The scope of the concept of the environment
Source: Swarbrooke (1999).

in urban areas (Williams, 1998). However, tourists are also particularly attracted to sites that are coincidentally fragile, such as cliff-tops, coasts and mountains (Ryan, 1991; Williams, 1998).

The nature of the activities tourists are engaged in will greatly influence the impacts they have. Some activities lead to minimal impact on the environment and are not resource consumptive. Sightseeing from a bus will have little effect on the actual environment travelled through (although the bus may contribute to pollution and traffic congestion). Off-road vehicles in a mountain or dune environment will have far more direct impact. Tourism involving hunting and fishing can also be heavily resource consumptive if not carefully controlled and, as indicated in Chapter 3, McKercher (1993) argued that tourism tends to over-consume resources.

The nature of the infrastructure that exists for tourism is significant in relation to impacts. It would appear that the effects of those involved in mass tourism on the French and Spanish Mediterranean coastal areas are potentially far greater than a small number of walkers in the Himalayan Mountains. However, if this form of mass tourism is well planned and the groups controlled, it can limit impacts to a minimum. Paradoxically, a small group of trekkers visiting a relatively remote area of Nepal, where there is little preparation for tourists, could be far more damaging to the environment (see Holden and Ewen, 2002).

In many parts of the world, tourism is a seasonal activity. Under these conditions, tourism may only affect the environment for part of the year. During the rest of the year the environment may be able to recover. However, in some areas despite only seasonal tourism affecting the environment, this impact is so serious that there is little chance for recovery. For example, there are certain areas of the Swiss Alps that are so heavily used for ski tourism that they cannot recover fully during the summer period. Over time the inability of a slope to re-grow sufficient vegetation means it is more susceptible to erosion (Krippendorf, 1987; Hopkins and Maclean, 2014).

In relation to tourism's impacts on the physical environment, an important term is ecology. Ecology is the study of the relationships between animals and plants. The relationships are often complex, involving soil, water, microorganisms, plants and animals. The individual components and the links between them are referred to as ecosystems and there are many of these across the globe, ranging from, at the small scale, a pond, up to those covering thousands of kilometres, such as the tropical rainforest. In some ecosystems, humans are of relatively minor importance, but increasingly all ecosystems are either directly or indirectly affected by human activity, including tourism (Mason, 1990; Holden, 2000). At the relatively small scale, ecological impacts of tourism include, for example, the effects on plants as a result of trampling by visitors and modifications to animal behaviour as a result of tourists being present in their habitat. An example of ecological impacts of tourism at a global scale would be atmospheric pollution caused by passenger airliners, the resulting contribution to global climate change and consequent effects on both terrestrial and marine ecosystems.

There is a relatively long history of the environment acting as a significant attraction for visitors, but there is also growing evidence of conflict between tourism activity and the wish to conserve landscapes and habitats. As with other impacts it is possible to sub-divide environmental impacts under the headings positive and negative. However, as with other impacts, the value position of the observer, or commentator on environmental impacts, will affect their assessment of whether these impacts are classified as positive or negative.

Conventionally, the following may be regarded as positive impacts:

● Tourism may stimulate measures to protect the environment and/or landscape and/or wildlife.
● Tourism can help to promote the establishment of national parks and/or wildlife reserves.
● Tourism can promote the preservation of buildings/monuments (this includes, for example, UNESCO's World Heritage Sites).
● Tourism may provide the money, for example, via entrance charges, to maintain historic buildings, heritage sites and wildlife habitats.

Conventionally, the following have been regarded as negative environmental impacts:

● Tourists are likely to drop litter.
● Tourism can contribute to congestion in terms of overcrowding of people as well as traffic congestion.
● Tourism can contribute to the pollution of water courses and beaches.
● Tourism may result in footpath erosion.
● Tourism can lead to the creation of unsightly human structures such as buildings (for example, hotels) that do not fit in with vernacular architecture.
● Tourism may lead to damage and/or disturbance to wildlife habitats.

Figure 6.2 shows a number of impacts of tourism on the environment and it indicates a somewhat more complex situation regarding the effects of tourism than the lists above. Here, by comparing the positive and negative effects of tourism in relation to particular key themes, a form of balance sheet has been created. Figure 6.2 shows a far greater number of negative effects than positive effects, but this does not mean that negative effects are more important, as quantity of impacts does not necessarily equate with quality of impacts.

One of the key concepts in relation to environmental impacts of tourism is carrying capacity. This can be viewed as a scientific term, and it is therefore possible to measure carrying capacity. When used in a scientific sense it may relate to, for example, a plant or animal species that is threatened by the damage caused by visitors, and any increase will lead to more damage. In this way, it can be seen as a threshold measure, beyond which damage and possibly irreversible change may occur.

Area of effect	Negative impacts	Positive impacts
Biodiversity	Disruption of breeding/feeding patterns	Encouragement to conserve animals as attractions
	Killing of animals for leisure (hunting) or to supply souvenir trade	
	Loss of habitats and change in species composition	Establishment of protected or conserved areas to meet tourist demands
	Destruction of vegetation	
Erosion and physical damage	Soil erosion	Tourism revenue to finance ground repair and site restoration
	Damage to sites through trampling	
	Overloading of key infrastructure (e.g. water supply networks)	Improvement to infrastructure prompted by tourist demand
Pollution	Water pollution through sewage or fuel spillage and rubbish from pleasure boats	Cleaning programmes to protect the attractiveness of location to tourists
	Air pollution (e.g. vehicle emissions)	
	Noise pollution (e.g. from vehicles or tourist attractions:bars, discos, etc.)	
	Littering	
Resource base	Depletion of ground and surface water	Development of new/improved sources of supply
	Diversion of water supply to meet tourist needs (e.g. golf courses or pools)	
	Depletion of local fuel sources	
	Depletion of local building-material sources	
Visual/structural change	Land transfers to tourism (e.g. from farming)	New uses for marginal or unproductive lands
	Detrimental visual impact on natural and non-natural landscapes through tourism development	Landscape improvement (e.g. to clear urban dereliction)
	Introduction of new architectural styles	Regeneration and/or modernization of built environment
	Changes in (urban) functions	Reuse of disused buildings
	Physical expansion of built-up areas	

Figure 6.2 'Balance sheet' of environmental impacts of tourism
Source: Adapted from Hunter and Green (1995).

Carrying capacity also has a less purely scientific connotation, as it can be viewed as a term linked to perception. In this sense, the perceptual carrying capacity is in 'the eye of the beholder'. For example, what one observer views as a landscape virtually free of human activity, for another may be already too full with the evidence of people, past and present. This point about varying perceptions of carrying capacity is also important in relation to damage/disturbance in the environment. One commentator may perceive loss, or damage, or perhaps unsightliness, while another 'sees' none of these impacts.

Whatever the nature of perception by different individuals, it is clear some landscapes are more susceptible to damage from tourism than others. In an attempt to overcome this problem of differing perceptions, environmental or physical impacts can be separated from ecological impacts when discussing carrying capacity. As has been suggested, there is a third type of carrying capacity, perceptual carrying capacity. These three forms of carrying capacity are summarized below:

- *Environmental (or physical) carrying capacity* usually refers to physical space and the number of people (or the number of cars) in a particular place.
- *Ecological carrying capacity* is a threshold measure, which if exceeded will lead to actual damage of plants/animals/habitat.
- *Perceptual carrying capacity* is the level of crowding that a tourist is willing to tolerate before he/she decides a particular location is too full and then goes elsewhere.

The first two terms refer to actual measures and, in particular, ecological carrying capacity would be used in a scientific approach to the environmental impacts of tourism. Both environmental carrying capacity and ecological carrying capacity can be measured with scientific equipment and are likely to be significant measures in determining the point at which negative environmental impacts will occur. As perceptual carrying capacity is a subjective assessment of environmental effects, it is not a strictly scientific term as it requires individuals' views. The way in which it would be assessed in a given setting is through the use of a questionnaire survey or interview. The case study of Waitomo Caves in New Zealand indicates the significance of perceptual carrying capacity.

Case study: Waitomo Caves, New Zealand

Waitomo Caves are located in the North Island of New Zealand. They are a part of a system of limestone caves and underground rivers. The key feature of the system is the Glowworm Cave. The area is part-owned by a local Maori group, but is also part government-owned and the responsibility of the Department of Conservation (DOC). The Glowworm Cave itself and a number of associated commercial activities are currently leased to a commercial operator, Tourism Holdings Ltd (THL) and form part of the village of Waitomo (population approximately 500). The site is regarded as one of considerable aesthetic and ecological significance and, with over 500,000 visitors per year in the early twenty-first century, is one of the most important visitor attractions in New Zealand.

The Glowworm Cave operates as a 'traditional' attraction in which tour groups are guided through various parts of the cave system. The high point of the visit (for the great majority of tourists) is the viewing of the glowworms from a small boat on an underground river in almost complete darkness. As the glowworms hang from the roof of the cave they look like overhead stars in the night sky. Tours of the Glowworm Cave last approximately 40 minutes and visitation is subject to diurnal and seasonal fluctuations. The peak season is November–April and 11 am–2 pm is the busiest time of day. In the mid-1990s, the main visitor groups were as follows: Japanese 27 per cent, Korean 26 per cent, Taiwanese 9 per cent, Australian 8 per cent and New Zealander 7 per cent.

THL regards the Glowworm Cave very much as a 'money maker', and it is considered by most speleological (caving) circles as a 'sacrificial' site, that is, it concentrates activity so that other, more environmentally significant, sites remain relatively undisturbed. An important environmental problem of the cave is carbon dioxide, as excessive amounts of it lead to corrosion of the limestone. The cave licence specifies that carbon dioxide should not exceed 2,400 parts per million. This is equivalent to 300 people per hour. There is no accurate measurement of visitor numbers at the cave, but anecdotal evidence suggests that the limit of 300 people per hour is regularly exceeded. It would appear that the glowworms are unaffected by visitor numbers (although the use of flash photography can change behaviour). However, a perception that commercial interests were overriding ecological and experiential factors, led to DOC conducting research. This study focused on visitor experience with respect to crowding, and whether perceptions of crowding were affecting the experience and hence its sustainability.

The results of the study indicate a number of differences in perception of crowding and satisfaction with the visit between New Zealanders and the various international visitor groups. New Zealanders registered the highest perception of crowding, although they were generally not dissatisfied with the visit. Although Koreans registered amongst the lowest levels of crowding, they were dissatisfied with the number of groups in the cave at any one time and having to wait for other groups. As many as 71 per cent of visitors in summer registered some form of crowding, but this fell to 40 per cent in winter. Australian and Japanese visitors tended to view the cave system as relatively crowded, more so than the Korean visitors, but less so than the New Zealanders. Another important finding was that New Zealand visitors were being 'squeezed out' by high-volume international short-stay visitors. This was largely a result of aggressive promotion to the 'Asian market'.

In conclusion, this study suggested that the search for social carrying capacity at the Glowworm Cave necessitates the introduction of the issue of who decides on appropriate levels of crowding and to which visitor groups it should be applied. The research also revealed that the concept of social or perceptual carrying capacity was unworkable without some clearly defined value positions that management could employ. This study therefore shows the potential and real conflict facing a tourism operator when market driven management and a strong marketing policy clash with the localized sensitivities of culture and heritage.

(Adapted from Doorne, 2000.)

The Waitomo study indicates that perceptual carrying capacity is difficult to assess; however, even in relation to ecological and environmental carrying capacities, measuring is far from straightforward. Capacities are also likely to vary according to whatever management strategies are in place. To overcome this problem, other measures have been developed and applied. The limits of acceptable change (LAC) technique was developed in the United States. This has been used in relation to proposed developments. It involves establishing an agreed set of criteria before the development and the prescription of desired conditions and levels of change after development (Williams, 1998). However, this approach suffers from technical difficulties in agreeing some of the more qualitative aspects of tourism development. The LAC approach also assumes the existence of rational planning, which, as is discussed in Chapter 7, should not necessarily be assumed to be occurring in any given context!

Another technique is that of the environmental impact assessment (EIA), which has become a particularly common process in the last 25 years or so. In relation to assessing tourism's impacts, the EIA is similar to the use of the LAC and the key principles of EIA are summarized in Figure 6.3. EIAs are also used in relation to other industries and they provide a framework for informing the decision-making process. A number of different methods and techniques can be used in an EIA, including impact checklists, cartographic analysis simulation and predictive models (Williams, 1998).

Discussion of carrying capacities, LACs and EIAs raises one of the key factors in relation to environmental impacts. This is the importance of scale. Footpath erosion, for example, may appear a small-scale impact and may easily be alleviated by re-routeing. In this case, both impacts and management attempts to alleviate will be limited to a small area. However, in the case of coastal pollution that has been caused by raw sewage being pumped into the sea from a hotel complex, this is very likely to spread widely and attempts to alleviate this will require access to an extensive area.

- Assessments should identify the nature of the proposed and induced activities that are likely to be generated by the project.
- Assessments should identify the elements of the environment that will be significantly affected.
- Assessments will evaluate the nature and extent of initial impacts and those that are likely to be generated via secondary effects.
- Assessments will propose management strategies to control impacts and ensure maximum benefits from the project.

Figure 6.3 Key principles of EIA
Source: Adapted from Hunter and Green (1995).

As the Waitomo Caves case study indicates, the environment is a key tourism draw in New Zealand. It is certainly a major tourist attraction, if not the major attraction. This is linked to the idea of the 'clean green image', which is used in marketing New Zealand to international tourists. For a relatively long period until the early 1980s New Zealand felt sheltered from negative impacts of tourism on the environment. Part of the reason there is a growing concern about environmental impacts of tourism in New Zealand, is that the country needs to maintain its 'clean green image' to sell holiday experiences. The New Zealand Tourism Board (1992) indicated that, in 1991, natural attractions accounted for 29 per cent of visits to New Zealand and 55 per cent of all overseas tourists visited a national park in that year. Natural attractions accounted for almost one-third (31 per cent) of all visits to New Zealand in 2003 (New Zealand Tourism Board, 2004) and 29 per cent in 2012 (TourismNewZealand, 2013).

There are two important ideals in the relationship between tourism and the environment in New Zealand: these are the notions of first, wilderness and second, equality of access to the countryside. However, with increasing numbers of both domestic and international visitors these ideals may become incompatible.

Coastal areas and offshore islands, lakes and rivers and high country and mountain areas were identified approximately twenty years ago as the most environmentally sensitive areas in New Zealand (New Zealand Tourism Board, 1996). In relation to impacts on ecosystems, native bush areas are threatened by introduced species, native animals are vulnerable to disturbance and construction of facilities can cause problems particularly if too much vegetation is removed as poor drainage of sites results and the ground becomes unstable.

As Maori own more than 50 per cent of the privately owned native bush-land in New Zealand, their role is very important. However, many Maori people see growth in environmental concern as being detrimental to them. This can lead to conflict as a result of different Maori attitudes to the environment compared with white (pakeha) views. Nevertheless, there is some evidence in New Zealand that tourism can promote preservation and, of particular relevance to Maori values, tourism can help promote protection of sites of cultural significance.

Large areas of Australia are often regarded as wilderness or semi-wilderness. Their use for all forms of development in the past has tended to ignore that such areas are finite resources. However, coastal areas are the most developed in Australia and the case study of Julian Rocks considers the scale of environmental impacts of tourism in Australia in a marine environment.

Case study: Julian Rocks, Australia

The Julian Rocks Aquatic Reserve is close to the township of Byron Bay and located approximately 2 km off the northern part of the New South Wales (NSW) coast in Australia. This is a popular holiday spot on the NSW coast and the main attraction is the surfing beach. Scuba diving is also a very significant activity. The great majority of visitors are Australian domestic visitors. Backpackers comprise the fastest growing visitor segment and there are increasing numbers of international backpackers.

Julian Rocks comprise a nature reserve and the surrounding waters (within a 500 m radius) have been an aquatic reserve since 1982. The aims of the aquatic reserve are to protect, manage and conserve the environment and existing uses of the area and to ensure ecological diversity and significance are maintained. Julian Rocks has been described as one of the best diving locations on the east coast of Australia. Although not part of the Great Barrier Reef, over 10 per cent of the reserve is made up of coral. The area contains a diverse range of habitats including rock reefs, caves, tunnels, steep rocky slopes and sandy areas. There are many fish species, some of which breed here as well as marine turtles and grey nurse sharks.

Julian Rocks is a popular and heavily used scuba diving site. The peak diving season is November–January (the southern hemisphere summer) and also at Easter. Diver numbers in December are double those of June. There were in excess of 20,000 dives in 1993, 86 per cent of which occurred in two specific locations. These sites are used as intensively as all but two of those on the Great Barrier Reef, but they are smaller in area than the leading two on the Great Barrier Reef. The number of divers has increased steadily since the mid-1980s. In 1985, there were only two dive operators, who ran normally three, or at most, four vessels. By 1994, there were four operators using up to ten boats. Each of these vessels can carry up to twelve divers. In 1994, the vessels made 3,800 launches at the local boat launch ramp. This suggests that there was the potential for over 40,000 dives per year (double the actual usage in 1993).

By the mid-1990s there were reports that the site had declined since the early 1980s. Damage was largely attributed to boat anchors, although this was not only from dive vessels but also fishing boats. Research in the early 1990s indicated that a key contributor to environmental damage was overcrowding at the two most visited sites. Some of the damage was inflicted directly by divers coming into contact with sensitive submarine material, in particular coral. Fins, coming into contact with living coral, were a cause of damage; although most of this was not serious damage, hard coral suffered more than other organisms. This research also noted that the majority of damage resulted from inexperienced divers. There was also conflict between divers and recreational anglers. Divers complained about damage caused by anchors, destruction of corals by snagged lines, the catching of non-target fish and the incidence of turtles and sharks with fish hooks in their mouths.

It is very difficult to define the carrying capacity for an area such as Julian Rocks. A major problem is the lack of baseline data on the ecology of the area. There is also a lack of information on attitudes of divers to crowding. Nevertheless, a study conducted at a site in the Caribbean with some similarities to Julian Rocks, although with more sensitive coral, suggested an upper limit of 5,000 dives per year. Each of the two most popular

(*continued*)

Case study: Julian Rocks, Australia (continued)

sites at Julian Rocks had double this number in 1993. Because of this lack of baseline data it is also difficult to assess the LAC. However, anecdotal evidence would suggest that the great majority of divers would conclude that no change was acceptable. Apparent or potential degradation was a primary reason for declaring Julian Rocks a marine preservation area, implying that any further change was unacceptable. User perception of the area suggests that levels of change related to social values such as crowding are likely to be as significant as environmental change. Hence, even if management practices led to an improved environment, social factors might impose an upper limit on user numbers that could be below a threshold limit above which environmental damage would occur.

(Adapted from Dervis and Harriot, 1996.)

Summary

The environment is a key resource for tourism. It is possible to sub-divide the environment into the human (or built environment) and the natural environment. The environment provides some of the significant attractions for visitors. Hence, any damage to the environment may contribute to a reduction in visitor numbers.

Tourism can have important negative impacts on the environment, including footpath erosion, river and marine pollution, litter, traffic congestion, overcrowding and the creation of unsightly structures. It can seriously affect ecosystems. However, it can have beneficial impacts by contributing to an awareness of the need to conserve valued landscapes and buildings, and revenue generated from visitor charges can be used to preserve and maintain threatened sites.

In relation to assisting with planning and management of environmental impacts, the concept of carrying capacity is particularly useful. Environmental and ecological carrying capacity are both scientific terms and hence lend themselves to scientific forms of measuring. The concept of perceptual carrying capacity is no less important in relation to management of environmental impacts, although it may be more difficult to assess in a given context, as it is a more subjective term.

As visitor numbers continue to increase, and virtually nowhere on Earth remains free of tourists, the need for carefully planned and managed tourism in relation to environmental impacts has become, and continues to be, a critical issue.

Student activities

1   In relation to a tourism activity in your area, identify the environmental impacts. Classify the impacts under the headings 'positive' and 'negative'. Note which of these two lists of impacts is the longer. Why do you think there are differences in the content and length of these two lists?

2   Which areas of your region/country are particularly susceptible to environmental impacts of tourism?

3   What are the major types of environmental impact of tourism in your country/region?

4   How can tourism negatively affect ecosystems in your area?

5   How might environmental impacts on a heavily visited small tropical island vary from those on the interior of the mainland of Europe?

6   Explain why carrying capacity is an important concept, but a problematic one.

7   What does the case study of Waitomo Caves reveal about the concept of carrying capacity and its practical application?

8   What are the environmental impacts of tourism at Julian Rocks, Australia and why is tourism difficult to control there?

9   Select a location in your area and indicate how you would assess the following:

- environmental carrying capacity;
- ecological carrying capacity;
- perceptual carrying capacity.

Conclusions to Part I

The three preceding chapters (Chapters 4–6) have indicated the importance of different types of tourism impact. These impacts have been classified under the headings: economic, socio-cultural or environmental. However, as stated in Chapter 3, in a real setting, impacts are not that easy to separate and classify under these headings. Tourism impacts are, in fact, multi-faceted. A number of the case studies in Chapters 4–6 may have suggested this, although this may not have been asserted overtly.

In any given situation, it is likely that there will be a combination of different impacts, with some being considered more significant than others. It is also likely that the impacts of tourism will vary over time. The theories of Butler and Doxey suggest how tourism impacts may change over time. It is therefore possible and indeed very likely that, for example, where economic gain is noted at the earliest stages of tourism, it will be the case, several years later, that socio-cultural effects are becoming more apparent and environmental consequences may also be noted. By this stage in the development of tourism, the initial positive economic impacts of tourism may be replaced, or diminished, by growing social unease between the residents and tourists, as well as mounting concern about tourism's environmental impacts.

It is important to note that when considering tourism impacts, the environment in which impacts are taking place usually comprises complex systems in which there are inter-relationship between the environmental, social and economic aspects. Impacts often have a cumulative dimension in which

> secondary processes reinforce and develop the consequences of change in unpredicted ways, so treating individual problems in isolation ignores the likelihood that there is a composite impact that may be greater than the sum of the individual parts.
>
> (Williams, 1998: 102)

Williams (1998) argued for a holistic approach to tourism impacts and, in addition to the point made above, he suggested that such an approach enables a more balanced view of these impacts to be obtained and in this way, positive aspects of tourism impacts will be recognized as well negative views.

Adopting a holistic approach also makes us aware that the word environment embraces a diversity of concepts – built environments, physical environments, economic environments, social environments, cultural environments and political environments – and tourism has the potential to influence all of these, albeit in varying degrees.

PART II

Tourism planning and management: concepts, issues and players

Chapter 7

Tourism planning and management: concepts and issues

Learning objectives

At the end of this chapter you should be able to:

- understand the meaning of planning;
- understand the meaning of management;
- understand the relationship between planning and management;
- understand the meaning of both tourism planning and management;
- understand the meaning of policy and the nature of tourism policy;
- understand some preliminary ideas on tourism planning, management and sustainability.

Introduction

The first section of this book considered the growth, development and impacts of tourism. This and the following chapters consider planning and management issues in relation to the development and impacts of tourism. This first chapter in the second part of the book discusses, initially, the nature of planning and management in general terms. It focuses on tourism planning and management and considers the relationship between tourism planning, policy and management.

Modern Western-style planning can be traced back at least 200 years to town planning in the United Kingdom (Gunn, 1988; Williams, 1998). However, the physical planning of the layout of urban areas dates back to the Greek era (Gunn, 1988). Modern town planning of the past 200 years or so emerged when the population became increasingly urbanized and was, largely, a response to the increasing 'evils' of urban living in terms of social and environmental impacts (Gunn, 1988). Those involved in planning for utopian cities to replace the rapidly built unplanned creations of eighteenth century Britain, however, were still concerned primarily with the physical appearance of cities.

In the early twentieth century, almost all urban planning in Britain was linked to a number of central government planning acts and there was additionally focus from the 1930s onwards on rural areas with a succession of Town and Country Planning Acts (Mason, 2013a). In federal countries such as the USA, Canada and Australia, state governments are the bodies which have usually exercised rights over private property and specific laws and regulations restrict the places where particular activities can take place. In New Zealand, the planning system which affects land-use activities, including tourism, is embedded within the Resource Management Act of 1991 (Mason, 2013a).

If early attempts at planning were to create order in response to social and environmental degradation, this is still an important rationale for planning today. As Williams (1998) suggested, without planning there is the risk that an activity will be unregulated, formless or haphazard and likely to lead to a range of negative economic, social and environmental impacts. Gunn (1988) made a similar point when he claimed that the absence of planning may result in serious malfunctions and inefficiencies.

In its early stages, modern planning may have been largely reactive, but, as Gunn (1988) suggested, by the late twentieth century it was far more proactive and future oriented. Although planning experiences vary from country to country and place to place across the globe, some form of official planning has taken place almost everywhere.

Key perspectives

The nature of planning

According to Williams (1998) the aim of modern planning is to seek optimal solutions to perceived problems and it is designed to increase and, hopefully, maximize development benefits, which will produce predictable outcomes. Williams (1998: 126) claimed planning 'is an ordered sequence of operations and actions that are designed to realise one single goal or a set of interrelated goals'. Hence, according to Williams, planning is, or should be, a process: for anticipating and ordering change; that is forward looking; that seeks optimal solutions; that is designed to increase and ideally maximize possible development benefits; and that will produce predictable outcomes.

However, planning is a very difficult term to define, particularly as it can be used in a variety of contexts. Hence, it can be used in connection with individuals, groups, organizations and governments. It can be used in relation to different geographical settings, such as urban and rural, as well as being applied at different scales such as local, regional and national. A plan can mean, for example, little more than partially thought through ideas that are barely articulated, or a complex, carefully considered and presented document. Hall, P. (1992: 1) suggested that this is where part of the problem with the concept of planning arises. As he stated: 'Although people realise that planning has a more general meaning, they tend to remember the idea of the plan as a physical representation or design.'

This focus on the plan as a physical design has probably contributed to the failure to recognize the importance of the processes involved, i.e. the processes that have led to the creation of the actual physical plan. However, a focus on planning as a process, rather than with a consideration of its product, can lead to planning being considered rather vague and abstract (Gunn, 1988). Nevertheless, it is the process element of planning that is particularly important. McCabe *et al.* (2000) argued strongly that planning is a process when they suggested a plan provides direction. As they indicated:

> A plan . . . enables us to identify where we are going and *how to get there* [emphasis added] – in other words it should clarify the path that is to be taken and the outcomes or end results. It also draws attention to the stages on the way and . . . helps to set and establish priorities that can assist in the scheduling of activities.
>
> (McCabe *et al.*, 2000: 235)

One of the key elements of the process of planning is decision-making (Veal, 1994; Hall, 2000a). As Veal (1994: 3) stated, 'planning can be seen as the process of deciding'. Hall (2000a) suggested that this process is not straightforward, as he claimed these decisions are interdependent and systematically related and not just individual decisions. The process of planning involves 'bargaining, negotiation, compromise, coercion, values, choice and politics' (Hall, 2000a: 7).

Hall (2000a) stated that decision-making is part of a continuum that follows directly from planning and this, in turn, is followed by action. Gunn (1988) believed that action was a very important part of planning and employed the ideas of Lang (1985) to differentiate between strategic planning and conventional planning. Lang (1985) suggested that conventional planning separates the planning from the implementation stage, has only vague goals, is reactive rather than proactive, periodic rather than consistent and fails to consider the values of those individuals and organizations involved. Strategic planning, however, according to Lang is action-oriented, focused, ongoing, proactive and considers the values of those involved.

Wilkinson (1997) suggested that a plan provides the rationale for and details of how implementation will take place within a country or region, and sets this within a wider economic and social context. He also indicated that planning involves not only the formulation of plans and their implementation, but also their supervision and review.

Hall (2000a) argued that the most important aspect of planning is that it is directed towards the future. He used the ideas of Chadwick to support this. As Chadwick (1971: 24) suggested, 'planning is a process, a process of human thought and action based upon that thought – in point of fact, forethought, thought for the future, nothing more or less than this is planning'. Gunn (1988: 15) also indicated that planning is clearly forward looking when he stated it requires 'some estimated perception of the future'.

Planning and policy

Planning and policy are closely related terms. Wilkinson (1997) linked planning and policy when stating planning is a course of action, while policy is the implementation of the planned course of action. Policy is usually created by and emanates from a public body or organization. Such public policy is a major concern of government activity. As Wilkinson (1997) indicated, policy is a course of action adopted by an agency, such as a government body. Public policy is, therefore, what governments decide to do or not to do (Dye, 1992).

However, it is important to note that planning is not just a process conducted by government. Private sector organizations (in tourism this would include, for example, tour operators and airlines) prepare careful plans and usually have a number of policies through which they operationalize these plans. Hence, as Elliot (1997) indicated, planning covers private as well as government and public enterprise.

Public policy, by definition, is in the public domain, while the policies of individual organizations are often protected because of commercial concerns and may not be so easily discerned. In relation to public policy, it is important to recognize that it is not created in a vacuum, but is greatly influenced by the social, economic and environmental context in which it is created, as well as the governmental structures and nature of the political regime. Therefore, it is important to realize that policy results from political structures, value systems, institutional frameworks, the distribution of power and the decision-making process (Simeon, 1976; Hall and Jenkins, 1995).

Values and planning

The section above on policy and planning suggested that values are important in planning. As Hall (2000a) argued, the standpoint or value position in relation to planning must not be ignored. A similar view was put forward by Healey (1997: 29) who indicated that public policy and planning are 'social processes through which ways of thinking, ways of valuing and ways of acting are actively constructed by participants'.

Both Gunn (1988) and Veal (1994) suggested that planning for recreation and tourism relies heavily on values, and each argued that community values are particularly important. Therefore, it is essential, they claimed, that a recreation and/or tourism policy should reflect the values of stakeholders and interested parties.

However, if planning is intended to represent the views of all stakeholders and interested parties, then it should be obvious that there will not automatically be unanimity and homogeneity in values and views. Nevertheless, Wilkinson (1997) claimed that much thinking and writing about planning tends to assume that it is a straightforward, virtually value-free, scientific process. He noted in relation to conventional definitions of planning that:

> emphasis [is] on a straightforward approach that accepts the (positivist) possibility of comprehensive rationality. Such a process assumes several factors: consensus on objectives, lack of uncertainty, known alternatives, a high degree of centralised control, and ample time and money to prepare a plan.

> (Wilkinson, 1997: 24)

Wilkinson argued such factors rarely exist in any planning situation, and are unlikely to be found in tourism planning. Similar views were put forward by Cullingsworth (1997) who indicated the implications of the meeting of differing value systems in the planning process. As Cullingsworth (1997: 5) claimed:

> Rational planning is a theoretical idea. Actual planning is a practical exercise of political choice that involves beliefs and values. It is a laborious process in which many public and private agencies are concerned. These comprise a wide range of conflicting interests. Planning is a means by which attempts are made to resolve these conflicts.

Wildavsky (1987) also stressed the importance of recognizing that planning is not a rational activity. Hall, P. (1992) argued very strongly that planning is not a tidy process as posited by theorists of the activity. He indicated that a key problem is trying to predict the future when there are conflicts of values. He added to this that there is the problem of the interaction of decisions made in different spheres of public policy, and there is the clash of organized pressure groups with the defence of vested interests. Hence, Hall, P. (1992: 246) argued: 'The systems view of planning is therefore a condition to which planners aim but will never be the reality.'

Several of the processes referred to by Hall are related to conflict resolution and can be seen as very much part of a wider political process. Jenkins (1997) also indicated that planning is very much a political process. As he stated, a plan is: 'a document that has been the focus of political debate and is available to the public' (Jenkins, 1997: 25). The relationship between planning and policy in relation to differing values and the wider political context is discussed in the next section.

Planning and policy in leisure, recreation and tourism

Leisure planning

As tourism is a recreational activity that takes place in leisure time, planning in the leisure area usually includes both recreation and tourism (Spink, 1994; Veal, 1994; Hall and Page, 1999). Therefore, tourism planning can be seen to fit within the wider context of leisure planning and the planning framework for tourism can be seen to fall within leisure. However, tradition-ally there has been a split between outdoor recreation and tourism provision, with the former being provided by the public sector and the latter by the private sector (Hall and Jenkins, 1995). However, from the mid-1980s onwards this distinction began to disappear in Western countries (Hall and Page, 1999). Today, in relation to tourism provision, there is much overlap between the public and private sectors in many countries. However, this tends to create com-plications in terms of responsibilities for planning.

The planning process adopted in the leisure field tends to display the same characteristics as those found in planning more generally, in that it is often disjointed and reactive. However, it is complicated by the fact that the process may involve a variety of land-owners, public bod-ies and private providers, as well as different user groups (Glyptis, 1994; Veal, 1994; Williams, 1998). This means that the process is complex and at times difficult to operationalize. Within the British context, Veal (1994) identified three phases of leisure planning: the 'demand phase' (1960–1972) which was in response to a rapidly growing population base; the 'need phase' (1973–1985) which saw the focus on the needs of particular groups; and the 'enterprise phase' (from 1985 to the mid-1990s) which saw the rise of private providers, with the govern-ment seeking to distance itself from leisure provision.

Spink (1994) introduced the concept of leisure action spaces, which range from the home, through the local neighbourhood and the region, to national and international levels. Within these spaces, individuals have the choice of pursuing various leisure options, including visiting heritage sites, resorts and the countryside. With a focus on the United Kingdom, he argued that most leisure/recreation activities take place within urban areas, including the urban fringes such as country parks, green-belt areas, footpaths and bridleways.

However, by definition, those classified as involved in leisure/recreation activities in their home area will be residents of the area; those who have travelled into an area will be classi-fied as tourists (see Mason, 1995; Cooper et al., 1998). Therefore, planning for tourism is likely to be targeted at different visitor groups and involve different processes (Mason, 1995). The nature of tourism planning is discussed next.

Tourism planning

In the early 1980s, the key aims of tourism planning were summarized in the following way: 'to ensure that opportunities are available for tourists to gain enjoyable and satisfying experiences and at the same time to provide a means for improving the way of life for residents and of destination areas' (Matthieson and Wall, 1982: 186).

In the late 1990s, Williams (1998) suggested a number of general aims for tourism planning. He indicated that it can help to shape and control physical patterns of development, conserve scarce resources, provide a framework for active promotion and marketing of destinations and can be a mechanism to integrate tourism with other sectors. More specifically, Williams (1998) suggested that tourism planning has a number of key objectives. These are, he suggested, as follows:

- The creation of a mechanism for the structured provision of tourist facilities over quite large geographic areas.
- The coordination of the fragmented nature of tourism (particularly in relation to accommodation, transport, marketing and human resources).
- Certain interventions to conserve resources and maximize benefits to the local community in an attempt to achieve sustainability (usually through a tourism development or management plan).
- The redistribution of tourism benefits (the development of new tourism sites or the economic realignment of places that tourists have begun to leave).

Williams also considered that tourism planning, as part of an integrated plan involving other human activities, gives tourism a political significance and hence provides legitimacy to an activity, which has not always been accorded this status. Planning can also be an attempt to match supply and demand for tourism services/activities (Williams, 1998).

Much early tourism planning was very site specific and linked to the supply side (or destination end) of tourism activity (Gunn, 1988). This geographical focus helps to explain the rationale often provided for tourism planning. Williams (1998) provided such a rationale when he stated that there is now enough evidence around the world to suggest that unplanned tourist destinations are those associated with negative impacts. In seeking to justify a rationale for tourism planning, Jenkins (1991) argued that all countries should have a planning process in place, to make use of resources in a wise and efficient manner.

However, planning for recreation and tourism has not necessarily been a straightforward process (Gunn, 1988; Spink, 1994; Veal, 1994; Coccossis, 1996; Williams, 1998). Williams (1998) suggested that a major problem of tourism planning is that it encompasses many activities and although it may address physical, economic, environmental and business concerns it does not necessarily blend these together well. Coccossis (1996) concurs with this view and argued that one of the activities relating to tourism planning, environmental conservation, was seen as being a threat to economic and social development for most of the period up until the mid-1990s and still is viewed in this way, particularly by some sections of the tourism industry (Mason, 2013a). Similar concerns are associated with outdoor recreation planning, where the increasing pressures on limited environmental resources have led to environmental degradation (Chavez, 1997; Hammitt and Cole, 1998) and conflict between different user groups (Moore, 1994; Hendricks, 1995; Ramthun, 1995; Watson, 1995). Reference to conflict infers that tourism planning is a political process. Hall (2000a) supported this view when he argued that tourism policy is what governments decide to do or not do about tourism. Gunn (1988) and Veal (1994) also confirmed that tourism planning is very much a political process.

Fennell (1999) argued that tourism planning requires a policy, which states the aims and objectives to be implemented in the planning process. This is similar to Gunn's (1988) view and he went on to suggest that for plans to be implemented governance is required. Fennell (1999) further stated that implementation is usually done by governments. However, Lickorish (1991) claimed that government has often viewed the responsibility of tourism policy as lying with the private sector. Williams (1998) and Hall and Jenkins (1995) also discussed this problem, and indicated that recreation and tourism planning increasingly involves both public and private sector bodies. Gunn (1988) suggested that this mix of private and public sector responsibility for planning is one of several reasons why tourism planning has not been as effective as planners may have wished.

As with policy in generic terms, tourism policy involves a number of ideas and statements that can be implemented via a tourism plan (Wilkinson, 1997). However, Hirschmann (1976) suggested tourism policy is different from many other policies created by government and suggested that one of the reasons tourism policy is different from other forms of policy is that unlike agrarian reform and some industrial policies that are forced on government, tourism policy is chosen. It is also different from policies like industrial policy because there tends to be little conflict, at least not in the initial stages (Hirschmann, 1976). An industrial policy of restructuring may involve job losses, environmental change and attempts to relocate industry. This will clearly lead to at least controversy and possible conflict and strife. This is not the way tourism policy has been perceived, as, Hirschmann claimed, unlike industrial policy, tourism policy is not linked to major problem solving such as the economic and social changes associated with, for example, the closure of a coal mine or steel works.

Almost 80 years ago, Lasswell (1936) indicated that the core issues in politics are who gets what, where, when, how and why. This view is still highly relevant today, but Richter (1989) argued that tourism policies have rarely been conceived of and scrutinized in terms of Lasswell's core political issues. Hence, tourism policy may be viewed as 'simple' by those whose job it is to create and implement it (Wilkinson, 1997). However, as Cooper et al. (2005) suggested, the process of tourism planning is not simple, although it may well follow a systematic approach. Cooper et al. (2005) indicated that tourism planning in many developed countries and some developing countries follows a number of stages, which are fairly consistent, and these are shown in Figure 7.1. A discussion of each of these stages follows.

In Stage 1 of Figure 7.1, there needs to be recognition by the planning authority, which is often a government body, but may be a private industry, that tourism is a desirable development option, and also recognition that there are likely to be constraints to development. Once this has been achieved there needs to be a clear understanding of the objectives of the plan (Stage 2). These could include the following: to distribute economic benefits to as many as possible in the host community; to increase employment in tourism; to develop a tourism product which attracts a good cross-section of both domestic and international tourists; to aid the development of peripheral regions; to preserve cultural and natural resources. These goals need to be clear, not conflicting, and achievable.

In Stage 3, in terms of surveying existing data, as Cooper et al. (2005) indicated, it is often the case that data of a tourism nature are held by bodies that are not specifically concerned with tourism. This means that searching for relevant secondary data in as many locations as possible is necessary. Once the existing data are known then new surveys can be planned if, as is likely, they are required. The requirements of tourism planning are likely to be comprehensive and therefore surveys in Stage 4 may include: tourist attractions, tourist travel patterns, tourists' socio-demographic characteristics, accommodation facilities and services, environmental indicators, socio-cultural characteristics, education and training needs.

In terms of the analysis of both secondary and primary data in Stage 5, Cooper et al. (2005) suggested that there are usually several major themes. Asset evaluation involves an examination

Stage 1 Recognizing the need for a tourism plan/strategy
What is the issue/problem being addressed by the plan?

Stage 2 Setting objectives/goals for a specific planning strategy
Why do we need (this type of) tourism development?

Stage 3 Survey of existing data
What do we already know from our sources of information?

Stage 4 Implementation of new surveys
What new information do we need and how shall we obtain it?

Stage 5 Analysis of secondary and primary data
What have we learned from our research?

Stage 6 Initial policy and plan creation

Stage 7 Recommendations of the plan

Stage 8 Implementation of the plan

Stage 9 Monitoring, evaluation and re-formulation

Figure 7.1 The process of planning in tourism, showing stages and related questions

of what tourism assets currently exist and how these can be developed, but also the possible constraints to development. The infrastructure for tourism would also be included in this evaluation. Market analysis is an attempt to find out the type of tourists currently visiting and why they come. The particular geographical entity being planned may need to be compared with other similar competing locations. Impact analysis will be an attempt to examine the likely effects the planned development will have on the local community, the environment and economy. This may lead to the creation of an instrument for forecasting likely changes. In this phase, there is also a theme which is concerned with the timing of the actual development and will involve issues such as funding for the development, the number of staff (foreign and domestic) and the organizational structure. Stage 6 is the plan creation and formulation, according to Cooper *et al.* (2005). It is most likely that the analysis of secondary and primary data will lead to a number of possible development options and not just one. The alternative plans would then be evaluated according to specific criteria such as economic benefits, socio-cultural and environmental impacts. Some form of cost–benefit analysis of each possible development strategy would then be conducted, which would probably lead to a 'preferred' plan. In Stage 7, this preferred plan would then be sent for comment to relevant authorities or a possible a set of recommendations would be provided. Discussions would then take place between the planners and authorities and this should lead to a final development plan.

It is most likely that the method of implementation of the plan will have been considered well in advance of actual implementation (Stage 8), Cooper *et al.* (2005) suggested. Hence the regulatory and legislative controls will be brought into effect at this time. Mechanism for public debate and discussions about the planned development would also be in place. The final stage of the plan in action is monitoring and evaluation (Stage 9). Monitoring is partly to examine if there have been any deviations from the original plan, particularly to investigate if this leads to a diversion from the initial objectives, and also to understand the effects of unexpected events including outbreaks of diseases, natural hazards such as volcanic explosions or tsunamis, as well as warfare and terrorism. The implementation team can then react to any unexpected changes and feed back this information to bodies such as government to ensure that the plan stays on target.

Cooper *et al.* (2005) also stressed that to ensure that the planning process is successful, the nature of the team of planners is very important. They will need a good deal of expertise and experience, they suggested. The team should contain physical planners, economists, market planners, social scientists, environmental scientists, engineers, draughtsmen and legal experts (Cooper *et al.*, 2005).

Figure 7.1 can be viewed as a summary of what the stages of tourism planning are likely to be in general terms, but the following case study provides more specific details on the nature of tourism planning. It shows the ways in which local communities in Northern Canada are provided with information on the processes of tourism planning, by a government body. This case study is based upon advice given by the Ministry of Canadian Indian and Northern Affairs to local communities that wish to either establish new forms of tourism, or gain greater benefits from existing tourism activities.

Case study: developing a tourism action plan for a local community

A tourism action plan defines the who, what, where, when and how of making tourism happen. It provides the framework for businesses, local government and other organizations to analyse tourism resources and concerns and to encourage development in your community.

There are five main components to the action plan:

1 *Attractions*: natural and built features.
2 *Promotion*: marketing tools and promotional activities.
3 *Infrastructure*: transport, water and power, community facilities.
4 *Services*: hotels, motels, shops, restaurants, campsites.
5 *Hospitality*: this influences tourists' perception of their stay and whether they are likely to return.

The processes of developing the plan are outlined next.

Phase 1: *identify present tourism markets*

A community needs reliable information on what the current state of tourism actually is. As well as identifying facilities for tourists that currently exist it should ascertain why tourists visit, where they stay, how long they stay, how they travel to the community and how much money they spend.

Phase 2: *develop market profiles*

This is to gather accurate data on precisely which types of tourist come to the community and their relative importance to the community. The tourism assets of the community should be recorded using the five main components above (attractions, promotion, infrastructure, services and hospitality). In addition concerns about tourism development should be recorded under headings such as negative assets and liabilities. New ideas about possible assets/liabilities may also emerge at this time.

(continued)

Case study: developing a tourism action plan for a local community (continued)

Phase 3: *determine potential markets*

This involves looking at possibilities for increasing existing tourism, by clearly identifying strengths, weaknesses, opportunities and threats based on current knowledge and specifically using the five key components of the plan (see above).

Phase 4: *state tourism goals and objectives*

These should be clear statements on the type of tourism the community wants. They are likely to contain phrases such as: 'to improve tourism . . .'.

Phase 5: *develop action steps*

These are the specific action steps to achieve the goals and objectives.

Phase 6: *involve your community*

The draft tourism plan should be sent to members of the community to review and discuss.

Phase 7: *implement the action plan*

This should only be done after it has received support from the local community, elected officials, private industry and relevant groups and individuals outside the local community, including consultants and experts.

Phase 8: *monitor the results*

Procedures for monitoring success or failure of the plan should be in place before implementation begins. Monitoring should be conducted in relation to specific goals and objectives and should be done on a regular basis.

(Based on Indian and Northern Affairs, 2004.)

Although this case study is located in Canada, and is targeted specifically at local communities, it reveals many similarities with the generic planning approach discussed by Cooper *et al.* (2005), particularly in terms of the nature and sequencing of the planning stages and the actual processes occurring within each stage.

A key issue with tourism planning is that it operates at a number of scales, from national, through regional down to the local level. This can contribute to problems of coordination. Hence, in relation to the Canadian case study above, it may be relatively easy to create and operationalize a plan at the local level, but at regional and national levels this can be far more difficult. The following case study discusses planning at the national level, using New Zealand as the example, and provides an indication that the process of tourism planning at the national level is not that straightforward.

Case study: tourism planning in New Zealand

Planning in New Zealand

The key piece of legislation relating to planning in New Zealand is the Resource Management Act (RMA), which became law in 1991 and replaced 59 previous resource and planning statutes. The RMA provides a legislative framework for planning for and managing land, air, water, coastal, geothermal and pollution issues under one umbrella. The overall aim of the RMA is to promote sustainable management, whilst at the same time it is developing and protecting resources which enable social and economic well-being (Gow, 1995).

Under the RMA, planning for and the management of natural and physical resources is delegated to regional and local authorities. Locally, the district or city councils are responsible for developing a district plan, which identifies community objectives over a 10-year period and specifies the processes for achieving these (Page and Thorn, 1997). The Conservation Act 1987 requires the Department of Conservation (DOC) to prepare management plans for all the land under its jurisdiction, which currently is around one-third of New Zealand. This is important because a significant amount of outdoor recreation and tourism takes place on the DOC land. In some areas of New Zealand, DOC land is adjacent to local or regional council land, which may require some cooperation between agencies in terms of the policies and practices adopted in each area.

Leisure planning and tourism in New Zealand

Much leisure planning in New Zealand has been associated with the provision of sport and recreation facilities in the form of playing fields, recreation centres and swimming pools (Department of Tourism, Sport and Racing, 1994). However, whilst local government allocates money to managing these recreation facilities and open spaces, only a small amount tends to be invested in planning. This has resulted in an ad hoc approach to leisure planning, rather than one which involves integrating a number of information sources, so as to ensure policy decisions are based on informed decisions (Department of Tourism, Sport and Racing, 1994). Since the early 1990s, issues associated with sustainability have emerged in recreation planning. Accompanying the socio-economic and political changes occurring in urban and regional areas of New Zealand, have come questions of not only environmental, but also social and economic sustainability. It is argued, therefore, that leisure planning needs to be seen in the wider political context and integrated with local and regional planning, rather than be regarded as an optional extra (Department of Tourism, Sport and Racing, 1994).

Most initial approaches by recreation and tourism providers are made to local councils, as they are responsible for determining the effects of land use under their jurisdiction according to the RMA. Page and Thorn's (1997) study suggested that research with respect to tourism is undertaken by over half of all councils in New Zealand. The majority of this research focused on visitor numbers, with little being conducted in the area of resource sustainability or visitor satisfaction. Dymond (1997: 289) came to similar conclusions in his research and his findings suggested that 'local resident satisfaction is only being measured within a third of local authority areas . . . indirect sources are dominant, for example local authority strategic plan consultations and resident satisfaction surveys'.

(continued)

Case study: tourism planning in New Zealand (continued)

He concluded that more research needed to be centred on supply related issues, which consider the sustainability of the tourism resource base.

In relation to tourism planning, it is often regarded as something that appears to be conducted retrospectively rather than in a proactive manner. In the New Zealand context, Page and Thorn (1997: 70) suggested 'that tourism is identified as an activity requiring promotion, rather than something which requires strategic planning'. Similar approaches to tourism planning have been noted in other parts of the developed world (see Butler, 1991; Dymond, 1997). Furthermore, the RMA encourages a focus on individual project impacts, which in turn has meant that local recreation and tourism planning often takes place on an 'as required' basis, rather than as part of an integrated approach (Page and Thorn, 1997).

Of particular importance in New Zealand is that the nature of regional and local planning rarely falls squarely into either urban or rural contexts. More often than not, local councils have to address planning issues associated with semi-rural or semi-urban environments. This in itself requires councils to take a broader approach to planning issues associated with their area, than may be the case in, for example, the United Kingdom or other European countries.

Whether the planning issue under consideration in New Zealand is recreation or tourism focused, urban or rural, it appears that there is a need for an integrated proactive approach to planning. The RMA has only been in existence for nearly a quarter of a century and may be the appropriate vehicle for more integrated planning. As Page and Thorn (1997: 64–5) suggested, 'the RMA should encourage public sector planners to adopt a more holistic view of development and the way in which tourism affects the environment and population within a sustainable framework' (see Photo 7.1).

Photo 7.1 The Lido, Palmerston North, New Zealand. Swimming pools are usually designated as part of the remit of planning in leisure. They tend to be in public ownership and serve a local market. However, they also cater for tourists and may be in private ownership. This indicates just one of the problems of planning for the leisure/tourism field.

(Adapted from Mason and Leberman, 1998.)

Planning and management

The case study of New Zealand gives an indication of specific links between tourism planning and tourism management. This section discusses the links between planning and management in generic terms, and is followed by a discussion in greater detail on tourism planning and management.

As with the term planning, management also has a number of different definitions. Gilbert *et al.* (1995: 8) defined the activity in the following way: 'Management is a goal-oriented process that involves the allocation of resources and the coordination of the talents and efforts of a group of people.'

Gilbert *et al.* (1995) indicated a major link between planning and management. As they noted, one of the key activities involved in managing is planning. They suggested that managing is the first part of a process that also involves organizing, empowering and controlling. They further elaborated their ideas on managing by suggesting that it is in reality a cyclical process, with a link back from controlling to planning. They also argued that each of activities in any given situation may be ongoing simultaneously and therefore each is not an entirely discrete process.

Similar views on the nature of management and its links with planning have been expounded by Doswell (1997). Doswell suggested that there is a well-established way of looking at the functions of management, and this is based on one of the earliest thinkers in management theory, the French writer Fayol.

Doswell indicated the functions of management are as follows: planning, organizing, giving direction, providing coordination and monitoring. Doswell claimed planning is about what one is trying to achieve, organization is concerned with mobilizing and deploying resources, giving direction relates to the provision of leadership and maintenance of a sense of purpose, while coordination is the provision of a unifying force and monitoring is a control function achieved through the reporting and analysis of results.

Hall and Page (1999) also recognized this link between planning and management. They suggested that strategic planning can be regarded as a process that involves concurrently integrating planning and management. In essence, this means that the proactive approach of planning should be intertwined with the – frequently reactive – reality of management. However, even this relationship is not that straightforward. As Mason and Leberman (2000) indicated, there is evidence that planning policies have been put in place without considering the issue in detail beforehand. Hence, they noted, planning, in many cases, is reactive rather than proactive, particularly when policy documents are often prepared for a 5–10-year period. This means that the information in the plan is dated by the time it takes effect and new issues may have arisen in the interim.

If management is perceived as a goal-oriented process, then it is necessary to have some measure of its effectiveness in relation to these goals (Gilbert *et al.*, 1995). The performance of management is therefore part of the management process and is in effect a measure of the quality of management. As Gilbert *et al.* argued, there are two factors that should be measured in relation to the quality or effectiveness of management. These are as follows: how well has the process been aimed at appropriate goals and how well has the process been managed in terms of use of resources (Gilbert *et al.*, 1995: 19)?

Tourism management

Many standard works on management refer to the activity being about people. Such works are usually concerned with the management of businesses or companies and one important aspect of tourism management has a specific focus on people who work in tourism. This is usually referred to as functional management and can be seen as a part of strategic management (see Moutinho, 2000). However, tourism management is also concerned with ways to manage the resources for tourism, the interaction of tourists with physical resources and the interaction of tourists with residents of tourist areas (Mason, 1995). This focus of tourism management is concerned primarily with tourism impacts in resort areas or tourism destinations. It is in such areas that the supply side of tourism (physical resources, built environment and resident population) interacts with the demand side (often summarized as the market side, but which is made up of tourists, travel agents, tour operators, transport operators, tourist boards and tourism developers). It is this aspect of tourism management, the management of tourism impacts, rather than the management of people in tourism businesses, with which this book is primarily concerned.

The definition of tourism management that is particularly useful in this book is that produced by Middleton (1994). Middleton's definition is as follows: 'Strategies and action programmes using and coordinating available techniques to control and influence tourism supply and visitor demand in order to achieve defined policy goals' (Middleton, cited in Middleton and Hawkins,1998: 84).

To a great extent, it is possible to say that tourism management is what tourism planners are, or should be, engaged in (Doswell, 1997). However, as Doswell indicated, tourism planning and tourism management are often treated as separate activities. Doswell claimed that this is due to planning being linked to physical planners. In this case, planning is not seen as an ongoing process of management, but a one-off activity which precedes the construction of whatever was planned (Doswell, 1997). In the context of developing countries, Doswell indicated that such a one-off plan is likely to be a master plan. Doswell distinguished between master plans and ongoing planning and argued that a master plan is created prior to construction and may not involve any ongoing monitoring. Doswell also argued that only ongoing planning in tourism is likely to be satisfactory in relation to tourism management. As he stated:

> The whole concept of a planning process means there is no end as such, only a beginning. It means that things, once studied and agreed, can start to be implemented. Action can be taken from the start. It also means that committees and working groups, organised to consult on an initial plan, can be left in place to play an ongoing role.
>
> (Doswell, 1997: 184)

In practical terms, Middleton and Hawkins (1998) indicated tourism management is concerned with procedures to influence five variables that are as follows: location, timing, access, products and education. Middleton and Hawkins suggested in relation to location that there may be too few, or too many, visitors and tourist businesses in a particular destination. In relation to timing, they indicated there may be too many or too few visitors, at particular places at particular times of the day, week or month. They indicated that access relates to the relative ease or difficulty and associated cost of reaching chosen places. They suggested that there could be too many or too few products in a particular location and perhaps a lack of infrastructure to support certain products. Education is concerned with the awareness of the cumulative behaviour of visitors and tourism businesses and awareness of residents' wishes for the destination, Middleton and Hawkins (1998) indicated.

Middleton and Hawkins (1998: 85) provided a good summary of tourism management in practice when they stated: 'Tourism management focuses on ways and means to influence visitors' choices of location, access, timing and product provision, and to develop local understanding and knowledge.' The reality of 'influencing visitors' choices' means ways to persuade tourists and tourism businesses to voluntarily change their naturally occurring behaviour where 'naturally occurring behaviour ' is what people do when exercising their instincts and choices in a free society (Middleton and Hawkins, 1998). Changing this behaviour may require selected inducements, or by obliging people and businesses to change through the imposition of regulations, controls, taxes or penalties of various types (Mason and Mowforth, 1996; Middleton and Hawkins, 1998).

In most countries, controlling visitor numbers at destinations is beyond the influence of either public sector bodies, such as tourist boards, or private sector organizations. In some cases control can be exerted by such methods as high entrance charges to attractions and/or limited car parking spaces. However, in the majority of destinations, such draconian measures are not employed. Instead, what Middleton and Hawkins (1998: 85) term 'selective influences and control' are used. These are designed to achieve stated and quantified objectives at destinations. They are as follows:

- making judgments on carrying capacity;
- selecting and targeting particular market segments or groups;
- identifying partner organizations in planning and marketing for tourism;
- developing a variety of management techniques for visitor segments and products;
- systematically monitoring results and making any required changes.

These selective influences and controls are shown in Figure 7.2. The left-hand column shows examples of mainly public sector resource constraints, while the right-hand column shows controls as market forces, which are primarily associated with the private sector.

A major concern in relation to the use of selective influences and controls is having the relevant information to make appropriate decisions. Research information for targeting and monitoring at the local level is vital (Mason and Leberman, 2000; Leberman and Mason, 2002). However, much planning and management in the recreation and tourism fields would appear to take place without the required information (Mason and Leberman, 2000). Mason and Leberman argued that it is necessary to start the planning process by gathering information about the issue concerned. This process should involve conducting proactive wide-ranging research and in particular consulting with relevant stakeholders, which then enables a decision to be made based on the information collected, they suggested. The gathering of data as a significant part of tourism management is also advocated by Middleton and Hawkins (1998).

Resource constraints (supply orientation) mainly public sector	Market forces (demand orientation) mainly commercial sector
Regulation of land use	Knowledge of visitor profiles, behaviour, needs and trends
Regulation of buildings	Design of visitor products (quality and satisfaction)
Regulation of environmental impacts	Capacity (products marketed)
Provision of infrastructure	Promotion (image/positioning)
Control by licensing	Distribution of products/access for customers
Provision of information	Provision of information
Fiscal controls and incentives	Price

Figure 7.2 Resource constraints and market forces: tourism management controls and influences at destinations

Source: Based on Pearce (1989) and Middleton (1994).

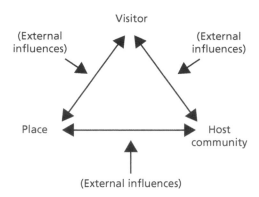

Figure 7.3 The triangle of three major components in tourism management
Source: adapted from ETB (1991).

In the early 1990s, the English Tourist Board (ETB) produced an influential report on the relationship between tourism and the environment (ETB, 1991). The report included a triangle which can be considered to be at the heart of all approaches to tourism management. This triangle is shown in Figure 7.3 and indicates that the three major components to be taken into consideration in tourism management are as follows: the visitor, the host community and the environment. Figure 7.3 shows how these three factors are inter-related and significantly impact upon each other. Although the triangle is relatively simplistic, it does 'neatly encapsulate the three main focal points for management decisions' (Middleton and Hawkins, 1998: 86).

However, the situation is somewhat more complex than this. There are more than just visitors and residents interacting with the environment (Middleton and Hawkins, 1998). In addition, there are elected representatives and appointed officials, as well as tourism-related businesses that need to be taken into account. The elected representatives and appointed officials are responsible to residents for the goals and management of a destination. Businesses involved include accommodation providers, cafés, restaurants and hotels as well as transport providers and visitor attractions. Middleton and Hawkins (1998) also indicated that residents will be made up of different interest groups and visitors will possibly comprise a number of different market segments. They stressed the importance of recognizing this variety of stakeholders or the nature of the 'players' in tourism, particularly with reference to attempts to achieve sustainable tourism practices.

Swarbrooke (1999) produced a very similar set of stakeholders in tourism management to that suggested by Middleton and Hawkins. In addition to the 'players' provided by Middleton and Hawkins, he also included the voluntary sector, particularly pressure groups and professional bodies, as well as the media.

Much of this discussion concerning tourism management has implied a major separation between the public and the private sector. However, there is significant evidence of the importance of partnerships in tourism management (Bramwell and Lane, 2000). Such partnerships may involve the voluntary sector as well as links between private organizations and public bodies (Mason *et al.*, 2000b). Partnerships are likely to be particularly significant in future attempts to achieve sustainable tourism practices (Bramwell and Lane, 2000). While the private sector is likely to have the best information about demand and also influential marketing techniques, the public sector should be most aware of acceptable levels of tourism impacts and be able to apply sanctions in relation to agreed resource capacities.

Tourism planning, management and sustainability

Many publications and much research in the last decade of the twentieth century and the first years of the twenty-first century focusing on tourism planning and management, were concerned with issues relating to planning, management and sustainability. The concept of sustainability emerged from ideas on sustainable development (Fennell, 1999; Holden, 2000). One of the more influential early statements came at the World Conference on Environment and Development (WCED) in 1987 in which it was stated that sustainable development 'meets the goals of the present without compromising the ability of future generations to meet their own needs' (WCED, 1987: 43).

One of the first public action strategies on tourism and sustainability came from the Globe 90 conference held in Canada. Conference delegates suggested five goals of sustainable tourism. These are as follows (Fennell, 1999: 14):

1   to develop greater awareness and understanding of the significant contribution tourism can make to environment and economy;
2   to promote equity and development;
3   to improve the quality of life of the host community;
4   to provide a high quality of experience for the visitor;
5   to maintain the quality of the environment.

However, the concept of sustainable tourism did not remain constant, but changed during the last decade of the twentieth century and early twenty-first century. Depending on the author, the target audience and the context in which statements have been made, emphasis has been placed on environmental factors, social factors or economic factors. For some commentators, sustainable tourism relates primarily to community issues, for others it is about jobs and the tourism industry, yet others are more concerned with conserving threatened environments. These changing approaches have contributed to a realization that attempting to sustain jobs, host communities and the local environment are potentially conflicting aims and, hence, are not necessarily achievable (Holden, 2013).

The concept of sustainability has also been applied in tourism at a variety of scales and in both the public and private sectors (Holden, 2000). Therefore, there is now a significant literature on sustainable tourism but much of this is theoretical and there is often a large gap between theory and practice. As long ago as the early 1990s, Butler (1991) made a sobering observation when he argued that whatever its origins and aims, all tourism tends towards mass tourism and as Fennell (1999) argued, despite the rhetoric, it would appear that few sustainable tourism projects have withstood the test of time. Adding to this is the contribution that disasters (either natural or human induced) can make to supposedly carefully constructed tourism plans (see Faulkner, 2001) and these may challenge concepts of long-term sustainability. The significance of crises and disasters in relation to planning and management is examined in Chapter 18, which focuses on sustainability issues, as despite concerns raised above they remain a key focus for much writing and research in tourism.

Summary

This chapter has indicated that modern planning is a forward-looking, future-oriented activity. In the past, planning was often a largely reactive process in response to perceived problems, but more recently, planning has become a proactive activity. Tourism planning is concerned specifically with ideas on the future of tourism and is, or at least should be, a coherent process of ordering change with the intention of deriving maximum benefits, while minimizing negative effects. Tourism policy is the implementation of a tourism plan. Tourism management involves the day-to-day, ongoing overseeing and monitoring of the effects of a tourism plan and tourism policy. This may suggest a linear relationship, which begins with planning, is followed by policy and this in turn is succeeded by management. However, the relationship between planning and management is somewhat more complex. One of the key roles of managers and therefore important as a major process of management is planning. Hence, planning activities and management processes are likely to be taking place simultaneously in a given context.

Tourism planning and tourism management take place in the real world, where there are different individuals and groups, different value systems, varying and often conflicting interests and the processes of negotiation, coercion, compromise and choice all conspire to ensure that these activities are not necessarily rational or straightforward.

In the last decade of the twentieth century, planning and management in tourism became increasingly linked with ideas on sustainability and this link remains very significant today. However, despite a growing literature in this field, there is still a significant gap between theory and practice.

Student activities

1   What is the relationship between planning and management?
2   What is the relationship between planning and policy?
3   How is tourism planning and management (a) similar to planning and management in general; (b) different from planning and management in general?
4   Compare the information provided in Figure 7.1 and the case study concerned with developing a tourism action plan in Canada. What similarities and what differences are there between the stages and processes shown in Figure 7.1 and the case study?
5   Study the case-study material of New Zealand and indicate why tourism planning in New Zealand is not a straightforward process.
6   Use local media to investigate a planning issue in your local area that has a tourism dimension. Consider the following:

   ● What are the main issues?
   ● Who is involved?
   ● What are the views of those involved?
   ● What are the planning processes?
   ● How does the tourism dimension fit?
   ● What are the links between policy and planning?
   ● What are the links between planning and management?
   ● What are the possible outcomes?
   ● What is your preferred option?

Chapter 8

The key players in tourism planning and management

Learning objectives

At the end of this chapter you should:

- be aware of the key players in tourism management;
- be aware of a number of introductory issues in relation to the key players in tourism planning and management; viz. tourists, the host community, the tourism industry, government agencies, the media and non-governmental organizations (NGOs).

Introduction

Discussion of tourism management requires consideration of a number of factors, including:

- Who is managing?
- What is being managed?
- How is it being managed?
- Where is it happening?
- When is it happening?

These questions are clearly linked and it may be difficult to separate, for example, the 'who' from the 'how' and the 'when' and the 'where'. This chapter concentrates on 'who' is involved.

In relation to those involved, consideration needs to be given to individuals and organizations acting as managers, including government bodies, as well as members of the tourism industry. Tourism management clearly relates to the tourists themselves and will also need to consider the host or resident population. Later chapters present in-depth discussions on the management of tourism, in relation to key players and related issues focusing on:

- the management of tourists/visitors;
- the role of the host community;
- the management of resources for tourism (in particular environmental, social and cultural resources);
- the management of the tourism industry;
- partnerships in tourism planning and management;
- destination management.

Key perspectives

Key players in tourism management

It is possible to suggest that the key players in tourism planning and management are as follows:

- the tourists themselves;
- the host population;
- the tourism industry;
- government agencies (at local, regional, national and international level).

Less obvious players, but nevertheless having very important roles, are voluntary organizations/ NGOs (including charities and pressure groups) and also the media (Swarbrooke, 1999).

The 'ETB triangle' (ETB, 1991) (see Figure 7.3) stresses the importance of both the tourist and the local or host community when discussing the factors influencing management issues in tourism. This chapter initially provides a discussion of the involvement of tourists in relation to planning and management of tourism prior to a discussion of host communities. This is followed by a consideration of the role of government agencies and the tourism industry itself. Finally in this chapter, the focus is on the media and NGOs.

The tourists

Tourists are obviously of key importance in the management of tourism. Unfortunately, tourists are often viewed as the major cause of the problems of tourism. If they are perceived as one homogeneous group, then tourists are a relatively easy target for the so-called evils of tourism. They are 'outsiders' and can be blamed by 'insiders' (the local people) for negative consequences of tourism. When the outward appearance of tourists and their behaviour is in marked contrast to that of the local population, it is also easy to point the finger of blame at them. However, this is rather a simplistic picture. It is possible to argue that tourists have both rights and responsibilities (Swarbrooke, 1999). Figure 8.1 indicates a number of basic responsibilities of tourists and also some others that are linked to the concept of sustainability in tourism, while Figure 8.2 suggests some rights of tourists.

Although there are a number of laws and regulations relating to the operational aspects of the tourism industry, there are few regulations pertaining directly to the behaviour of tourists (Mason and Mowforth, 1996; Swarbrooke, 1999). Hence, the notion of tourists' responsibilities can be seen as rather an alien concept. However, there have been a number of attempts to influence the behaviour of tourists. These usually take the form of voluntary codes of conduct (Mason and Mowforth, 1996) and/or the use of more overt educational approaches (Mason and Christie, 2003; and see Orams, 1995 on the efficacy of such approaches).

Basic responsibilities
- The responsibility for obeying local laws and regulations.
- The responsibility for not taking part in activities which while not illegal, or where the laws are not enforced by the local authorities, are nevertheless, widely condemned by society, such as sex with children.
- The responsibility for not deliberately offending local religious beliefs or cultural norms of behaviour.
- The responsibility for not deliberately harming the local physical environment.
- The responsibility to minimize the use of scarce local resources.

Extra responsibilities of tourists in relation to sustainable tourism
- The responsibility not to visit destinations which have a poor record on human rights.
- The responsibility to find out about the destination before the holiday and try to learn a few words of the local language, at least.
- The responsibility to try to meet local people, learn about their lifestyles and establish friendships.
- The responsibility to protect the natural wildlife by not buying souvenirs made from living creatures, for example.
- The responsibility to abide by all local religious beliefs and cultural values, even those with which the tourist personally disagrees.
- The responsibility to boycott local businesses which pay their staff poor wages, or provide bad working conditions for their employees.
- The responsibility to behave sensibly, so as not to spread infections such as HIV and hepatitis B.
- The responsibility to contribute as much as possible to the local economy.

Figure 8.1 Responsibilities of the tourist
Source: Swarbrooke (1999).

The rights of the tourist	Those who are responsible for protecting these rights
The right to be safe and secure from crime, terrorism and disease	• The host community • Government agencies (e.g. security services and health authorities)
The right not to be discriminated against on the grounds of race, sex or disability	• The host community • The tourism industry • Government agencies (e.g. immigration departments)
The right not to be exploited by local businesses and individuals	• The tourism industry • The host community • Government agencies (e.g. police)
The right to the fair marketing of products through honest travel brochures and advertisements	• The tourism industry • Government agencies (e.g. the advertising regulators)
The right to a safe, clean, physical environment	• The host community • The tourism industry • Government agencies (e.g. environmental bodies and policy departments)
The right to free and unrestricted movement providing that they cause no damage The right to meet local people freely The right to courteous and competent service	• Government agencies (e.g. security services) • Government agencies (e.g. security services) • The host community • The tourism industry

Figure 8.2 The rights of tourists and the responsibilities of the host community, government agencies and the tourism industry. The left-hand column presents the rights and the right-hand column who is responsible for protecting them

Source: Swarbrooke (1999).

Attempts to educate tourists have frequently been linked to concerns about the real and potential impacts that they are perceived to have on the environment and/or the community at the destination. Such attempts have been usually closely linked to what has been termed 'alternative' or 'responsible' tourism, which was developing in the late 1980s (Mowforth, 1992). Creating more responsible tourism was also linked with the growth of ecotourism in the late 1980s (Mason and Mowforth, 1995; Fennell, 1999), which can itself also be viewed as a form of alternative or responsible tourism (Mowforth, 1992)

The use of the term alternative requires an explanation of to what it is an alternative. However, this is not always made clear. Generally the term is attached to forms of tourism that are an alternative to large-scale mass tourism. Hence, alternative tourism would be small scale, non-packaged and involving relatively few people. Such tourism has also been referred to as 'good' tourism (Wood and House, 1991). In the early 1990s, being a 'good' tourist involved travelling independently, out of season, to relatively unknown areas, buying local produce, enjoying local traditions and cultural activities and getting to know local people, as well as taking an interest in the local environment and wildlife (Wood and House, 1991).

An important problem arises here in that such notions of 'good tourism' imply, explicitly or implicitly, that the form of tourism under discussion is better than mass tourism. Clearly a value judgement is being made here. There are a number of criticisms of this anti-mass tourism, pro-'good' tourism stance. As Swarbrooke (1999) claimed, if there is a 'good' tourist then there must be an 'evil' tourist to contrast with the 'good', who either intentionally or accidentally causes harm. In this way, the concept is divisive. Further criticisms include the suggestion that the type of tourism favoured by the good tourist, or at least commentators on good tourism, only appeals to a minority (Wheeler, 1993). Additionally it is argued that as a minority activity, such tourism offers little to established destinations where there are large numbers of visitors and many people are already employed in tourism (Swarbrooke, 1999). Wheeler (1993) also suggested in relation to ecotourism, which he renamed 'egotourism', that it is more likely to make the ecotourist feel better about their involvement, than actually bring benefits to the environment and local communities. Also, there has been little compelling evidence to support the idea that supposed 'good' tourism is any more sustainable in the longer term than mass tourism. Indeed, as Butler (1998) suggested, all forms of tourism tend, over time, towards mass tourism. Therefore, terms such as responsible tourism and ecotourism may be little more than convenient labels which appeal to certain self-righteous consumers and this in turn may help sell more holidays (see Mason and Mowforth, 1996; Fennell, 1999). If this is so, it runs entirely contrary to the principles upon which these forms of tourism are based!

An important factor that this discussion of various forms of tourism has demonstrated is that, unlike what is stated in much popular commentary on tourism, tourists are far from one homogeneous group. There are important demographic variables; for example, it is only necessary to consider 'seniors' travel in comparison with '18–30' activities to grasp this point. Tourism marketing media reveals that different types of holidays are targeted at male and female, heterosexual and homosexual tourists. Tourists engage in very different types of pursuits. Some forms of tourism are very active – sport tourism, for example – while other types are relatively passive, such as sightseeing from a coach. Some activities consume resources and have marked economic, socio-cultural or environmental impacts (McKercher, 1993), while others have minimal consequences. Tourists to one resort may vary according to seasonal factors; skiing in winter and walking in summer in a mountain environment, for example. Additionally, an individual tourist may appear in one particular holiday location, or a number of destinations, in a variety of guises over a period of a week, a month, a year or a life-time.

Regulation of tourist behaviour, the application of codes of conduct, the use of tourist education within tourism planning and management and the nature of ecotourism are discussed in more detail in subsequent chapters.

The host community

Such terminology as 'host community' may be somewhat misleading as it implies that there are guests to complement the supposed hosts. However, as tourists are not always welcome, a more appropriate term could be local community, resident community or destination community. Nevertheless, the term host community is now commonly used in tourism literature and so it is employed here.

As has been indicated in Chapter 5, the host community can act as a major attraction for tourists. More often than not, it is the cultural manifestations of the community, including craft and art works, as well as less tangible factors such as music, dance and religious festivals that act as important attractions. In some cases, actually meeting members of a particular community and staying with them is a key motivation for certain types of tourist. However, as several of the earlier case studies and discussions have indicated, there are a number of dangers that may result from the contact between tourists and host communities, particularly in terms of erosion of host community values and possible loss of cultural identity.

An important aspect of any discussion of host communities is that it would be wrong to assume that there is such a thing as a host community. As has been discussed above in relation to tourists, the host community is heterogeneous not homogeneous. A host community can be made up of long-term indigenous residents and recent domestic as well as international migrants. In addition to obvious variations in gender and age, a host community is likely to have individuals and groups with several different value positions, political persuasions and attitudes to socio-cultural phenomena, including tourism.

Some definitions of host communities refer to a specific geographical area. This would seem a sensible way to define a host community. However, there are problems with this. The geographical extent of the community has to be decided upon. It may be relatively simple when considering a small town or village. In this situation, a local political boundary may serve as the boundary of a community, but even here it is quite possible for one community to spread over several geographical and political boundaries. For example, in New Zealand it is possible to talk about the 'Maori community', which could be all of those with some Maori ancestors in New Zealand. However, the term could refer only to those living in one specific settlement. At the international level, all Maori in the world could be viewed as part of the 'Maori community'.

This discussion may lead to the conclusion that the most appropriate way to define a community is by the values and behaviour that it shares. This approach is, however, problematic as many geographical settlements are made up of majority and minority groups in any one community. Hence, geographical settlements, including many tourist destinations, exhibit variations of community in terms of ethnic background, length of residency, age of residents and levels of income.

In relation to tourism planning and management, if it is acknowledged that communities are heterogeneous, then the importance of different groups and vested interests needs to be recognized. The acceptance of the notion of heterogeneous communities brings with it the realization that the planning and management of tourism is a more complex and yet even more necessary task (see Mason and Cheyne, 2000). In accepting that communities are heterogeneous, Swarbrooke (1999: 125) suggests that they could be divided up in terms of:

- elites and the rest of the population;
- indigenous residents and immigrants;
- those directly involved in tourism and those not involved;
- property owners and property renters;
- younger people and older people;
- employers, employees, self-employed;
- those with private cars, those relying on public transport;
- affluent and less well-off residents;
- majority communities/minority communities.

The preceding discussion may have implied that host communities are passive recipients of tourists. This is not necessarily the case. There are many examples, particularly in developed countries and increasingly in the developing world, where local residents in a tourist destination are actively involved in the provision for tourism and also its planning and management.

By the late 1990s, there was a groundswell of opinion that communities should be involved actively in planning for tourism (Middleton and Hawkins, 1998) and this has continued for the first years of the twenty-first century. However, this is not a particularly recent development. In fact, as long ago as the mid-1980s, Murphy (1985) had argued that as tourism makes use of a community's resources, then the community should be a key player in the process of planning and managing tourism. Swarbrooke (1999) suggested that the rationale for community involvement in tourism is as follows: it is part of the democratic process; it provides a voice for those directly affected by tourism; it makes use of local knowledge to ensure decisions are well informed; and it can reduce potential conflict between tourists and members of the host community.

Nevertheless, the actual involvement of a community in tourism planning and management will depend on a number of factors. These include the following: the nature of the political system at national and local level; the degree of 'political literacy' of the local population; the nature of the particular tourism issue; the awareness of the tourism issue in the community; how the tourism issue is perceived by members of the community; the history of involvement (or lack of it) in tourism-related issues; and the attitudes and behaviour of sections of the media.

Discussions of the involvement of communities in tourism planning and management and illustrations through case studies are provided in subsequent chapters that are concerned with, respectively, host communities, natural resources for tourism and codes of conduct.

Government agencies

Government agencies are frequently referred to as the public sector of tourism. They are not commercial organizations intent on making a profit, but are organizations that are meant to represent the views of tax payers and electors. Government agencies are funded from taxes and in most developed countries are run by democratically elected representatives supported by paid civil servants. In some parts of the world, particularly some developing countries, governments are headed by unelected dictators or military rulers and in such cases the rationale suggested for the involvement of the public sector in tourism is not necessarily that provided below.

In many developed countries there are a multiplicity of government bodies that have a bearing on tourism planning and management. These bodies exist at different scales from national, through regional, down to local. A number of countries in Europe, such as France and Spain (two of the major destinations in Europe for international visitors), have national bodies for tourism in the form of a Ministry, or Department, of Tourism. The United Kingdom, also a significant tourism destination in Europe, has an Under-Secretary of State for Tourism, but in 2015 subsumed this relatively minor role, and its public sector national tourism functions, within the Department of Culture, Media and Sport, which is under the control of the Secretary of State for Culture, Media and Sport. At the local and regional level, in the United Kingdom as well as many other developed countries, there are not necessarily government agencies focusing specifically on tourism or government representatives with tourism knowledge and experience (Middleton and Hawkins, 1998). Such factors will have a significant impact on the ability of the public sector to influence the course of tourism development in a particular tourist destination.

The main reasons for the involvement of the public sector in tourism are as follows:

- The public sector is mandated to represent the whole population and not just one set of stakeholders or interest group.
- The public sector is intended to be impartial, with no particular vested or commercial interests.

- The public sector can take a longer-term view of tourism development than, for example, the private sector (Swarbrooke, 1999: 87).

However, the public sector in many developed countries has what may appear at face value to be contradictory roles. Governments may not only attempt to regulate tourism, but they also have a role in marketing tourism (Mason and Mowforth, 1995; Seaton and Bennett, 1996: Page and O'Connell, 2009). Marketing is usually associated with promoting tourism, hence not controlling or regulating it. However, there are examples when marketing is used as a controlling measure. Such an example is that employed by what was previously the government agency, and now a charitable trust, English Heritage and the NGO the National Trust of England. These organizations work together in the marketing and management of two prehistoric sites in England. Stonehenge is the most visited prehistoric stone circle site in the United Kingdom. Approximately 30 km away is a similar prehistoric stone circle at Avebury. Stonehenge received approximately 1 million visitors per year in the first 12 years of the twenty-first century, while Avebury received one-fifth of this total (approximately 200,000 visitors) per year (Kuo and Mason, 2013). The main reason for this great difference in visitor numbers is that Stonehenge is very strongly marketed to both domestic and international tourist groups. However, Avebury is deliberately not marketed to overseas visitors and there is also only a limited attempt to market it within the United Kingdom. There is further discussion of the management of Stonehenge and Avebury in Chapter 9.

In the discussion that follows, it is also suggested that the ability of the public sector to regulate tourism is relatively restricted. This is due partly to the fact that there is only a limited amount of legislation directly affecting tourism. Governments in a number of European countries, such as the United Kingdom, for example, have legislation relating to land use and also building controls, as we have seen in Chapter 7. Such governments may also have certain official standards and these may be backed by international standards established by the International Standards Organization (ISO). The ISO has standards in relation to, for example, vegetarian food and there are likely to be national standards in relation to, for instance, food hygiene or hotel accommodation.

Governments tend to operate at a number of different levels in any one country. Hence, there are at least national, regional and local level government bodies. For example, as is revealed by the case study in Chapter 7, in New Zealand the main legislation relating to land use planning is the Resource Management Act (RMA). The RMA was introduced in 1991 and provides a legislative framework for managing land, air, water, coastal, geothermal and pollution issues under one umbrella in New Zealand (Mason and Leberman, 2000). As the New Zealand case study reveals, the overall aim of the RMA is to promote sustainable management whilst at the same time developing and protecting resources which enable social and economic well-being. Under the RMA the management of natural resources is delegated to regional and local authorities. Locally, the district or city councils are responsible for developing a district plan. The Department of Conservation (DOC) in New Zealand is also charged with the preparation of land management plans, and in the early years of the twenty-first century such plans cover approximately one-third of the New Zealand land area.

Governments in most developed countries and increasingly in developing countries are also involved in setting aside areas that are designated for special protection for environmental or cultural reasons. This has led to the creation of national parks in individual countries and when countries collaborate internationally this has led to the establishment of World Heritage Sites, such as Kakadu National Park in the Northern Territory of Australia and the Tonagariro National Park on the North Island of New Zealand. Governments may also require Environmental Impact Assessment (EIA) to be conducted when a new tourism venture is to be developed. As Middleton and Hawkins (1998) suggested, an EIA is an attempt to prevent environmental degradation by giving decision-makers information about the likely consequences of development actions. EIAs usually require the completion of an evaluation form prior to a development. This would cover a number of environmental resources and the likely impact of the tourism development upon them. The EIA would consider not only whether there is likely to be an impact but also its intensity.

However, as Swarbrooke (1999) indicated, there is virtually no tourism legislation concerning certain key areas of significance to tourism planning. These key areas include: socio-cultural impacts of tourism, environmental impacts of tourism; impacts of tourism on wildlife; the carrying capacity of areas and sites; tourist behaviour; and the wages and working conditions of tourism industry employees. This has meant that public bodies and government organizations have tended to rely on the tourism industry regulating itself. However, there is no reason to believe that the tourism industry will be any more responsible for its actions in regard to the environment and social impacts than any other industry (Mason and Mowforth, 1996).

The public sector has also tended to rely on the education of tourists in an attempt to modify their behaviour in relation to potential and real impacts. Such voluntary efforts often involve codes of conduct targeted at visitors or sectors of the tourism industry in an attempt to regulate behaviour. Educating tourists through interpretation at visitor sites is another commonly adopted approach. Tour guides can also play a role in the education of visitors. The use of codes of conduct and the education of visitors as tourism management approaches are discussed in some detail in later chapters, in Part III of the book. However, there is a good deal of evidence that attempts at self-regulation are only achieving moderate success and there is likely to be a need for the introduction of externally imposed, government-backed legislation pertaining to certain sectors of tourism (Swarbrooke, 1999; Mason, 2005). Government legislation aimed at controlling tourist behaviour is also a possibility.

The preceding discussion has focused on the public sector playing a mainly reactive role in terms of attempting to regulate and control tourism. However, public bodies can be proactive and play a positive role in tourism planning and management. Governments may own or at least administer certain key assets for tourism, such as valued natural or semi-natural environments, as well as built environment attractions such as museums and historic buildings. These can be marketed and/or regulated in such a way that they provide models for private operators. Governments can also develop the infrastructure necessary for both public and private sector tourism activities. If the public sector can do this in a way that is more sustainable than previous attempts, it may give a lead that is then followed by the private sector tourism operators.

Much of the writing concerned with the role of governments in tourism implies that in developed countries government involvement will be far more extensive than in developing countries. This is because governments in developed countries are likely have a number of roles, the most significant of which is usually to promote tourism, largely for economic reasons, but they may also regulate aspects of tourism, mainly for legal reasons such as on the grounds of health and safety. However, it is not just in Western democratic countries that governments are actively involved in tourism development. In the Middle East, Dubai provides a very good example of how a developing country that had virtually no tourism activity 25 years ago is now using tourism as the major approach within its development strategy. The following case study examines tourism growth in Dubai and the role of government within this.

Case study: tourism development in Dubai and the role of government

Dubai is one of seven Middle Eastern states that make up the United Arab Emirates (UAE). It is the second most powerful state after Abu Dhabi. Traditionally the Emirates have been dependent on oil revenue. This has made both Abu Dhabi and Dubai very wealthy. However, in the early 1990s, there was a realization that oil revenue would not continue indefinitely. Within the Emirates, Dubai was given a certain amount of leeway to plan its future and the country's rulers (the Al Makthoum royal family) opted for tourism as the key component of a strategy which also involved establishing Dubai as a centre for media and telecommunications, finance and real estate. In this way the government hoped to move swiftly from an economy based on wealth derived from extractive industries to one based on the service sector. The importance of tourism as part of this strategy can be seen in the fact that in the early 1990s the then Crown Prince of Dubai made himself Head of the Department of Tourism and Commerce Marketing, which subsequently developed the plans for tourism in Dubai. Tourism was selected as the key element of strategic planning partly on the basis that Dubai was much more liberal than many other Arab states and more than half of its residents were expatriates.

The original strategic plans were to make Dubai a major tourism hub by 2010. This was to be achieved as part of a rapid push towards economic growth, involving industry partnerships and the creation of unique visitor experiences. The intention in the mid-1990s was to receive 15 million international visitors in Dubai by 2010.

In terms of the desire to be a major tourism hub, by 2003, Dubai was receiving 18 million air passengers per year (although some passengers were only in transit) and it was the major Middle East air hub. This was made possible by the upgrading of the international airport. Emirates airline, based in Dubai, was the major Middle Eastern airline by 2004. In 2001 a cruise ship terminal was opened and in 2003, 26 international cruise ships visited Dubai. Dubai has tried to position itself between expensive long haul destinations such as the Maldives, the Caribbean and Australia and cheaper short haul destinations such as Turkey, Morocco and Egypt. Receipts from tourism overtook oil receipts in 2003.

Dubai has concentrated on the top end of the accommodation spectrum and there were 275 hotels and 96 apartment hotels opened by 2004, which accounted for 75 per cent of all such accommodation in the UAE. The plan was to have 80,000 hotel bedrooms by 2010. Major hotel developments include the Palm and Dubai Tower and Dubai already has what for many is the Middle East's tourism icon, the sail-shaped Burj al-Arab hotel.

Initially tourism was 'sun, sea, sand' based, but more recently desert-based activities, including safaris, four-wheel drive and camel-based excursions have been developed. In addition, Dubai has become a major shopping destination with the Mall of the Emirates opened in 2005, the biggest indoor shopping complex outside North America. There is also an indoor ski slope in this shopping complex. Future plans include a major theme park, Dubailand, as well as small scale ecotourism ventures. Heritage tourism, based on traditional Arab culture, is also intended to be expanded.

Visitor statistics reveal the rapid growth of tourism. In 1990 Dubai had only 0.6 million visitors. This had risen to 1.6 million by 1995. The most rapid growth came after the mid-1990s, so by 2000 there were 3.1 million visitors and in 2003, 5.8 million (WTO, 2005). In 2003, approximately half of the visitors came from other Arab countries in the Middle East, about a quarter from the Indian sub-continent and 15 per cent from Europe (WTO, 2005).

However, a number of challenges face the Dubai government. The rapid rate of expansion has put huge pressure on resources, particularly water. Traffic congestion is now a major problem and environmental damage including pollution of Dubai Creek, around which Dubai city is expanding, is increasingly threatening potential ecotourism development. Although not directly affected by terrorism or warfare, Dubai is very close to areas of the Middle East where conflict is common. New aircraft technology may mean that it is no longer necessary for medium and long haul flights to stop over in Dubai for refuelling. Cruise ship expansion is limited by religious laws preventing gambling on ships visiting Dubai. Hotels have tended to be at, or near, the luxury end of the market, which means there is a lack of cheaper accommodation, so 'low-budget' travellers are unlikely to visit. Although Dubai can offer almost guaranteed winter sun and comfortable temperatures at this time for visitors from Europe, its summer temperatures of 45–50 °C may be seen by many potential visitors as too high. The rapid rate of tourism growth has already deterred some tourists who see Dubai as a 'massive building site'. It is also difficult to see how Arab heritage and the natural environment can be conserved with planned visitor numbers reaching 40 million by the end of 2015.

(Based on Henderson, 2006.)

The material in the case study of Dubai was written before the economic downturn of 2008 and the problems that this has caused have resulted in yet one more challenge for Dubai in terms of maintaining its level of tourism development.

However, Dubai was not the only country whose government was affected by the economic downturn as it was a global phenomenon. Indeed, there have been attempts by governments to overcome the economic problems caused by the downturn and an increasing number of international links and intergovernmental treaties that attempt to create more sustainable forms of tourism. One important development at the international level at the end of the twentieth century was the application of Agenda 21 (developed at the 1992 Rio Environment Summit) to tourism. Figure 8.3 shows the actions identified for travel and tourism companies from Agenda 21. It is possible that such intergovernmental cooperation, as envisaged by Agenda 21, will lead to fairer, more equitable and more sustainable forms of international tourism.

The tourism industry

The tourism industry should be a key player in tourism planning and management, but it is not easy to define, as it is complex and has many dimensions. As Middleton and Hawkins (1998) argued, the industry is so large and diverse that some tourism companies would not see themselves as part of the same industry. In Chapter 1, Leiper's systems model of tourism is shown in Figure 1.4. This shows three sectors: the generating zone, the transit zone and the

Actions identified for travel and tourism companies, with the main aim of establishing systems and procedures which incorporate sustainable development at the core of the decision-making process for business operations. (Applies also to public sector business operations.)

    (i) Waste minimization, re-use, and recycling
   (ii) Energy efficiency, conservation, and management
  (iii) Management of fresh water resources
  (iv) Waste water management
   (v) Management of hazardous substances
  (vi) Use of more environmentally friendly transport
 (vii) Land-use planning and management
(viii) Involving staff, customers, and local communities in environmental issues
  (ix) Design for sustainability
   (x) Developing partnerships for sustainable development

Figure 8.3 Agenda 21 for the travel and tourism industry

Source: Press release of February 1997 issued by WTTC/WTO/Earth Council.

destination zone. Each of these zones, or sectors, contains tourism industry organizations. In the generating zone are travel agents, tour operators and marketing agencies. The travel media also operates from here. The transition zone contains the carriers such as airlines and rail companies. The destination zone contains the greatest variety of tourism industry organizations as there are various types of accommodation including hotels, and there are restaurants and other food providers. The destination zone also has different forms of hospitality and entertainment providers as well as visitor attractions, transport providers, tourist information offices and other infrastructure organizations that support tourism. It should be noted that some of the so-called industries within tourism, such as Tourist Information Centres, are in fact public sector organizations. However, one of the key differences between the private sector of the tourism industry and the public sector is that the private sector responds directly to market forces (Middleton and Hawkins, 1998).

The tourism industry has often been blamed for causing damage to destinations and showing little willingness to be involved in planning for long-term viability of tourism development (Mason and Mowforth, 1995). However, the complexity of the tourism industry makes it difficult to point the finger of blame directly at the cause of problems. Nevertheless, the tourism industry has been accused of:

- Being mainly concerned with short-term profit, rather than long-term sustainability.
- Exploiting the environment and local populations, rather than conserving them.
- Being relatively fickle and showing little commitment to particular destinations.
- Not doing enough to raise tourist awareness of issues such as sustainability.
- Only getting on the sustainability wagon when it is likely to achieve good publicity.
- Being owned and controlled by large transnational corporations, which have little regard for individual destinations (Swarbrooke, 1999: 104–5).

Despite the fact that there are a large number and range of tourism businesses, there are many linkages between apparently different sectors. For example, travel agents and tour operators often work closely together, and some agents may be owned by operators. Under these circumstances, agents may strongly market the brands of the operator they are linked with. Operators may also have a stake in hotels and carriers. These linkages can also be seen in what are termed distribution channels (Ujma, 2002). These channels are the ways that the industry tries to reach its customers to sell its products (Lominé and Edmunds, 2007). The link between tour operators and travel agents is an example of a traditional distribution channel. Linkages in the industry are becoming more common. Even apparently competing organizations may be linked. In the 1990s, for example, Qantas linked with British Airways and other international airlines to offer a global service. In an attempt to gain customer loyalty they established 'Frequent Flyer' (an 'air miles' scheme) which provided 'free' travel as reward for collecting sufficient points. Following this link up of the two airlines, other similar 'air miles' type schemes which are, in effect, loyalty schemes have been established by other airlines that previously competed with each other.

The major way in which members of the tourism industry manage their operations is through what is known as the marketing mix (Middleton and Hawkins, 1998). The marketing mix can be summarized under four headings, each of which begins with a 'p'. These are as follows: product, price, promotion and place. Middleton and Hawkins (1998) add one other 'p' to this list, that of 'people'. The marketing mix can be used by the tourist industry to manage the consumer, in this case the visitor or tourist.

The private sector provides the bulk of most tourist products at tourist destinations. This is particularly so with visitors staying in commercial accommodation. However, even those staying with friends and relatives are likely to make some purchases in a destination. The number and type of visitors in a destination is therefore strongly influenced by decisions taken by commercial tourism operators in terms of the products they have to offer there. However, this is only partially the case as a major part of the tourism product is the tourist experience and the public sector has a role here. This experience is obtained within the wider context of the destination environment. Evidence suggests that few tourism operators in a destination have paid much regard to the wider environment in which tourism takes place. Small businesses, in particular, expect visitors to be provided with free access to the environment around them, but such operators have generally not accepted any responsibility, for example, for increased traffic congestion, pollution and litter that tourists may cause (Middleton and Hawkins, 1998). However, if the quality of the environment declines, customers may go elsewhere. It is more often than not, the public sector that makes attempts to improve the quality of the environment, which tourists, purchasing from the private sector, have contributed to damaging.

The strongest influence that the private sector has for determining the level of demand for their product is price (Middleton and Hawkins, 1998). The price of a holiday is largely determined by commercial judgements of what the market will bear. Hence, the private sector largely determines products and prices, the segments to be targeted and the volume of products to be offered. When commercial decisions on product and price are made, there has been until very recently little attempt to factor in environmental costs or socio-cultural impacts (Swarbrooke, 1999). As Middleton and Hawkins (1998) argued, it would require some form of external regulation and/or private sector collaboration to ensure that such factors applied equally across all those competing in the same market.

Commercial operators can influence the behaviour of tourists by promotion. Promotion involves publicity and usually this is an attempt to increase product awareness and ultimately sell more holiday experiences. The promotion of products is often seen as the key marketing role of commercial operators (Seaton and Bennett, 1996). However, the public sector also has an important role in marketing destinations (Middleton and Hawkins, 1998). It is frequently carried out by local council officials and staff at Tourist Information Centres as well as via a number of publicity media. As promotion is a key way that both the private and public sector can influence tourists' behaviour, it can be a very important tool in tourism planning and management.

The fourth 'p' in the marketing mix is place. In tourism marketing terms, place means the point at which tourists can gain convenient access to information about the various tourist products on offer. The obvious place to obtain this is the destination itself, but another place is a travel agency. Distribution of information ensuring the appropriate potential consumer receives the material is important. Increasingly, tourists are gaining access to marketing information via the Internet, which means the role of traditional travel agencies is declining and the concept of place in the marketing mix is changing.

As indicated above, Middleton and Hawkins (1998) added a fifth 'p' to the traditional marketing mix. They suggested that people are vital within marketing. They referred specifically to those providing tourist services, both within the destination and beyond. Clearly, the relationship between hotel staff and visitors can greatly influence a tourist's view of a destination. There are also people who have very little or no direct involvement in tourism, such as bank staff and health workers, but who can influence a tourist's experiences of a resort.

As has been previously stated, few operators, until very recently, have been concerned with the impacts of taking tourists to destinations on the environment or society of the destination. However, by the early twenty-first century a number of tourism companies had become involved in initiatives and this suggests a growing awareness and concern with such impacts. These include recycling, promoting 'green' holidays, providing information on environmentally sound activities for tourists and donating money to local charities. Some operators are also using guides selected from local communities and are involved in partnerships with local community groups.

It would appear that most industry action to date has been designed to show that the industry can regulate itself. One interpretation of this could be that industry does not wish for external control and regulation and hence voluntary self-regulation is preferable (Swarbrooke, 1999; Mason, 2007a). Another interpretation is that the industry is aware that regulation will eventually come and that it wishes to appear proactive rather than reactive, as this may soften the blow of external regulation (Mason and Mowforth, 1996). Some industry bodies have taken voluntary self-regulation to the point of designing and implementing voluntary codes of conduct. These operate at the individual company level – the Canadian Chateau Whistler Hotel Group has such a code of operation. Voluntary codes are also found at supra-national level and examples include the Pacific Asia Travel Associations Code for Environmentally Responsible Tourism (Mason and Mowforth, 1996). Such codes are generally welcomed by commentators on tourism (Mason and Mowforth, 1996; Malloy and Fennell, 1998), but may be, in reality, little more than clever marketing devices, which when they make environmental claims that cannot be supported by evidence, are examples of what is known as 'greenwashing' (Mason, 2005; Fennell and Malloy, 2007). These codes may, however, succeed in providing tourists with a 'feel good' factor, while doing little to change industry practices in relation to the environment and society of tourist destinations.

Other players

Two other sets of actors are important in terms of tourism planning and management. These are voluntary sector organizations and the media. The voluntary sector is made up of a number of different groups. These include pressure groups, voluntary trusts, some of which have charitable status, and industry associations. Pressure groups can be further subdivided into those whose membership is primarily public and those whose members come largely from within the tourism industry.

A major pressure group in the United Kingdom is Tourism Concern. The original members of Tourism Concern were individuals who were concerned mainly about the social impacts of tourism, particularly in developing countries. Tourism Concern has mounted and run campaigns targeted at, for example, child prostitution and the enforced displacement of local people as a result of tourism development. Tourism Concern has widened its focus to encompass economic and environmental issues, and now has many members who are academics and students, but it has few members from the tourism industry. It has, however, frequently found itself in conflict with the industry. Given this lack of involvement of industry, its effectiveness has been limited, although it has almost certainly raised levels of awareness.

There are also organizations that act as pressure groups, but are not part of the voluntary sector. However, neither are they part of the tourism industry. Such organizations are termed non-governmental organizations, or NGOs, and they usually have a far wider brief than just tourism, but run events/campaigns and/or plan projects that have important tourism dimensions. In the United Kingdom, one NGO, the World Wide Fund for Nature (WWF), has been active since the early 1990s in campaigning for more 'environmentally friendly' forms of tourism. WWF has been active in connection with tourism issues in several areas globally and a particular project of theirs, the WWF Arctic Tourism Project, is discussed in Chapter 13. Another NGO, Friends of the Earth, has also campaigned for preservation of the environment in relation to tourism development. In the United States, the Audobon Society has performed a somewhat similar role to that of WWF, in terms of tourism issues.

A number of non-profit-making trusts exist in developed countries and they are targeted at one particular issue or purpose. In the United Kingdom, for example, the National Trust is a non-profit-making organization involved in conserving historic buildings and heritage landscapes. In New Zealand, the organization Forest and Bird fulfils a similar role in terms of landscape conservation. At the local scale, a non-profit-making trust aimed at heritage preservation in New Zealand is the Napier Art Deco Trust. Due largely to rebuilding after the 1931 earthquake, the New Zealand North Island town of Napier has one of the most complete set of art deco buildings anywhere. The trust was established in 1985 to both conserve this heritage and make it available to visitors.

The tourism industry also has a number of pressure groups. The World Travel and Tourism Council (WTTC) is such a pressure group and receives support from major tourism companies. It lobbies on behalf of the tourism industry. There are also a number of professional bodies that represent the tourism industry. In the United Kingdom, for example, there is the Association of British Travel Agents, and also the Association of Independent Travel Operators. In relation to Australia and New Zealand, the Pacific Asia Travel Association is a major regional professional body for the tourism industry.

The media has potentially a key role in tourism planning and management issues. Much of the media deals directly or indirectly with tourism. In Australia, New Zealand and the United Kingdom, a number of the main terrestrial television channels regularly show 'travel shows'. These tend to be relatively uncritical 'travelogue' style programmes, whose aim is to promote holidays to particular destinations. A number of newspapers in each country use a similar approach. There are also significant numbers of travel-related magazines and radio programmes and much travel information is now available on the Internet. Probably the oldest form of literature concerned with travel is the guidebook. Many types of television programme and several magazines have an indirect travel component; those focusing on wildlife and natural history are within this category. The media has even created tourist attractions, as the following case study indicates.

Case study: how the media can create a tourist attraction

Ian reckons that he has got a lot to thank his 10,000 sheep for. On his rolling 500 hectare farm in the heartland of the Waikato region of the North Island of New Zealand, he says it was his woolly flock and the way that they kept the pasture trimmed that attracted the interest of the *Lord of the Rings* film scouts. The scouts were searching for the tranquil green Shire, the mythical land of the hobbits in Tolkien's famous trilogy.

Three main attributes attracted the scouts: the farm's neat pastures, the lack of visible signs of modern human settlement such as houses, roads and power lines, and the big pine tree on the edge of a lake that became the Shire's party tree.

The film-makers finally decided to use the farm in March 1999. But from then on it was a case of tight security as Ian and his family were sworn to secrecy. However, word that the farm was the secret location for filming quickly spread. Media interest grew with newspapers phoning repeatedly only to be told that Ian could not say a thing! The army was then contracted by the film company to build a road into the Shire. This was followed by the film crew digging hobbit holes, planting gardens and landscaping the area. Filming of *Lord of the Rings* finally got under way in late 1999, but was not completed until early 2001.

The first part of the trilogy, *The Fellowship of the Ring* was shown to cinema audiences in late 2001 and just before the second part, *The Two Towers*, was reaching cinemas in December 2002, Ian was released from his contract with the film-makers. He is just beginning to offer guided tours of the remnants of the set.

Although some visitors would like to see the site restored to how it was in the movie, Ian says this is unrealistic. However, the virtually bare site (there are a dozen or so hobbit holes, including the remains of Bag End) has not deterred fans like Dave and Di from Hampshire, who booked for the 2-hour tour at NZ$50. 'I knew all about it from the book and the film and I thought the tour was very good. Excellent', said Di.

(Source: the *Manawatu Evening Standard*, 18 December 2002.)

Twelve years after the release of the first *Lord of the Rings* film, as a tourist it was still possible in 2013 to visit 'The Shire' in Waikato (TourismNewZealand, 2013). However, the Waikato region is just one of many in New Zealand that were used in the making of the *Lord of the Rings* film trilogy. All three parts of the trilogy were very successful at the box office. This success was used to gain publicity for tourism to New Zealand. One way in which the film trilogy and tourism have been closely linked is through the publication of a book, in late 2002, which specifically identified and promoted just under 100 locations in New Zealand that were used in the filming. More recently the director of *Lord of the Rings* has adapted Tolkien's *The Hobbit*, which is closely linked to the *Lord of the Rings* trilogy, for the big screen. *The Hobbit* was released in three parts in 2012, 2013 and 2014. This has helped maintain publicity, not just for the different locations involved in the filming of *Lord of the Rings* and *The Hobbit*, but New Zealand as a whole.

Until recently, most media concerned either directly, or indirectly, with tourism was largely promotional and lacked a critical perspective. By the early twenty-first century this situation was gradually changing. Consumer 'watchdog' television and radio programmes have investigated travel and tourism 'stories', while some newspapers, such as *The Independent* in the United Kingdom, have focused specifically on important issues such as those relating to tourism sustainability. Guidebooks have also tended to become more discerning and critical in the past decade or so. The 'Good Tourist' series (see Wood and House, 1991), discussed above, is one indication of this attempt to provide alternative perspectives.

It is likely with advances in satellite and cable television and as the Internet reaches more potential consumers that the power of the media will grow. Nevertheless, there is no real reason why the media should adopt a critical perspective to tourism issues and assist in planning and management through the promotion of more sustainable forms of tourism.

Summary

This chapter has introduced a discussion of the key players in tourism planning and management. The major players are the tourists themselves, members of host communities, representatives of the travel industry and government agencies. NGOs and the media are also important players in relation to tourism planning and management.

In relation to tourists and host communities, it is important to note that neither group is homogeneous. However, the heterogeneity of tourists and host communities is often ignored in much tourism literature, including that on planning and management. This heterogeneity contributes to the complexity of planning and managing tourism. The government role in tourism is often viewed as promotional rather than regulatory, although government at various levels fulfils both these roles. The tourism industry, although it is multi-faceted, is frequently viewed as being in need of external regulation in relation to tourism impacts. However, recently, some sectors of the industry have made attempts to regulate themselves. NGOs and the media have been important in relation to tourism planning and management. Historically, the media has tended to act in a largely promotional role, but more recently, particularly through its focus on issues and the mounting of campaigns on tourism themes, a more critical stance has been developed.

Student activities

1 Consider the key players in tourism planning and management and produce a table that summarizes the key roles of each player.
2 Consider how the key players in tourism planning and management are able to interact with each other in a formal context. What obstacles exist in relation to both formal and informal interaction between the key players?
3 In relation to the role of government and the case study of tourism development in Dubai, what are the advantages and disadvantages of the direct involvement of the Dubai government in the development of tourism?
4 Compare the role of government in its involvement in tourism in your locality/region/country with that of the government in Dubai.
5 How influential is the media in tourism?
6 Consider a location that you know well that has been used by the media in terms of a TV programme, film or radio production. How has this been exploited for tourism purposes and what further could be done? What are the potential issues resulting from the media's involvement in promoting specific locations for tourism?
7 Conduct a group debate with the motion 'Tourists comprise the single most important players in tourism planning and management.'

Chapter 9

Visitor management

Learning objectives

At the end of this chapter, you should be able to:

- demonstrate a general understanding of what constitutes visitor management;
- demonstrate an understanding of various attempts at visitor management and the advantages and disadvantages of these processes;
- indicate the problems of the lack of adequate data in relation to visitor management;
- define in your own words the term interpretation in relation to visitor management;
- define in your own words the term education in relation to visitor management;
- define in your own words the term regulation in relation to visitor management.

Introduction

Managing visitors is one of the important ways of managing the impacts of tourism, particularly impacts on the environment, but in addition managing socio-cultural and economic impacts. Visitor management has been viewed in the past 30 years or so as a significant way to attempt to reduce the negative impacts of tourism. Often, this has been through attempts to divert tourists from areas with large volumes of tourists, the so-called 'honey pots'. Another approach has been to minimize the negative impacts at popular site by 'hardening' (e.g. resurfacing paths and footpaths), or by schemes such as 'park and ride' which keep cars out of the immediate environment of a popular attraction. However, there is a danger that by attempting to improve the site, this only encourages more visitors who in turn cause more damage (Swarbrooke, 1999; Mason, 2005).

This introductory statement indicates that visitor management can be viewed as a way to regulate visitors. Hence, regulation may relate to such factors as preventing (or indeed allowing) access to particular areas or sites. Regulation is also likely to involve the provision of information and instructions on what can and cannot be done. In most cases, regulations relating to tourism are likely to be voluntary, of a self-regulatory nature, and unlikely to be backed up with laws. There are, however, legal regulations of relevance to tourism relating to transport, health and safety, and hygiene.

As well as regulation, managing visitors can also involve education. Education frequently involves the process of interpretation. This educational process may not only involve the dissemination of information about a particular site, but is also likely to involve more general education about social and environmental factors. In certain situations, a combination of education and regulation is used in an attempt to manage visitors. Education and regulation in relation to visitors are discussed in greater detail in Part III of this book. This chapter considers the overall framework in which visitor management takes place and presents a number of management issues via an investigation of selected examples.

Key perspectives

Visitor management has been used by a number of different agencies and organizations, at different scales and in a variety of locations. In some countries, it has become a major tool in an attempt to control visitor flows. In the United Kingdom, for example, a government task force produced a tourism report that had visitor management as a key strategy. This report, Maintaining the Balance (referred to in Chapter 7), from the UK Ministry of Environment/ Department of Employment and published in 1991 (and republished as ETB, 1991), focused on the relationship between the environment and the visitor and suggested that there are three main ways of managing visitors. These are as follows:

- controlling the number of visitors – either by limiting numbers to match capacity, or spreading the number throughout the year, rather than having them concentrated in time in a focused 'tourist season';
- modifying visitor behaviour;
- adapting the resource in ways to enable it to cope with the volume of visitors, and hence become less damaged.

In relation to the first of these three methods, that of controlling the numbers of visitors, the report suggested that the initial task is to determine the carrying capacity. The report then cites the following threshold levels at which the ambience and character of the place is damaged and the quality of the experience is threatened. These are as follows:

- a level above which physical damage occurs;
- a level above which irreversible damage occurs;
- a level above which the local community suffers unacceptable side effects.

In addition to this approach to controlling the number of visitors, the report also discussed the ways of managing traffic. It argued for positive routeing of vehicles, clear parking strategy, park and ride schemes, the use of public transport, road closures, traffic calming and traffic control systems.

The report also made a number of suggestions on modifying visitor behaviour. These are as follows:

- marketing and general information provision;
- promotion to bring visitors out of season, to help spread the load;
- promotion of alternative destinations;
- niche marketing, to attract particular types of visitors;
- providing visitors with specific information;
- the use of signs, Travel Information Centres and information points/boards;
- the use of codes of conduct to enable a combination of education and regulation in the interpretation process.

In addition, the report made suggestions on modifying/adapting the resource as a part of the process of visitor management. It indicated that this approach acknowledges there will be some wear and tear of the tourism resource. Minimizing damage through an adaptation of the resource in an attempt to promote protection is the key aim of this approach. The report suggested the following approaches:

- The use of wardens, guides and even guards to watch over and/or supervise. This is to prevent unruly behaviour, theft or deliberate damage.
- Restricting the use of the site (e.g. cordoning off areas, to prevent access, allow re-growth).
- Protective measures (e.g. coverings over valuable carpets, stones, reinforcement of footpaths, the wearing of slippers/shoe covers to protect floors).
- The building of replicas (e.g. there was a suggestion in the past to create a 'Foam Henge' to prevent damage to Stonehenge, a prehistoric monument in the south of England, which is discussed in more detail in a case study in this chapter).

New Zealand provides a good example of possible conflict in relation to visitor management. The potential for real conflict is linked closely to traditional New Zealand attitudes to use of the environment (these were discussed briefly in Chapter 6). The New Zealand Government Ministry, the Department of Conservation (DOC), produced a report in 1994 and according to DOC there are potential points of conflict. These are as follows:

- The majority of New Zealanders view the environment as one to which they have free access and this is particularly so with the backcountry (remote mountain areas), even though they may visit such areas only infrequently. New Zealanders are therefore generally opposed to attempts to limit access.
- The New Zealand tradition of self-reliance means opposition to improving existing accommodation and increasing the number of huts and other facilities in the backcountry.

● International visitors generally demand easy access to facilities, and these need to be of a relatively high standard, particularly toilets and washing facilities. International visitors also demand good signage, clear notice boards, good maps and sufficiently well-serviced campsites. International visitor numbers are likely to increase significantly in the next 10–15 years, while domestic visitors will remain almost constant. Hence the pressure will be to improve and increase facilities for the international visitor, but this is likely to be opposed by domestic visitors.

● There will come a point when the visitor experience/satisfaction declines.

● This will occur when numbers reach a certain (as yet unknown) level. At this point there may well be conflict between, for example, international hikers and domestic mountain bikers.

● There is pressure for visitors to make a greater contribution and to pay more to help maintain the environment they are visiting.

● There is an increased desire by local communities and Maori communities to have a greater say in environment/conservation decision-making.

A major problem in relation to all types of visitor management is the lack of data about the impacts of tourism at particular sites that attract visitors (Shackley, 1998). In certain locations site records relating to details of visitors may not be kept at all, or records from one site may be combined with others. Some sites attracting visitors are not neatly contained within a limited geographical area. Given the problems of measuring visitor numbers, site managers may resort to guesswork (Shackley, 1998). However, as Shackley asserts, it is clear that visitors to many attractions are increasing. Nevertheless, visitor numbers are not spread evenly throughout the year in many destinations, but there are usually seasonal peaks and troughs. At the micro-scale, even during the peak period of visits, there is a variation in visitor numbers at a given site. Often, the weekly (and even daily) peaks and troughs are linked to the schedule of tour operators and carriers. Those organizing such visits seldom take into account issues of crowding, visitor preferences or visitor satisfaction levels (Shackley, 1998; Mason and Kuo, 2008).

An extreme case of this 'periodicity' of visits is that of a cruise ship. Visits by cruise ships to relatively remote attractions, for example, to Antarctica or the Arctic region, may take place infrequently. Several weeks may elapse between visits and when a ship arrives, the visit may have a duration of less than 1 hour (Mason *et al.*, 2000a). During this time, up to 10 per cent of annual arrivals may occur, creating enormous pressure on all shore-based facilities.

At particularly popular 'honey pots', crowding may not only contribute to low satisfaction levels, adversely affect the natural and/or built environment, but also may create safety problems. The Eden Project, involving the creation of biomes (plant worlds) in large domed glasshouses in a disused quarry, in Cornwall, England, was first opened in March 2001 (see Photo 9.1).

Photo 9.2 was taken a month later at Easter 2001 and shows the aftermath of the problems caused by queuing to enter. The attraction was planned to take a maximum of 5,000 visitors per day. On the day the photograph was taken, over 13,000 visitors came to the site. Queuing time for the car park at the attraction averaged 1.5 hours and the pedestrian queue added another 1 hour on average to a proposed visit. On this particular day, as is shown in Photo 9.2, police arrested a driver for alleged dangerous driving. The car was seen to overtake a line of queuing cars and drive in a hazardous manner, narrowly avoiding a car park steward and running over traffic cones. This form of tourism-related 'road rage' is clearly an undesirable consequence of overcrowding at an attraction.

Even relatively remote 'wilderness areas' including several in Australia are not without their visitor management problems. Issues relating to growing numbers of visitors and related visitor management strategies are discussed in the following case study that focuses on the World Heritage Site (WHS) of Kakadu National Park in Australia.

Photo 9.1 The Eden Project in Cornwall. The attraction opened in early 2001. During the Easter week of 2001, visitor numbers exceeded the planned maximum day targets by more than double. This caused huge traffic jams and contributed to the incident shown in the accompanying photograph.

Photo 9.2 Road rage at the Eden Project, Cornwall. Police carrying out an arrest for dangerous driving at the Eden Project at Easter 2001

Case study: visitor management in Kakadu Park, Australia

Kakadu Park is a WHS in the Northern Territory of Australia. It was established as a national park in the late 1980s. The establishment of the park was an attempt to reconcile the interests of conservation, mining, Aboriginal land rights and tourism. Kakadu achieved World Heritage status in 1992.

Kakadu has a tropical climate, with high temperatures all year round (with a mean between 30 and 37 °C). It has two seasons: a wet season from October to March and dry season from April to September. Heavy rainfall, particularly in January and February, causes widespread flooding in the riverine flood plains. The area has several large rivers and streams.

The climate supports a complex tropical ecosystem and the only recent arrival of Europeans and European-descended settlers means Kakadu is a major habitat for a large range of wildlife. Over one-third of Australia's bird life is found here, over 120 reptiles and amphibians, 50 different fish species, 55 types of mammal, 1,500 types of butterfly and moth and over 1,600 botanical species. In addition to the bird life, for many visitors the key attraction is the saltwater crocodile.

Aboriginal settlements in Kakadu date back at least 50,000 years. One of the major cultural components of the park is the large number of Aboriginal rock paintings. There are least 5,000 known sites of rock paintings and, probably, another 5,000 yet to be itemized. These are important living parts of Aboriginal culture, they are a repository of local knowledge, a source of teaching, manifestations of the spiritual made physical and a link between Aboriginal Dreamtime and the present. A number of these rock paintings are tourist attractions.

The discovery of gold in the nineteenth century and uranium in the 1950s led to the creation of a framework in which the interests of Aborigines, conservation and mining could be encompassed. The result was that title was invested in Aboriginal peoples under the 1976 Aboriginal Land Rights Acts. Jabiru town was established at this time as a mining centre.

Visitor management issues

Initially, tourism development was denied in some areas including Jabiru. By the late 1970s, with the establishment of the area as a national park, tourism infrastructure was allowed. Visitor numbers increased rapidly in the period from the early 1980s to the mid-1990s (46,000 in 1982 and 220,000 in 1994). Visitors tend to be well educated and better paid than the average Australian. The average length of stay was 3–4 days in the mid-1990s. One of the major destinations is Yellow River with over 75 per cent of tourists visiting. Here, the main tourist product is a wildlife experience, the opportunity to go bird watching and a scenic boat ride. Aboriginal involvement in tourism is significant, although not always direct. The most famous hotel in the area, the Gagudju Crocodile Hotel, is Aboriginal owned. The hotel owners also own Yellow River Boat tours, motels and camping grounds. In addition to the group that owns the Gagudju Crocodile Hotel, there are two other Aboriginal associations actively involved in tourism. Aboriginal groups obtain significant economic benefits from tourism. Considerable amounts of this benefit are ploughed back into sustaining the park and maintaining the traditional lifestyle.

(continued)

Case study: visitor management in Kakadu Park, Australia (continued)

The original intention when creating the park was to prevent tourism development in the town of Jabiru. However, Jabiru grew as shops, services and a town infrastructure developed and as a result it was decided to concentrate tourism here. Nevertheless, the town is zoned, with some areas focusing on tourism and in other areas tourism is excluded.

On the rivers in the park, there is a recommendation that boats should not travel faster than 10 kilometres per hour. This restricts bank erosion to only a minor scale. While the larger tour boats run by the Yellow River operation tend to comply with the recommendation, smaller craft have been reported as travelling faster.

Evidence was emerging in the late 1990s that tourism is affecting wildlife in the park. A number of bird species including the red-winged parrots, sulphur-crested cockatoos and shining flycatchers were recorded as being 'highly disturbed' when tourist boats passed them. This means they flew away but it was not known whether they regrouped after the departure of the tourists.

In Kakadu, it is possible for tourists to see rock art in situ. Sites are managed through the use of mainly Aboriginal guides. Guided walks are a popular part of the tourist experience in the park. Guides act as interpreters and also in an unofficial policing role, monitoring any unintentional damage or vandalism at sites. The park authorities also have a record of the sacred sites in the park, but these are not generally known to tourists or any other member of the public. The park authorities also have the power to deny access to certain sites.

In conclusion, in Kakadu National Park there has been an attempt to allow local indigenous people to retain their traditional lifestyle, promote their culture in the way they see fit, obtain employment and to allow tourists to see wildlife in a natural setting within the context of Aboriginal culture.

(Adapted from Ryan, 1998.)

The study of Kakadu National Park indicates a number of issues concerned with managing WHS where visitors go to a relatively remote area that contains important natural attractions. However, some WHSs are based on built attractions and the United Kingdom's prehistoric monument, Stonehenge, is such a site. It is the most visited prehistoric site in the United Kingdom and is one of the world's most important archaeological remains. The location of the site amongst other factors contributes to significant visitor management problems. These are presented in the following case study.

Case study: visitor management at Stonehenge

Stonehenge is a stone monument dating back at least 4,000 years and possibly as far back as 4000 BCE (hence, it may be 6,000 years old). What the monument was used for has caused much controversy over a period of several hundred years. This, in turn, has generated much literature, which has been a form of marketing to potential tourists. A number of theories exist:

- it is a prehistoric temple or religious site;
- it is a prehistoric calendar;
- it has astronomical significance helping to mark the position of stars.

It seems likely that it was probably a combination of all the three listed above, with compelling evidence that it was a calendar. The stones at Stonehenge mark the position of the sun at different times of the year, with mid-summer's day (June 21) and mid-winter's day (December 21) given particular prominence in the stone circle.

Stonehenge is a WHS. It had approximately 900,000 paying visitors in 2006 (plus at least 200,000 who looked from the road but did not pay). It is the most visited prehistoric site in the United Kingdom and has been consistently in the top ten UK visitor attractions since 1990. In 2003, as high a proportion as 73 per cent of visitors were from overseas (41 per cent of visitors from the United States) and 98 per cent of visitors arrived by car/coach. Most visitors stay for only 20–30 minutes and about half of these do not get beyond the visitor centre or car park so they do not actually go to the stones. It has been estimated that up to 500 visitors per hour could be accommodated in the stone circle if access was allowed, but there are up to 2,000 visitors per hour in the peak summer season of July and August. Up to late 2013, the facilities included a temporary visitor centre, a souvenir shop, a takeaway café/restaurant, temporary toilets and a large car park.

Stonehenge is owned by English Heritage (EH), an independent body set up in 1984 by Parliament to protect England's archaeological and architectural heritage. It is marketed globally, but particularly in the United States, by EH and the British Tourist Authority (VisitBritain). The interpretation of Stonehenge is almost exclusively by hand-held mobile phone-sized electronic devices, known as audio wands. These operate in a number of languages and provide a basic interpretation of the site, but have the option of more details. There are numbered stopping off points with a linked commentary in English, several different European languages and also Japanese.

There are several key management issues, which are as follows:

- The sheer number of visitors – on average about 1 million per year since 2003.
- There is the problem of possible damage to the monument. To prevent damage to the stones they are normally roped off. One of the reasons given is the potential damage caused by too many hands and feet. But another reason is that 'alternative' groups in Britain, those who claim to be Celtic priests (Druids) and others, usually referred to as New Age travellers, have tried to use Stonehenge for festivals and quasi-religious ceremonies. In the early part of the twenty first-century, access was granted for the use by 'Druids' on the summer solstice (21 June) and winter solstice (21 December). But as most visitors cannot get this type of access they may feel cheated.
- Authenticity of the experience and related tourist satisfaction is a key factor.

(continued)

Case study: visitor management at Stonehenge (continued)

- Entrance costs have been relatively low, averaging about £7.50 for adults and £5.00 for children, in the first decade of the twenty-first century, and with other concessionary fares for groups and senior citizens and students may encourage large numbers of visitors.
- The site is between two relatively major roads linking London with southwest England. The traffic noise, particularly in summer, is disruptive to the experience of the site. The busiest road is the A303 trunk road and over the past 25 years there have been several plans to build a tunnel to house this road, although by early 2015 none have led to its construction. The longer the tunnel is delayed the more it will cost to build.
- Up to late 2013, the visitor centre, which was initially planned to be only a temporary structure, was underground and there was an under-road bypass to get to the site. This was for safety reasons as there were road accidents in the past. The visitor centre was called 'a national disgrace' by the House of Commons Select Committee on Heritage in 1994. Over the period from 1990 to 2010, there were a series of plans to build a new visitor centre. Partly to do with construction costs, there was no building in that period. The final plan was for a visitor centre approximately 3 km north west of the nearest town of Amesbury and 1.5 km from Stonehenge itself.
- This new permanent visitor centre, with a café, toilets, car parking and interpretation centre, was finally opened in December 2013 and now provides an interpretation of the site of Stonehenge over a 10,000-year period. In preparation for the opening of the new visitor centre, in July 2012 work began on closure of a part of the A344 road. This involved grassing over the road between Stonehenge and the junction of the A344 and the A303 and the original pedestrian underpass (under the A344) to Stonehenge was also filled in at this time. This section of the A344 was closed in June 2013 and vehicle access was prohibited. Visitors, who wish, can travel by motorized 'train' (carriages pulled by English Heritage Land Rovers) to the actual site of the stones from this visitor centre. However, siting a visitor centre away from Stonehenge, and involving a 'train' journey to the actual site, has raised authenticity issues.
- Who actually owns the site, and for what purposes it should be used, is a major area of controversy. In the past 25 years or so, various groups have claimed that they should have access to the site, including New Age travellers for festivals and 'Druids' for religious purposes. As these groups have been viewed until very recently as outside the mainstream of society, it has been relatively easy for the police and authorities to get the support of locals to restrict access. However, in the mid-1980s, a number of clashes between police and New Age travellers led to serious injury to persons and property. Eventually, the police had to pay compensation and access to the site has been on the agenda ever since.

In the early part of the twenty-first century, Stonehenge has been roped off most of the time, although there have been occasions, such as mid-summer's day, when access has been allowed. Increasingly, private access is being allowed outside normal opening hours, particularly for scientific/educational purposes, but also in the past ten years, for corporate events where customers in groups pay a higher entrance charge. An important issue for future management relates to who is allowed regular access. Is it fair, for example, that scientists/archaeologists can gain easy access, but not those who claim they want to use the site for religious purposes?

Prior to the building of the new visitor centre, in an attempt to find answers to some of the questions concerned with the visitor experience and management issues, a questionnaire survey of visitors to Stonehenge, which gathered demographic information and posed Likert scale 'attitude' questions, was conducted in 2004 (see Mason and Kuo, 2008). The survey was conducted for 2 days towards the end of the main summer season. Visitors were questioned at a point just outside the main turnstile entrance to Stonehenge. The major results are presented below.

Approximately 40 per cent of visitors were British, whilst almost 60 per cent were from overseas with the single biggest group (29 per cent) from the United States. There were also a large number of visitors from continental Europe. Approximately three-quarters were first-time visitors and the remaining respondents who had visited more than once were nearly all British. In terms of motivational factors for visiting, the uniqueness of Stonehenge, its status as a WHS and its role in helping visitors' understanding of archaeology and prehistory were the most significant. In relation to the visitor experience, generally favourable responses were revealed, with interpretation at Stonehenge being viewed as largely satisfactory, and visitors were particularly pleased with the audio wands. However, the various facilities and amenities at the monument, such as the toilets and food kiosk, achieved mixed results. The survey suggested a desire by visitors to regulate visitation, so that Stonehenge can be conserved, to ensure future generations continue to enjoy the monument. But visitors also wanted Stonehenge to be available for all types of visitor and not just specialist groups.

Although there was generally little difference between male and female visitors' responses, female visitors felt more strongly about the uniqueness of the site and also felt more strongly than the males that not allowing visitors to touch the stones is necessary to conserve Stonehenge. There were differences between British and overseas visitors in relation to views on entrance charges. Overseas visitors supported more strongly than British visitors the entrance charge for adults. Overseas visitors also showed a higher acceptance of increasing entrance charges and using the extra income for resource protection. There were also some differences between first time and repeat visitors' views on entrance charges, who should be allowed access and whether visitors should be encouraged to go to the new visitor centre, which would, it was assumed in the question statement, be built away from Stonehenge, rather than Stonehenge itself. With reference to the statements concerned with these three issues, repeat visitors' Likert scale mean scores were lower than those for first-time visitors.

Although this survey was only a snapshot of views at a particular moment in time, the responses of the visitors reveal a variety of views, and a rather more complex picture than much of the rhetoric concerning Stonehenge. In summary, and largely contradicting the UK Government Report suggesting that Stonehenge is a 'national disgrace', the majority of visitors indicated that Stonehenge is a unique site, with good interpretation, a fair entrance charge, generally good value for money and, overall, an enjoyable experience.

The research conducted at Stonehenge, described in the case study above, took place before the building of the new visitor centre, which at the time of writing has been open for just over a year. It will be very interesting, in the next few years, to note what affect this centre has on, for example, visitor numbers, types of visitors and their attitude to their experience.

Stonehenge is located in the county of Wiltshire in the United Kingdom. This county has more prehistoric sites than any other in the United Kingdom. Only 30 km away from Stonehenge, at

Avebury, is another stone circle, albeit with a much larger diameter than that at Stonehenge. Another difference in appearance between Stonehenge and Avebury is that the site of Avebury includes a village located within the stone circle. The site has been used for continuous habitation for probably 5,000 years. This means there are somewhat different visitor management issues.

The site is owned by the National Trust (NT). This is a body set up just over 100 years ago (1895) as a charitable organization to preserve both natural and built heritage. It is the biggest membership organization in the UK and owns areas of land and many old country houses. Rather confusingly, the site is in the 'guardianship' of EH and is managed by the NT. Avebury, like Stonehenge, is a WHS (see Photo 9.3).

Because of the nature of the site, with a living community inside the stone circle, there are different management issues. These are as follows:

- There is no entrance charge, because a road cuts through the site and hence it would be very difficult to have one.
- There is a car park (see Photo 9.4) at some distance from the site, so visitors have to walk to the site itself, but there is only a relatively low parking charge here during the main season and not in winter at all.
- There is a museum that is also a visitor centre. There is no charge to NT members here, but there are many NT and EH publications, plus souvenirs on sale here. There is a small café. There is a public house, shops and cafés in the village, mainly catering for tourists.
- The stone circle is easily accessible and the stones can be touched. However, the land is also used for sheep grazing, dog walking and the circle is cut in two by a busy, relatively dangerous road. The road passing through raises questions of authenticity/satisfaction of tourists.
- Avebury is a living community, so there is potential for conflict, in particular the feelings of locals in relation to the satisfaction of visitors.
- Periodically in the last 25 years, a number of stones have been defaced by graffiti. This has led to arguments over whether there should be continued free access, or if the area should be roped off, as at Stonehenge.
- Unlike Stonehenge, there is no security team. This is viewed as not desirable as the site is part of a living community.

Photo 9.3 Prehistoric Avebury is a WHS in the care of the NT

Photo 9.4 Parking at Stonehenge (and nearby Avebury) is a major visitor management issue

The site at Avebury, unlike that at Stonehenge, is not marketed directly either to domestic or overseas visitors. It is largely by word-of-mouth, and a small range of publications, that it is known. This is part of a deliberate visitor management strategy, which has been used in the past in an attempt to limit the number of visitors (R. Henderson, personal communication, 8 January 2003). The strategy to date appears to have been successful, as Avebury received only 54,000 'official' visitors in 2000. However, these were visitors recorded in the Avebury museum and it is likely the number of visitors to the stone circle will have been at least three or four times this figure (R. Henderson, personal communication, 8 January 2003). This means that probably 200,000 to 250,000 visitors come annually to Avebury. It is not possible to know exact numbers, as the site has a permanent settlement in it and hence access is needed for residents and there is no entrance charge to Avebury stone circle itself, although a charge is made in the nearby visitor car park. Nevertheless, Avebury has not had the visitor management problems of Stonehenge and the different approach here suggests that such problems are unlikely to occur in the near future. Despite the low visitor numbers and scale of activities at Avebury, there is a cost to maintaining the site. Hence, a key question for the future remains: 'What economic contribution does the site make to its own upkeep?'

Table 9.1 provides a summary and comparison of the major tourism management issues at Stonehenge and Avebury.

Summary

Visitor management involves regulating and often educating visitors. Controlling visitor numbers and/or modifying their behaviour are important approaches. Adapting the resources used by tourists is another approach in visitor management. Various techniques, including interpretation and the use of codes of conduct, can be used in relation to these visitor management approaches.

In some locations, New Zealand is one such example, managing visitors is not straightforward. This relates to the attitudes to the use of the environment amongst domestic visitors – they

Table 9.1 Comparison of major tourism management issues at Stonehenge and Avebury in 2014

Stonehenge	Avebury
Continual increase in visitor numbers: currently over one million/year.	Visitor numbers in slight decline since 2010.
Well known domestically and internationally.	Lesser known domestically and very little known internationally.
Strongly marketed internationally.	Previously de-marketed (left off some tourist maps, not mentioned in some tourist guides).
High density of visitors in a small area.	Low density of visitors in large area.
Highly regulated and structured visitor experience: visitors reach site by 'train' and follow footpath encircling stones.	Open, unrestricted access to stones: visitors can also walk to nearby prehistoric sites e.g. Silbury Hill and West Kennet Long Barrow.
Visitor facilities in new £25 million visitor centre opened in December 2013.	A cluster of facilities including restaurant/café, National Trust shop, two museums and toilets (200m from car park). A public house and two shops serving village (as well as tourists).
Very large car park adjacent to visitor centre.	
Almost all visitors arrive by private car, coaches and tour buses.	Car park away from stones/village (200 m) 'Pay and display', £5 all day in summer 2012.
Incessant flow of visitors on site, but regulated by arrival and departure of 'trains'.	Almost all visitors arrive by private car, coach or bus.
Entrance charge 2014, adults £14.50 (£7.80 in 2012 before opening of new visitor centre).	No entrance fee to Avebury – a living community.
Interpretation through hand-held audio guides available in 10 languages in 2012.	Major road bisects circle – potentially dangerous hazard for visitors.
Detailed interpretation of Stonehenge and surrounding landscape at new visitor centre.	A trickle of visitors spread over a relatively large area.
Signage at site.	No on-site interpretation.
More than 250 archaeological exhibits in visitor centre, state-of-the art audio-visual presentation and reconstructed face of 5,500- year-old man found 2.5 km from site.	No on-site signage; brief panels at car park and leaflet from (seasonal) National Trust caravan/hut.
Some archaeological finds also displayed in museums in Salisbury and Devizes.	Significant archaeological finds displayed on site (Stables and Barn Galleries) and at Devizes museum.

Source: Based on Kuo and Mason (2013).

expect to have free, unhindered access to virtually all areas. Increasing numbers of international visitors will place greater strains on even the remote wilderness areas. At currently heavily visited attractions, such as Stonehenge in the United Kingdom, there are serious concerns about visitor satisfaction, although the results of the visitor survey suggest that these concerns may be exaggerated. Nevertheless, radical solutions, including preventing site access and the creation of replicas, have been considered there and in late 2013 a new visitor centre at a distance of 1.5 km from Stonehenge was opened. However, as the example of Avebury in the United Kingdom suggests, a deliberate policy of not marketing a site may assist in the process of visitor management.

Student activities

1   What are the three main methods of controlling visitors suggested in the 1991 ETB report *Maintaining the Balance*? Consider each of these methods in turn and discuss how effective they would be in the longer term.
2   Why are there particular problems in relation to visitor management in New Zealand?
3   With reference to the case study of Kakadu National Park, produce a table with three columns headed as shown below and then complete the table:

Visitor management issue	Possible solution	Likelihood of success of solution
(a)		
(b)		
(c)		
(etc.)		

4   What effects on the visitor experience may the building of the new visitor centre have had at Stonehenge?
5   The results of the questionnaire survey conducted at Stonehenge in 2004 suggest a more complex picture than many of the conventionally held views on visitor management issues there. How would you explain the results of the survey?
6   What are the possible long-term problems/issues with the visitor management approach adopted at Avebury?
7   In relation to Table 9.1, what are the main differences, in terms of the management issues, between Stonehenge and Avebury?

Chapter 10

Managing the natural resources for tourism

Introduction

As Figure 6.1 indicates (see Chapter 6), the environment has five components: the natural environment, natural resources, wildlife, the farmed environment and the built environment. The focus of this chapter is the natural environment, natural resources and wildlife, and how these, together, act as tourist attractions. In summary, the type of tourism discussed in the chapter can be termed 'nature-based tourism'. According to Blamey (1995), much nature-based travel is generally referred to as ecotourism. This chapter focuses on the relationship between tourism and nature, discusses the concept of ecotourism and considers a number of management issues in relation to ecotourism.

Key perspectives

The natural environment and tourism are inextricably linked. By the last decade of the twentieth century, the environment was being increasingly viewed as the key resource for tourism. Therefore, ensuring that the environment is not over-exploited, suffers irreversible damage or becomes excessively polluted as a result of tourism, is a major task for tourism planners and managers in the twenty-first century. However, management of the environment is not just about maintaining the status quo, or not letting the environment decline. In fact many consumers are demanding a better quality environment for their tourism experiences (Middleton and Hawkins, 1998; Holden, 2013). However, until as recently as the mid-1990s, the aims of environmental conservation and tourism development were viewed as incompatible (Coccossis, 1996). Therefore, to benefit the environment and in turn provide higher-quality tourism experiences, it would seem vital that the relationship between tourism and the environment should be improved.

Swarbrooke (1999) made a number of suggestions on ways to improve the relationship between tourism and the environment. He argued that it is vital to take a holistic view and indicated that it is necessary to see the environment as a complex web of interrelationships that are best expressed through the concept of an ecosystem. Such a view is also supported by Fennell (1999), Hall (2000b) and Holden (2000; 2013).

A way to avoid repeated damage to the environment is to raise awareness amongst tourists and also the tourism industry. However, as has been argued in Chapter 7, there is also a need to regulate, through land-use planning and building controls, to avoid or reduce some types of negative environmental impact. It is also necessary to keep a sense of proportion, as some negative environmental impacts of tourism are not that serious and can be remedied relatively easily. Nevertheless, it has been argued that there should be greater acceptance that tourism does damage the environment and that it costs money to ameliorate or solve the problems (Hall, 2000b; Holden, 2000; 2013). Hence, it may be sensible to argue that holidays should have a built-in charge to the tourist, which is used to remedy the damage they have caused. Swarbrooke (1999) suggested that good practice does indeed exist and this should be promoted to tourism developers. In the long term, he says, it is important to maintain a balance between conserving the environment and its development for tourism purposes, although this may not be a simple, straightforward task.

The following case study of the Great Barrier Reef provides an indication of the problematic relationship between tourism and the environment, and in particular, it also presents some of the management approaches in response to the environmental impacts of tourism.

Case study: the Great Barrier Reef, Australia

The Great Barrier Reef is one of the largest coral reefs in the world with over 600 islands, 300 cay islands and almost 300 submerged reefs. There are more than 15,000 species of fish, 4,000 mollusc species and 400 sponges, as well as over 350 different types of coral. Until the mid-twentieth century, because of its location off the eastern shore of Australia, it remained relatively undeveloped for tourism. From 1975 onwards, tourism developed rapidly. The number of traditional charter boats grew dramatically after this date and in the mid-1980s high speed catamarans were introduced. Between 1982 and 1992 visitor numbers increased 35 fold and visitors were visiting four times as many sites. By 1989 there were almost one million visitors, by 1996 this had reached 2 million and by 2004 over 2.5 million and a significant proportion by this date were international visitors. The standard trip to the reef did not change very much in the last 20 years of the twentieth century. Most visitors took a day trip by large catamaran, which was then moored to a pontoon anchored close to the reef. Some visitors travel to islands that are part of the reef. In addition to the overall growth there has been a substantial increase in international visitors. In the late 1990s, Japanese formed the largest single international group of visitors, with increasing numbers from Taiwan, Hong Kong and Singapore. The main activities in this period were snorkelling and scuba diving, as well as sightseeing from semi-submersibles and glass-bottomed boats.

By the late 1990s, there was evidence of significant environmental impacts, including physical destruction of reefs by anchors and divers' feet, localized water pollution from sewage and fuel. There were also changes in fish behaviour, largely as a result of boat operators' crews feeding fish to entertain tourists. There was also the taking of souvenirs – visitors removing pieces of coral as well as fish specimens. In 1975 the Great Barrier Reef Marine Park was established, largely to attempt to provide a framework for dealing with the effects of increasing numbers of tourists. The main strategy within the park management system is zoning. Three main categories of zoning were established:

- A General Use Zone (this accounted for approximately 80 per cent of the park in the late 1990s) where almost all activities are permitted providing they are ecologically sustainable.
- National Park Zones that allow only activities that do not remove living species.
- Preservation Zones which permit only scientific research.

Tourism was permitted in the first two of these zones, but not in the Preservation Zone. Nevertheless permits were required for both the first and second zones. Factors considered in relation to the granting of permits at the time were the size, extent and location of usage, access conditions, likely effects on the environment in general and ecosystems in particular and likely effects on resources and their conservation. A number of educational strategies including pictorial symbols, guides and codes of conduct were aimed at tourists and these were backed up with local controls and prohibitions depending on particular circumstances.

In 2004 the zones were revised and new zones introduced. Seven major zones were established:

- General Use Zone
- Habitat Protection Zone
- Conservation Park Zone
- Buffer Zone
- Scientific Research Zone
- Marine National Park Zone
- Preservation Zone.

In this new zoning scheme, the General Use Zone had the widest range of activities that was permitted, while the Preservation Zone was the most restricted in terms of usage. The permit system was maintained after 2004 as well as the targeting of visitors with a variety of educational strategies. Combined together, these are still the approaches being used to encourage responsible behaviour amongst tourists and conserve the marine environment.

(Source: Mason, 2013a.)

The particular management approach used in relation to the Great Barrier Reef, as indicated in the case study, is that of zoning. In this approach, each zone has one use, or several permitted uses, as well as potential uses that are not allowed. However, zoning in a marine environment will be particularly difficult in terms of demarcating specific zones, as the water-based environment is continually moving and changing. There is also an issue of monitoring the use of any zones and specifically those where tourism is either permitted or not permitted. The Great Barrier Reef covers a vast area – millions of square kilometres – so will be very difficult to monitor and there is also a lack of an adequate 'police force' to do this. Even in terrestrial areas, zoning is problematic due at least in part to demarcation and monitoring issues (Mason, 2013a).

The attraction of the Great Barrier Reef for many international tourists is the proliferation of plants and animals that cannot be seen 'in the wild' in the visitor's own home area. However, the most likely location for people to see the types of plants and animals found on the Great Barrier Reef in their home area is an aquarium. Aquaria are types of zoo, and for a large number of people, zoos are the first (and perhaps only) place that they encounter such 'exotic' flora and fauna. Zoos can therefore be considered as visitor attractions where natural resources are displayed to the public (Mason, 1999; 2007b).

However, despite the fact that the role of traditional zoos has been changing in the past 25 years – from being menageries to being conservation centres – they remain controversial. With growing concern for the welfare of wildlife in captivity, there has been a re-examination, in the last 20 years or so, of the traditional zoo's purpose and function (Davis, 1996). The following case study shows the views of visitors on the role of the zoo and provides an insight into the way animals as natural resources are managed for tourism purposes.

Case study: the role of the modern zoo

It is generally accepted that the major roles of modern zoos are as follows: amusement, education, scientific research and species preservation. In greater detail, it has been suggested that there are eight specific, yet related roles, which are as follows:

- educating people about animals;
- conserving endangered species;
- safeguarding the welfare of visitors;
- entertaining visitors to generate revenue;
- providing visitor facilities, such as catering and merchandising;
- breeding animals to halt decline in the wild;
- re-introducing captive breeds into the wild;
- carrying out zoological and veterinary research to improve animal welfare in the wild and in captivity.

To gain a better understanding of the public perception of the role of zoos, research was conducted with visitors to Wellington Zoo, New Zealand. Wellington Zoo was established in 1906 and is the oldest zoo in New Zealand. A questionnaire survey was designed for use with visitors to the zoo with the aims as follows:

- To investigate characteristics of the Zoo's visitors.
- To obtain visitors' attitudes to the roles of the Zoo.

A total of 270 Zoo visitors completed the questionnaire survey. In terms of demographic factors, the sample was similar to that for earlier surveys conducted at the Zoo. In relation to the specific roles of the Zoo, a number of statements were prepared. These statements were developed from other researchers' work in similar types of zoos and in addition were based on previous questions used in earlier Wellington Council surveys at the Zoo. Using a five-point Likert scale, visitors were provided with a number of statements in relation to the Zoo's roles. Results from this question are shown in the table below and they have been aggregated to 'Agree' and 'Disagree'. This aggregation has been achieved in the following way: results in the categories 'Strongly Agree' and 'Agree' have been aggregated to 'Agree' and those in the category 'Strongly Disagree' and 'Disagree' have been aggregated to 'Disagree'. This table shows that the respondents indicated the educational role was the most important, with breeding and conserving animals also significant, whilst a majority of respondents disagreed with the statement indicating that the Zoo is mainly a tourist attraction.

Likert-scale statements on the roles of Wellington Zoo

	Agree	Disagree	Don't know
It is an organization that mainly breeds rare animals	63%	15%	22%
It is an organization set up mainly to educate people	94%	3%	3%
It is an organization set up mainly as a tourist attraction	32%	53%	15%
It is an organization set up mainly to conserve animals	54%	24%	22%

Respondents also received another type of question concerned with the roles of the Zoo. Here they were given a number of statements and could circle as many as they viewed as appropriate. The responses in relation to this question about the roles of the Zoo are shown in the table below.

Wellington Zoo roles

Statement on role of Zoo	Percentage of respondents circling each statement
A place of relaxation?	73
A place for education?	79
A place where visitors can see animals entertaining them?	46
A place for research?	37
A place for conservation?	55
Other?	6

Note: respondents could circle as many statements as they wished

This table indicates that the most important role according to respondents was 'education', closely followed by 'relaxation'. Just over a half of respondents indicated that the Zoo was a place for conservation and just under a half that it was a place where animals would entertain them. Just over a third indicated that the Zoo was a place for research. In summary, visitors perceived that the Zoo's single most important role was that of education. The Zoo was viewed also as having an important recreational role. A majority of visitors indicated that the Zoo had important roles in the two related areas of conservation and breeding animals, but over a third (approximately 35 per cent) were not aware of these roles. Although the Zoo's roles of education and entertainment appear not to be currently in conflict, the lack of awareness of the Zoo's conservation role by over one-third raises questions about the future of the traditional zoo. In particular, should managers market Wellington Zoo as primarily a place for family relaxation, where 'passive' education occurs, or should they promote the Zoo as a place where all visitors can learn about the need for conservation through active educational experiences? The response to these questions will affect the way animals are exhibited, the day-to-day running of the Zoo and its overall goals and related management strategy.

(Based on Mason, 2007b.)

A number of authors (see Mason, 2000; Ryan and Saward, 2003) have suggested that, as zoos are nature-based visitor attractions, they may offer the opportunity for ecotourism experiences. Ecotourism is considered to be a form of tourism where there is a potentially beneficial relationship between tourism and the natural environment. The term ecotourism has emerged in the last 30 years or so and, particularly during the last decade of the twentieth century, this form of tourism grew very rapidly. Unfortunately, there is little agreement on what, precisely, it is. It has emerged as an alternative (to mass tourism) form of tourism (Mowforth, 1992). However, terms such as 'responsible' and 'sustainable' have also been linked closely with the term ecotourism (Cater, 1994).

What is clear, however, is that ecotourism is a form of nature-based tourism (Boo, 1990). The concept of ecotourism appears to have emerged from the work of the Mexican researcher Ceballos-Lascurain in 1987. He indicated that nature tourism could be defined as:

> Tourism that consists in travelling to relatively undisturbed or uncontaminated natural areas with the specific objectives of studying, admiring and enjoying the scenery and its wild plants and animals, as well as any existing (both past and present) cultural manifestations.
>
> (Ceballos-Lascurain, cited in Boo, 1990)

Ceballos-Lascurain also used the term 'ecological tourist' (this was probably the first time the term had been used) and said such a person was interested in a scientific, aesthetic or philosophical approach to travel. The concept of ecotourism developed and changed in the last decade of the twentieth century, as the following statements, which are set out in chronological order, indicate:

- A form of tourism inspired primarily by the natural history of an area, including its indigenous cultures. The ecotourist visits relatively undeveloped areas in the spirit of appreciation, participation and sensitivity. The ecotourist practises a non-consumptive use of wildlife and natural resources (Ziffer, 1989; 60).
- Ecotourism is travel to relatively undisturbed natural areas for study, enjoyment or volunteer assistance. It is travel that concerns itself with the flora, fauna, geology and ecosystems of an area, as well as the people (caretakers) who live nearby, their needs, their culture and their relationships to the land. It is envisioned as a tool for both conservation and sustainable development – especially in areas where local people are asked to forego the consumptive use of resources for others (Wallace and Pierce, 1996).
- Ecotourism is low-impact nature tourism which contributes to the maintenance of species and habitats either directly through a contribution to conservation and/or indirectly by providing revenue to the local community sufficient for local people to value and therefore protect, their wildlife heritage (Goodwin, 1996: 228).
- Ecotourism is a sustainable form of natural resource based tourism that focuses primarily on experiencing and learning about nature, and which is ethically managed to be low-impact, non-consumptive and locally oriented (in terms of control, benefits and scale). It typically occurs in natural areas and should contribute to the conservation or preservation of such areas (Fennell, 1999: 43).

In the early 1990s several researchers were attempting to classify ecotourists, and Mowforth (1992) synthesized a number of statements and used the criteria of age, method of transport, how the experience is organized, the size of budget and type of tourism activity to produce a classification of ecotourists. This is shown in Figure 10.1. As Figure 10.1 shows, according to Mowforth (1992), there are three types of ecotourist, 'rough', 'smooth' and 'specialist'.

At the end of the twentieth century, in their attempt to define ecotourism, Wearing and Neil (1999) discussed what can be considered as required aspects of this form of tourism. The 'essentials' of ecotourism they considered are summarized below:

- Ecotourism encourages an understanding of the impacts of tourism.
- Ecotourism ensures a fair distribution of benefits and costs.

Feature	The rough ecotourist	The smooth ecotourist	The specialist ecotourist
Age	Young to middle aged	Middle-aged to old	Young to old
Travelling	Individually or in small groups	In groups	Individually
Organization	Independent	Tour-operated	Independent + specialist tours
Budget	Low: cheap hotel/ b&b;local/fast food; uses buses	High: 3–5 star hotels; luxury cafés; uses taxis	Mid–high: cheap 3 star hotels; mid-lux. cafés; as necessary
Type of tourism	Sport and adventure	Nature and safari	Scientific investigation/ hobby pursuit

Figure 10.1 A classification of ecotourists
Source: Mowforth (1992).

- Ecotourism generates local employment, both directly in the tourism sector and in various support and resource management sectors.
- Ecotourism stimulates profitable domestic industries – hotels and other lodging facilities, restaurants, transportation systems, handicrafts and guide services.
- Ecotourism generates foreign exchange and injects capital and new money into the local economy.
- Ecotourism diversifies the local economy, particularly in rural areas.
- Ecotourism seeks decision-making among all segments of the society including local populations, so that tourism and other resource users can co-exist.
- Ecotourism incorporates planning and zoning, which ensure tourism development appropriate to the carrying capacity of the ecosystem.
- Ecotourism stimulates improvements to local transportation, communications and other community infrastructures.
- Ecotourism creates recreational facilities which can be used by local communities as well as domestic and international visitors.
- Ecotourism encourages and helps pay for preservation of archaeological sites, and historic buildings and districts.
- Ecotourism monitors, assesses and manages the impacts of tourism, develops reliable methods of environmental accountability and counters any negative effect.

It may appear that the list of essential elements of ecotourism produced by Wearing and Neil (1999) is aspirational rather than closely based on reality. Hence, there is a real danger that the term ecotourism can be misused or abused. If ecotourism is perceived by potential tourists as a more desirable form of tourism, then using the term as a marketing ploy has significant advantages for tour operators and other sectors of the tourism industry. This is compounded by the lack of agreement on the meaning of ecotourism. Therefore, it is possible for unscrupulous operators to use the label 'ecotourism' to draw in potential customers, increase the price of the holiday and in turn raise their profits while providing an experience which does nothing for environmental or cultural conservation (see Mason and Mowforth, 1996; Fennell, 1999). This type of activity has been termed 'greenwashing' (see Fennell, 1999; Fennell and Malloy, 2007).

One way to discover if ecotourism justifies its name and is not mere 'greenwash' is to find out if operators, actually, do what they say they do in their promotional material. Research into the nature of ecotourism operators in New Zealand was conducted by Bonzon-Liu in an attempt to reveal if companies practised what they preached. The results from this research are presented in the case study below.

Case study: ecotourism operators in New Zealand

Bonzon-Liu's survey of ecotourism operators in New Zealand investigated the particular practices of the operators in relation to sustainability issues. Bonzon-Liu was particularly interested to discover which practices were regarded as sustainable by operators and were adopted by them and which activities were regarded as unsustainable. The following were found to be the major response categories in relation to sustainability and each includes further comment/examples from the data:

- *Ethical matters*: operators should publicly display codes of conduct and guidelines, they should indicate that they put the environment before profit, they should provide leadership in conservation efforts, they need to promote conservation, and put into practice their sustainable philosophy.
- *Education*: enhancing visitor knowledge, providing written and verbal information, using knowledgeable and competent interpretation staff and guides are key components of education within ecotourism. The education component has a strong conservation message, and clients should leave with a greater concern for environmental matters.
- *Focus on nature*: interpreting the environment is at the centre of ecotourism. However, ecotourism neither requires consumptive activities such as fishing, nor is it necessarily environmental activity such as skiing, rock climbing or adventure tourism. Ecotourism involves appreciating the environment in the context of the environment, but does not necessarily involve intensive use of it.
- *Minimizing impacts*: ecotourism should minimize all forms of tourism impact. This can be achieved through limiting group size, leaving wildlife alone, keeping noise level to a minimum, minimizing the use of fuel, minimizing visual impacts, restricting over-development, attempting to prevent litter and other forms of pollution.
- *Proactive measures*: ecotourism is not just about restricting activities but promoting certain types of behaviour/activities. Ecotourism should contribute financially to the protection and conservation of the environment, make use of environmentally friendly products, recycle, re-use and reduce waste, actively involve participants in conservation projects, be actively involved in research and act as an advocate for the environment.

Bonzon-Liu asked about unsustainable practices and classified the responses received under three headings:

- *Ethical matters*: a short-term focus, profit put before environmental concern, the lack of codes of conduct, growth-orientated rather than enhancement-orientated.

● *Environmental impacts*: damage to flora and fauna, overcrowding, poor waste disposal, disturbance to wildlife habitats, the use of vehicles which create too much noise and/or damage the environment.

● *Organizational problems*: lack of an adequate infrastructure for tourism, poor communication channels, poor education provision, lack of fees gathered to assist in maintenance of tracks and huts, failure to recognize significance of codes of conduct, poor planning and management of natural areas, uncontrolled and rapid growth of tourism.

(Adapted from Bonzon-Liu, 1999.)

As stated above, ecotourism usually has been viewed not just as an alternative form of tourism, but as a preferable form, in terms of the impacts it may have and the supposed benefits it may bring. In this way it is often considered a 'better' form of tourism. However, this raises the question of how to assess whether ecotourism is 'better' than other forms of tourism. This is likely to be particularly important for tourists when they are comparing different tourism products, and especially significant for local residents and government officials in tourism destinations, who will want to know whether one form of tourism is better for the economy, society and the local environment.

However, assessing whether ecotourism has different effects to other types of tourism will not be straightforward. There is no fully accepted set of measures of tourism impacts. Nevertheless, one way of assessing impacts is to ask local residents involved in an ecotourism setting to give their views. In the context of Nepal, Nyaupane and Thapa (2004) attempted such an approach, when they conducted a comparative study involving two areas in the Annapurna Conservation Area. They deliberately attempted to compare communities that were all in nature-based tourism locations where the attractions were fairly similar. Four communities were researched: two were on a well-used trekking trail, the Annapurna Sanctuary Trail, and were traditional mountain communities that have been receiving significant numbers of tourists for several decades, the other two settlements were on a recently designated 'Eco-trek' trail, which had far less usage than the Annapurna Sanctuary Trail. Research involved a sample of residents in each of the four communities and was conducted via an 'on the spot' questionnaire survey, with the researcher recording responses due to high levels of illiteracy in the area. The results are particularly interesting as they can be seen, at least partly, to provide support for much of the rhetoric on ecotourism. The residents of the small-scale Eco-trek communities indicated far fewer negative consequences than residents of the Annapurna Sanctuary Trail communities. Those advocating ecotourism in preference to other forms of tourism have frequently used the argument that there will be fewer negative impacts in ecotourism, than in more conventional forms of tourism. However, more unexpectedly, the study indicated that there was less in the way of positive tourism impacts in the Eco-trek communities than in the Annapurna Sanctuary Trail communities. Hence, in summary, this research indicates that scale is very important in relation to ecotourism and by implication all forms of tourism, as small-scale tourism locations suffered less negative consequences but gained fewer benefits, whilst larger-scale tourism destinations had more of both positive and negative impacts.

The research approach used in the case study of New Zealand tour operators above, and that in the example from Nepal discussed in the previous paragraph, indicates a reliance on individual respondents answering questions and giving their opinion on the nature of ecotourism and its relation to other forms of tourism. However, there are also less subjective ways of evaluating ecotourism and these can result in more objective assessments of the activity to help distinguish it from other forms of tourism. This will usually involve using criteria that can be measured to verify the credentials of companies or organizations that make claims about their tourism products. One particular approach has been through the use of ecolabels. Ecolabels have been connected with a variety of tourism products and are intended to indicate the 'green' credentials of the product. Eco-labels are predicated on the concept of certification. Certification is a formal process in which an independent body certifies to interested parties, such as tourists, marketing bodies and regulators, that a tourism provider complies with a specified standard (Buckley, 2002).

Eco-labels have been in existence for over 25 years. In 1988 there were just three schemes globally, by 2000 at least 75 and today there are probably several hundred in the world. Eco-label awards have been given to destinations, tourism products, tour operators and tourism attractions. Labels can be classified according to whether they cover the whole world or are regional only, and also whether there is one uniform label or they are multi-tiered, in other words have a basic level and advanced level.

The first global tourism eco-label was Green Globe 21. It embraced all types of tourism products and destinations across the world. It was originally set up in 1994 as Green Globe by the World Travel and Tourism Council. However it remained almost unknown and ineffective, until it was then taken over in 1999 and became a not-for-profit company, known as Green Globe 21. It currently has three levels of membership: 'affiliated', 'benchmarked' and 'certified' (Weaver, 2006).

Although the tourism industry, like many other industries, is not always happy about external regulation, eco-labels offer certain advantages to private companies. The award of eco-label certification can lead to positive publicity, which is a form of free marketing. There is then the likelihood of more sales to 'green/discerning' consumers, as well as greater leverage to charge higher prices. A company can also claim there is external recognition of any sustainability claim it makes. It can also use the external verification of its claim to stave off government attempts to regulate it, by arguing it is not necessary as it already has independent verification of its activities (see Mason and Mowforth, 1996). There are many small and medium enterprises (SMEs) in the tourism industry and eco-label schemes may allow these SMEs to benefit from links with other (larger) companies that already have the certification. This will enable the SME to network with these companies and, hopefully, gain the certification themselves.

However, it is vital if eco-labels are to be successful that they are recognized and endorsed by consumer groups, government bodies and NGOs as well as by members of the tourism industry. Below is a case study of a particularly successful example of a European eco-label which was developed by an NGO, has been in existence for more than a quarter of a century, and has had a significant impact on coastal areas.

Case study: eco-labels – the Blue Flag award

Blue Flag is similar to many other eco-label initiatives as it is regional rather than international. It is Europe-focused and Europe-wide and concerned with beach quality and marinas. It is an example of an early eco-label as it first appeared in 1987.

Blue Flag is operated by the not for profit NGO 'Foundation for Environmental Education for Europe' (FEEE). It originally applied 27 criteria (now 32) to beaches and 22 (24) to marinas – these are under four headings: water quality, environmental education and information, environmental management, safety and services. Most of these criteria are obligatory and some are recommended, according to differing local circumstances.

The award is given annually, but for one year only. It was awarded to 2,264 beaches and 600 marinas in Europe in 2004. In 2012 it was awarded to 2,346 beaches and 690 marinas. The procedure for giving the awards involves initially a national jury in each country, made up of NGO representatives and staff from government agencies who conduct the first round of assessment. Successful beaches are then forwarded to an international committee, which has five representatives from the parent body, FEEE, and one each from the World Tourism Organization, United Nations Environment Programme, the European Union and the European Union for Coastal Conservation. This committee then conducts its own assessment and either accepts or rejects the beaches submitted by the national committees. The Blue Flag award can be withdrawn at any time if violation of criteria occurs.

The Blue Flag criteria are set out in the table below.

Water quality	Environmental management
The beach must comply with water quality sampling/frequency requirements.	The local authority must have a beach management plan.
The beach must comply with standards for water quality analysis.	The local authority must comply with all regulations affecting the beach.
No industrial wastewater sewage/discharges are allowed to affect the beach.	The beach must be clean.
The beach must comply with Blue Flag microbiological parameters for faecal coli bacteria (*E. coli*).	Algae/natural vegetation/natural debris must be left on beach.
The beach must comply with Blue Flag requirements of physical/chemical parameters.	Sufficient waste disposal bins must be available at the beach and be regularly maintained.
	Recycling facilities must be available.
	An adequate number of toilets must be provided.
	Toilets must be kept clean.
	Toilets must have controlled sewage disposal.
	No unauthorized camping/driving/dumping is allowed.
	Access by dogs is to be strictly controlled.
	Buildings/beach equipment must be maintained.
	Coral reefs (if any) nearby have to be monitored.
	A sustainable means of transport to the beach must be promoted.

(*continued*)

Case study: eco-labels – the Blue Flag award (continued)

Education/information	Safety and services
Information about Blue Flag must be displayed.	There has to be an adequate number of lifeguards/lifesaving equipment.
Environmental education activities must be offered and promoted to beach users.	First aid equipment must be available.
Information about bathing water quality must be displayed.	Emergency plans for pollution need to be in place.
Information about local ecosystems and environmental phenomena must be displayed.	There has to be management of beach users to prevent accidents/conflict.
A map of the beach showing different facilities must be displayed.	There must be safety measures to protect users.
A code of conduct linked to local laws about the beach/surrounding area must be displayed.	Drinking water must be available.
	At least one Blue Flag beach in a local authority area must have wheelchair/disabled access.

(Adapted from FEEE, 2012)

Summary

Natural resources include the natural environment and wildlife. Nature-based tourism has become very important in the last 15 or so years. A particular type of nature-based tourism that emerged in the late 1980s was ecotourism. Initially concerned primarily with the environment, ecotourism had changed by the end of the twentieth century to include cultural factors. Education is viewed as a key component of ecotourism and increasingly the host community is seen as having an important role to play. However, it is possible that ecotourism may tend towards mass tourism in terms of its impacts. Ecotourism can also be used as a convenient label, which may in fact lead to the promotion of more tourism. In this way, it can be argued that ecotourism may also contribute more to a feeling of satisfaction amongst participants in the activity, than actual conservation of the environment. However, the use of eco-labels is an attempt to make eco-tourism a more objective, measurable activity. Nevertheless, there is still a lack of conclusive evidence that ecotourism is necessarily a 'better' form of tourism than other forms of tourism.

Student activities

1   What are the visitor attractions of the Great Barrier Reef? What issues are there in relation to the planning and management of tourism to the Great Barrier Reef?
2   List the key components of ecotourism.

3 Summarize how the concept of ecotourism developed and changed during the 1980s and 1990s. How would you summarize the concept of ecotourism today? What is different about the concept of ecotourism today compared with the original definition from the 1980s?

4 Why do some tourists view ecotourism as a preferable option to mass tourism?

5 What reasons might tour operators give for their involvement in ecotourism?

6 Study the case study of New Zealand ecotourism operators. How does ecotourism differ from more conventional tourism according to the information in the case study.

7 Why is scale of activity important in relation to ecotourism?

8 In relation to the Blue Flag case study, working in groups of three/four, assume you are the national committee that has been asked to assess a beach in your local area. Discuss how you would go about this task and in particular focus on:

- what techniques you would use to collect data in the 'field';
- what documents you would need to access;
- the type of information you could access online;
- who you would question.

Also discuss any problems that you envisage could occur while involved in this task.

Chapter 11

Tourism planning and management and the host community

Learning objectives

At the end of this chapter you should:

- understand the role that host communities have in tourism planning and management;
- be aware of obstacles that impede the involvement of host communities in tourism development;
- be aware of opportunities for local participation in community tourism development;
- be aware of the attitudes of members of host communities to proposed tourism development.

Introduction

Increasingly, the host community is being recognized as a major player in decision-making about tourism management and the future direction of tourism. However, as has been stated previously, the term host community is not necessarily appropriate, as tourists are not always welcome in a destination and a more appropriate term could be local community, resident community or destination community. However, the term is employed below as it is now commonly used in tourism literature.

Key perspectives

It is very important to note that as with tourists, the host community is heterogeneous not homogeneous and hence there is no such thing as a host community. In addition to the obvious variations in gender and age, any host community is likely to be a mixture of individuals and groups with varied political persuasions and attitudes to tourism, and will include those with a vested interest in tourism.

This heterogeneity is not always recognized, particularly by tourists. Tourists, particularly from wealthy, developed countries, are often attracted by the products of a host community in a developing country, such as arts and craft as well as less tangible factors, including music and dance. Such manifestations may be the product of what is perceived as the 'traditional community' and tourists may be far less interested in other aspects of a heterogeneous community, as well as individual members of the community who are not viewed as being within the realm of the 'traditional'. Nevertheless, making direct contact with members of a particular community and staying with them can also be a major attraction for some tourists. However, as the earlier discussions have indicated, there are a number of problems that may result from the contact between tourists and members of host communities, particularly in terms of the demonstration effect, erosion of host community values and possible loss of cultural identity.

Partly because of the problems that result from contact between some international tourists and communities in developing countries, and in an attempt to ensure greater benefits to host communities, there has been a focus, recently, on community participation in tourism planning and development. As Mowforth and Munt (1998) argued, one of the criteria often agreed as essential to achieving sustainability in any new tourism scheme, is the participation of local people. However, until about 20 years ago, most tourism development lacked the direct involvement of local people (Mowforth and Munt, 1998). As Pretty (1995: 4) stated in relation to development projects in general: 'The terms "people participation" and "popular participation" are now part of the normal language of development agencies.'

However, as Pretty claimed, participation can mean different things to different people. Pretty created a typology of participation and this is shown in Figure 11.1. Pretty also included a critique of each form of participation. Figure 11.1 shows that in some forms of participation, such as 'manipulative participation', actual power lies with groups beyond the local community. In fact, in this typology, it is only under the headings of 'interactive participation' and 'self-mobilization' that local peoples are actively involved in decision-making.

Pretty's typology may appear to imply that it is always better to have local communities involved in making decisions about tourism development in their community. However, involving local communities in decision-making about development projects does not necessarily ensure their success (Mowforth and Munt, 1998). Holden (2000) cited two examples in which local participation in decision-making led to the choice of a tourism project with significantly

Typology	Characteristic of each type
(1) Manipulative participation	Participation is simply a pretence: 'people's' representatives on official boards, but they are unelected and have no power.
(2) Passive participation	People participate by being told what has been decided or has already happened: involves unilateral announcements by project management without any listening to people's responses; information shared belongs only to external professionals.
(3) Participation by consultation	People participate by being consulted or by answering questions: external agents define problems and information-gathering processes, and so control analysis: process does not concede any share in decision-making; professionals under no obligation to account for people's views.
(4) Participation for material incentives	People participate by contributing resources (e.g. labour) in return for food, cash or other material incentive: farmers may provide fields and labour but are not involved in testing or the process of learning: this is commonly called participation, yet people have no stake in prolonging technologies or practices when the incentives end.
(5) Functional participation	Participation seen by external agencies as a means to achieve project goals, especially reduced costs: people may participate by forming groups to meet project objectives; involvement may be interactive and involve shared decision-making, but tends to arise only after major decisions have already been made by external agents; at worst, local people may still only be co-opted to serve external goals.
(6) Interactive participation	People participate in joint analysis, development of action plans and strengthening of local institutions: participation is seen as a right, not just the means to achieve project goals; the process involves interdisciplinary methodologies that seek multiple perspectives and use systematic and structured learning processes. As groups take control of local decisions and determine how available resources are used, so they have a stake in maintaining structures and practices.
(7) Self-mobilization	People participate by taking initiatives independently of external institutions to change systems: they develop contacts with external institutions for resources and technical advice they need, but retain control over resource use; self-mobilization can spread if governments and NGOs provide an enabling framework of support. Self-mobilization may or may not challenge existing distributions of wealth and power.

Figure 11.1 Pretty's typology of participation
Source: Pretty (1995).

more damaging environmental effects than some other rejected possibilities. However, as Mowforth and Munt suggested, criticism of the failure of local people to make appropriate decisions about their future may come from those with a vested interest in a project, such as government officials or even development agencies. Nevertheless, as Middleton and Hawkins (1998) suggested, there is little evidence that effective community-led tourism has been implemented. They argued that even in Canada, where Murphy (1985) suggested that affluent local communities are better placed than many others in the world, this has not happened. Middleton and Hawkins suggested that there are those who will argue that community-led planning has never worked, because it has never really been tried. They reject this and argued that the main reason that community-led planning has failed is due to the fact a community does not really exist and hence obtaining a consensual view on tourism development is virtually impossible.

As Murphy (1985) indicated, it is relatively easy for a community to unite in opposition to a tourism development. However, it is far more difficult for a community to: 'Conceptualize, agree and then achieve its own long-run tourism future' (Middleton and Hawkins, 1998: 127).

Within the context of New South Wales, Australia, Jenkins (1993) indicated why this is a difficult process. He suggested that there are seven impediments to local participation in tourism planning. In summary, these are as follows:

● A lack of understanding amongst the public of complex and technical planning issues.
● The likelihood that the public will not have a good understanding of how the planning process operates or how decisions are made.
● The problem of attaining and maintaining the representation of all views in the decision-making process.

- Apathy amongst some, if not a majority of, citizens.
- The increased cost in relation to staff time and money.
- The fact that decision-making takes much longer as result of community participation.
- The overall efficiency (particularly in terms of time/money and the smooth running) of the decision-making process is adversely affected.

The following case study indicates some of the issues raised by Jenkins (1993). The case study is based on research that was conducted prior to the emergence of substantial tourism activity and is used to indicate how residents of an area view the potential impact of tourism on their community. The case study focuses on a relatively remote rural area in the North Island of New Zealand. Here, in the mid-1990s, there was little evidence of organized tourism, and hence it was possible to provide some form of benchmark of local residents' attitudes to the likely effects of a new tourism development.

Case study: resident attitudes to tourism development in the Pohangina Valley, New Zealand

The Pohangina Valley (see Photo 11.1) is a North Island New Zealand rural backwater, which has generally remained off the beaten track. The location could be described in tourism marketing language as 'undiscovered and unspoiled'. The area, originally native bush, was settled by Europeans from the late nineteenth century onwards. A number of small settlements (each with only dozens rather than hundreds of people) grew up and the region reached its peak population in the 1930s and then declined until the early 1980s.

The development, which was the focus of the field research, caused much local interest and controversy. In July 1996, a proposal to develop an old school house in the township of Pohangina was put forward. After some opposition to the use of a local community facility for a private enterprise, the proposal was withdrawn. However, community sentiment had been disturbed. A new proposal was submitted in January 1997. This involved

Photo 11.1 The isolated Pohangina Valley, New Zealand, setting for the controversial planned tourism development

(*continued*)

Case study: resident attitudes to tourism development in the Pohangina Valley, New Zealand (continued)

the establishment of a café/bar using an existing private house at a distance of 6 km from the Pohangina township. However, this proposal led to death threats for some of the intended developers, a group of eight local individuals. This, in turn, contributed to much media interest, particularly from the local evening paper, which for several days ran front-page stories about the proposal and related issues. The proposal was submitted to the local district council and after a 1-month objection period had elapsed it was granted planning permission. The questionnaire survey, which was the main research instrument, was distributed in the week following the granting of planning permission. The response rate of 47 per cent provided a demographically representative sample according to local council staff. The results of the survey were as follows:

- As tourism was at such an early stage, residents could not even be considered to be at the euphoria stage of Doxey's (1975) Irridex theory. Generally, residents were in favour of the proposed development, but a significant minority (approximately a quarter), were opposed to it. The study indicated that this community, like many others, is made up of groups and individuals with mixed views in relation to the perceived impacts of tourism. In other words, the community was heterogeneous not homogeneous in its views on tourism.
- Respondents provided their views on the development based on perceived impacts. They tended to view these impacts from their own perspective, without necessarily any reference to tourism, which is probably not surprising given the general lack of tourism development in the area. Residents believed positive impacts would be the establishment of a meeting place, provision of a place close to home to obtain a meal and drink and the related reduction in travelling time to such locations. Some responses made reference to tourism when indicating the proposed development would create jobs, attract other businesses and promote the area for tourism. The negative impacts of the development were that it would contribute to more drunken driving, generally cause traffic problems and create more noise.
- There was some indication of gender differences in response to a number of survey questions. Women tended to be more opposed to the establishment of the café/bar (see Photo 11.2) and gave as reasons such concerns as increases in drunkenness and issues of road safety. Men were more in favour of the development. In relation to tourism dimensions, a number of women who supported the development gave consideration to impacts in a rather different way from the men who supported it. The women indicated the proposal would create tourism-related jobs and business opportunities more than the men. Such differences may be a product of the different world views of the male and female respondents to the survey (see Pearce *et al.*, 1996).
- The survey revealed a high degree of community attachment to the area. However, the length of residency did not appear to affect the strength of views held. The research supports the findings of McCool and Martin (1994) and Williams *et al.* (1992) that both 'old-timers' and new comers can have strong attachments to an environment and their views are more 'place dependent' than based on social networks.

Photo 11.2 The café/bar in the Pohangina Valley which was the focus of much controversy prior to development in 1997

- The research suggested, as has been found by several other studies, that the smaller the community the more visible the tourism development and the stronger the views held.
- The research provided a benchmark of community views as it took place prior to any significant tourism development and hence should be helpful in the planning process.
- The study suggested that the large-scale studies of tourism impacts and attitudes to tourism conducted in New Zealand in the last two decades of the twentieth century, mainly by the New Zealand Tourist Board, which produced largely positive attitudes to tourism, should be read with particular care and be subjected to more critical interpretation.

(Adapted from Mason and Cheyne, 2000.)

Despite the mixed views of respondents in the Pohangina study, the café/bar opened in 1997. In the summer of 2014 it was still open. Although no formal research has taken place since its opening, as far as is known, there has been no evidence of increases in drunken driving, violence and excessive noise. It would appear that the café/bar is used by some members of the local community, predominantly farmers, as a meeting place. It is also used by some women from the local community as a meeting place and attracts a significant number of tourists from many parts of New Zealand and even international visitors. Many of these tourists come in groups (often rugby teams) to visit a relatively 'remote New Zealand country pub' (G. White, pers. comm. 2014).

In some parts of the world, there is evidence to suggest that local communities can be actively involved in tourism development and achieve benefits. One of the longest running tourism projects, which has actively involved the local community, is in Lower Casamance, Senegal, West Africa (De Kadt, 1979, 1988). The original aim of the project was to create a more meaningful exchange between local people and tourists than was then being experienced along the

Senegalese coast. Here, there were large hotel resorts built with foreign capital, and the resorts were protected by security guards and high walls. By the early 1990s, 13 tourist camps had been built with loans from l'Agence de Co-operation Culturelle et Technique (Gningue, 1993). The tourist accommodation is simple lodges, built in local architectural styles with local materials by local people. The number of guests is limited to a maximum of 40 at any one time in any lodge. Lodges have only been constructed in villages with over 1,000 inhabitants. Tourists eat local food cooked using local recipes. Public expenditure of the revenue gained from tourism is controlled by village cooperatives. The scheme has been viewed as a success as it has aided development and social stability, improved health care and education facilities, and, of great importance, provided jobs for the young which has discouraged them from migrating to the larger towns in search of work (Gningue, 1993).

Within the context of nature-based tourism, Drake (1991) suggested a model of local participation in tourism development. Drake argued that local participation referred to the ability of local communities to influence the outcomes of development projects that had an impact upon them. Drake created a nine-phase model, which is presented in Figure 11.2.

There is more chance of community development projects being accepted by local people if it is realized that there are different groups in a community with different views (Fennell, 1999). Jurowski (1996) was particularly interested in trying to get tourism developers to recognize that there are a variety of individual values in a community and tourism developers will only be successful in developing a project if they are aware of this and act accordingly. Jurowski identified a number of unique groups in a community, with three major categories. One major group he termed 'attached residents'. These were either long-term residents or older community members who loved the community because of its social and physical benefits. They also liked to have control over the form and function of the community. Jurowski suggested that tourism planners can gain the support of this group in a community if they emphasize heritage themes, indicate that the project has social and ecological benefits to the community and establish a focal point and common theme for a tourism project. The second type of community members that were identified by Jurowski, he termed 'resource users'. Such people are typically recreationists. They are ambivalent about the economic benefits of a tourism development. Developers can gain their support by providing opportunities for their interests, supporting schemes that provide skill development for young people in the community, protecting 'their sites' for participation and allocating some tourism funds to support facilities and services these people want. Jurowski's third group he referred to as 'environmentalists'. He acknowledged that this group will tend to see negative impacts of any development. Jurowski suggested that developers should, however, pay special heed to this group. Hence, developers should provide information on the following: how the project will protect the environment; how to build in ecological education programmes; how to actively involve environmentalists in the development; and how to inspire community members to develop education programmes for tourists.

According to Fennell (1999), leadership is a key principle in the process of community development. However, as Mabey (1994) suggested, this is not 'old style' leadership, but an approach that requires power to be devolved to others in the community and will involve collaboration and partnerships. In this situation, the leadership is not held constantly by one individual or a small group, but passes between different community members and these people will play the role of leader or follower according to circumstances. Fennell (1999) stated that this will occur if there is a shared common purpose and under these conditions, community members will be empowered. He argued that this is the situation in which community members will be 'holding the will, resources and opportunity to make decisions within the community' (Fennell, 1999: 221). Under such conditions, Fennell asserted, it will be possible for people both internal and

- Phase 1: Determine the role of local participation in the project. This includes an assessment of how local people can help.
- Phase 2: Choose research team. The team should include a broad multidisciplinary approach.
- Phase 3: Conduct preliminary studies. The political economic and social conditions of the community should be studied, via documents and surveys. The following should be identified: needs, local leaders, community commitment to the project, media involvement/interest, traditional uses of land, role of women, type of people interested in the project and why, likely managers and financiers of project, land ownership and cultural values.
- Phase 4: Determine the level of local involvement. This will be somewhere along a continuum from low to high intensity.
- Phase 5: Determine an appropriate participation mechanism. This is linked to the intensity of involvement, the nature of existing institutions and characteristics of local people. It is likely to involve consultation and sharing.
- Phase 6: Initiate dialogue and educational efforts. The use of the press is important in this phase as a means by which to build consensus through public awareness. Key community representatives can be used in this process. The team should explain the goals and objectives of the project, how the project will affect the community, the values of the area, and history of threats and the benefits of the project. Workshops or public meetings could be organized to identify strengths and weaknesses of the project.
- Phase 7: Collective decision-making. This is a critical stage that synthesizes all research and information from the local population. The project team present the findings of their research to the community, together with an action plan. Community members are asked to react to the plan, with the possible end result being a forum through which the team and local people negotiate to reach a final consensus based on the impact of the project.
- Phase 8: Development of an action plan and implementation scheme. In this phase, the team and community develop an action plan for implementing solutions to identified problems. They may develop a variety of positions to be occupied by local people including gift shops, résearch positions, park management positions and private outfitting companies for the local people. This local action plan must then be integrated into the broader master plan of the project.
- Phase 9: Monitoring and evaluation. Monitoring and evaluation, although often neglected, should occur frequently and over the long term. The key to evaluation is to discover whether goals and objectives set out early in the project's life cycle have been accomplished or not.

Figure 11.2 Local participation in nature-based tourism: Drake's (1991) nine-phase model

external to a community to provide assistance, while local people will actually be able to shape and control the pace of tourism development.

A relatively new feature of host population involvement in tourism planning and development is the participation of indigenous people. As Weaver (2006: 145) indicated, this is not just involvement but 'the growing empowerment and assertiveness of indigenous people, which can be likened to an indigenous renaissance'. This process can be observed in the United States and Canada where there is the movement towards self-government and native controlled reserves and reservations (Weaver, 2006). One important difference between planning of tourism inside and outside a reserve is that local state or municipal planning laws and regulations do not usually apply inside a reserve. This has led to establishment of, for example, casinos on native reserves in the USA, when they are not allowed in the non-indigenous parts of the actual state in which the reserve is located (Weaver, 2006).

Another indication of the growing empowerment of indigenous communities is evident in the management of Uluru (formerly known as Ayers Rock) in Australia. During colonial times the land on which Uluru National Park is located was taken from the local Aborigines. Ownership of the national park has now reverted to descendants of the original Aboriginal owners of the land, and the park has a joint management scheme of non-indigenous and Aboriginal representatives. The land has been leased back for 99 years to the Northern Territories authorities (Hall, 2000a). In the joint management organization, Aborigines are in the majority and this has meant a much stronger Aboriginal influence on management policy (Weaver, 2006). For visitors to Uluru in the early part of the twenty-first century the major difference they would experience compared with that of the early 1990s is that, although visitors are not prohibited, they are actively discouraged from actually climbing Uluru, as this is deemed inappropriate by the joint management organization (Weaver, 2001).

Summary

Until approximately 15 years ago, little regard was paid to the views of host communities in relation to tourism development. By the end of the twentieth century, host communities were viewed as having an increasingly important role in tourism planning and management. There are, however, a number of obstacles to the involvement of host communities in tourism planning and management. In addition to a community's possible lack of understanding of the complexity of the planning process, there is the problem of obtaining the representation of a range of views. Also, involving the community takes time and thus is costly and may adversely affect the overall efficiency of the planning process. Nevertheless, if tourism is to be a more sustainable activity it would seem essential to involve host communities in planning and management processes.

Student activities

1   Why have local communities not been actively involved in tourism planning and management until comparatively recently?
2   Apply the Drake nine-phase model (Figure 11.2) to the case study of the Pohangina Valley, New Zealand. Which phases of the model appear to have been employed and which not applied in the project?
3   Identify a tourism project in your local area or one elsewhere of which you are aware. Apply the Drake nine-phase model to this project and indicate which phases of the model appear to have been employed and which not applied in the project. Explain why the model applies, or does not apply, as the case may be.
4   What are the benefits to tourism planning and management of the greater involvement of indigenous groups and what are the possible disadvantages?

Chapter 12

Tourism planning and management and the tourism industry

Introduction

As suggested in earlier chapters, the tourism industry is made up of a great variety of both private and public sector organizations and businesses. For example, there are travel agents, tour operators, carriers such as airlines and rail companies, as well as various types of accommodation including hotels, restaurants and other food providers, the latter being found largely in the destination area. The destination zone also has entertainment providers as well as visitor attractions, transport providers, tourist information offices and other infrastructure organizations that support tourism. Here in the destination are also located Tourist Information Centres, which are public sector organizations. This chapter provides a case study of the attitudes of representatives of a number of sectors of the UK outbound tourism industry and also focuses on the actions of tour operators and accommodation providers in relation to tourism planning and management issues.

Key perspectives

As stated above, there is no clearly definable 'tourism industry'. As a result, one of the key problems that has restricted the involvement of the 'industry' in tourism management, and in the development of more responsible forms of tourism, is that tourism businesses in specific sectors of the industry have not seen this as their responsibility. In fact, the 'industry' has tended to view government as being responsible for any regulations relating to tourism. Also, particular tourism businesses while operating in a free market situation have shown little inclination to impose upon themselves, or wish to have imposed on them, anything they perceive as preventing them from having a competitive edge over other tourism businesses. Many businesses therefore perceive that regulation for environmental or social protection will interfere with business performance (Forsyth, 1995).

Either as a result of the tourism industry not seeing it as their responsibility, or because of the perception that the industry does not care about the environment in which it operates, but only its profits, the industry is often viewed as causing significant negative impacts.

Tour operators are a key element in the tourism system but are an example of an industry sector that has a reputation for causing negative impacts and creating problems. Mass-market operators tend to have only low profit margins per customer so need to ensure there are large volumes of tourists. Mass-market tour operators usually send tourists to the 'honey pots' (the more popular destinations). As Middleton and Hawkins (1998) argued, mass package tourism has been traditionally 'supply side' or 'product-led' tourism. Holidays developed under such conditions in the past were done so on an understanding of customer needs, but with virtually no regard for the so-called 'externalities' (i.e. the impacts of the activity).

Large-scale operators in the United Kingdom, for example, have traditionally worked according to three basic concepts: maximum aircraft loads, lowest possible prices and perceived advantage of market share (Middleton and Hawkins, 1998). This approach could be summarized as 'pile 'em high and sell 'em cheap', in other words, financial viability of the operator lies in selling more holidays. Generally, tour operators working under these conditions have paid little regard to the environment of the destination. In fact, the environment frequently suffered as a result of the activities of these operators. If, at one point in time, they sent large numbers of tourists to particular destinations, then the only way they could maintain or possibly increase their profits at a future point was to send even more, was the prevailing view.

However, as discussed in Part I of this book, destination areas have finite resources and compounding the problem of too many tourists is that large tour operators also have the reputation for not staying loyal to specific destinations. Hence, when a resort becomes no longer popular (which may be the direct result of too many tourists visiting in the past), the tour operator shifts allegiance to other locations. Such tour operators have also tended to use their own employees as guides rather than hire local staff. Not only does this deprive the locals of jobs, but also the knowledge of the foreign employees is likely to be far less than that of the locals. Therefore, tourists may often be misinformed about the places they are visiting. Large tour operators also negotiate contracts with local suppliers to keep costs low for the tourists, but this approach gives little economic return for the locals.

There are a number of ways in which tour operators can assist in the better management of tourism, particularly at destinations. Swarbrooke (1999) suggested what he termed a three-pronged strategy to help tour operators play a more effective role in the development of more sustainable forms of tourism. He suggested the following: local communities should develop their own tour operation enterprises; destinations should try to ensure that as much as possible of their inbound tourism be handled by small specialist operators; and mass-market operators should be encouraged to act more responsibly.

Travel agents can also make significant contributions to better planned and managed tourism. In Australia, a prominent body is the Australian Federation of Travel Agents (AFTA). This body, formed in 1957, represents the distribution agents of Australia. In the late 1990s it had almost 2,000 members, comprising 1,500 travel agencies and almost 500 allied members. This organization has emphasized professionalism amongst travel agents. Professionalism here refers to effective management, ethical behaviour and fair trading (Pearce *et al.*, 1998). AFTA has a code of conduct that is intended to bind all its members and protect the interests of the consumer. As Pearce *et al.* (1998) indicated, this code is a long-standing initiative in the world of travel. Its details are as follows:

- *Accuracy*: AFTA members will be factual and accurate in the information they provide and will not use deceptive practices.
- *Affiliation*: AFTA members will not falsely represent a person's affiliation with their firm.
- *Compliance*: AFTA members will abide by all federal, state and local laws and regulations.
- *Confidentiality*: AFTA members will treat all client transactions in confidence.
- *Conflict of interest*: AFTA members will not allow any preferred relationship with a supplier to interfere with the interests of their clients.
- *Consumer protection*: AFTA members will use every effort to protect their clients against all attempts at fraud, misrepresentation or unethical practices.
- *Cooperation*: AFTA members will cooperate with any inquiry conducted by AFTA.
- *Delivery*: AFTA members delivering tours will provide all components as stated in their brochure, or written confirmation, or provide alternative services if required.
- *Disclosure*: AFTA members will provide details about terms and conditions of travel service including cancellation fees, before accepting payment for bookings.
- *Notice*: AFTA members will promptly notify clients of any changes in price itinerary of service provided.

- *Qualifications and professionalism*: AFTA members must employ staff with appropriate qualifications and are committed to continuing professional development.

In the last decade of the twentieth century, there was some evidence that tourism businesses were starting to manage their operations with the concept of sustainability in mind. For example, Forsyth (1995) conducted research into the practices of tourism enterprises in Britain, and their attitudes to sustainable tourism. Forsyth's sample comprised 69 tourism businesses including tour operators, travel agents, hotel chains, airlines, tourism associations, national tourism offices, consultancies and also included one sea cruise operator. He used key informants in each organization and conducted semi-structured interviews with them. The aims of the research were as follows: to identify the awareness of environmental and social problems resulting from tourism and practices adopted to overcome these; to identify the main obstacles to the adoption of such practices as perceived by the industry; and to find out what the industry saw as priorities for future action for sustainable tourism. A selection of the results are shown in the case study below. The results presented in the case study are those Forsyth obtained from the tour operators, travel agents, hotels, carriers, tourism associations and consultancies. Responses were ranked and only the more important from Forsyth's research are presented here, with the top five ranked topics shown in each of Tables 12.1, 12.2 and 12.3.

Case study: business attitudes to sustainable tourism – practices, obstacles and priorities

Table 12.1 Practices of sustainable tourism currently adopted*

Ranking	Practice	Frequency of response
1	Providing 'ecotips' and advice in brochures	13
	Giving donations to local charities and schools	13
2	Sponsoring research into impact/management of tourism	9
3	Promoting specialist 'green' holidays	8
	Lobbying of destinations to improve infrastructure, etc.	8
	Recycling brochures	8
	Advising companies on short- and long-term basis	8
4	Recycling paper and brochures	6
	Advising members on sustainable tourism	6
	Training or briefing industry representatives	6
	Conducting research	6
5	Monitoring fuel emissions, noise, sea waste management	5
	Developing links with research charities	5

Note
* Responses are ranked by frequency of response.

Table 12.2 Perceived obstacles to adopting practices of sustainable tourism*

Ranking	Perceived obstacle	Frequency of response
1	The belief that others are responsible, especially governments	18
2	The fear of taking steps not matched by competitors	12
	Difficulties in educating tourists	12
3	The belief that operators are powerless to produce change	8
	Apparent lack of demand for sustainable tourism in the British market	8
	Perceived intransigence and corruption amongst host authorities	8
4	The simplistic marketing of holidays to promote only one aspect of holiday locations	7
5	The belief that travel agents are powerless to produce change	6
	The false idea that sustainable tourism must be a niche product	6

Note
* Responses are ranked by frequency of response.

Table 12.3 Perceived priorities for action*

Ranking	Practice	Frequency of response
1	Increase awareness of sustainable tourism amongst tourists	13
	Increase awareness amongst host governments	13
2	Increase the quality and therefore value of holidays	9
3	Increase the awareness of tourists	8
	Increase the awareness of governments	8
4	Train staff in tour operators, hotel and travel agents	7
	Enforce government controls on tourists and tourism development	7
	Long term marketing to achieve a differentiation in the standard holiday package to allow competition on more than price	7
5	Increase range of holidays	5
	Develop mechanisms for tour operators to re-invest in destinations	5

Note
* Responses are ranked by frequency of response.

(Adapted from Forsyth, 1995.)

Forsyth's results indicate that although members of the tourism industry are prepared to act to bring about more sustainable tourism, the obstacles they perceive to achieving this fit well with the generally held views about them. It would seem that industry representatives view it as largely somebody else's role and responsibility to create more sustainable tourism. In particular, the full results of Forsyth's work indicated that it was tour operators and travel agents who seemed to want others to take responsibility and they suggested this should be primarily government, although tourists and host communities are also perceived by industry representatives as having a key role here.

Forsyth's survey was conducted 20 years ago. Since then, it might be expected that the industry would have modified its activities in relation to pressure for more sustainable tourism and the case study below discusses to what extent this has occurred in relation to one sector of the tourism industry.

One of the most rapidly growing sectors of the industry of the past 20 years or so has been cruise ships and the case study investigates the nature of this form of tourism and specifically discusses the amount of waste that cruise ships create and the response of the industry to increasing calls for them to become more environmentally friendly.

Case study: cruise ship waste

Cruise ships are massive floating hotels that provide a range of different forms of entertainment and amenities, including shops, as well as food and accommodation. The largest ships are over 350 m (a quarter of a mile) in length and act as a home for as many as 6,500 people for the duration of their trip. They also consume a very large amount of energy and create waste on the scale of a small city. The waste consists of sewage, grey water (water from sinks and showers), solid waste, oily waste, bilge water and hazardous waste. They also create air pollution as most are powered by diesel engines.

Cruise ships have an advantage over cities in that they can minimize waste disposal costs as a result of being on the move – so they can dump waste in the open ocean. The problem of ocean dumping has been significant for several decades. The solid waste produced by a cruise ship includes glass, cardboard, paper, steel and aluminium cans and plastics. Such waste, if disposed of in the oceans, can pose a threat to marine organisms, wildlife, people and coastal communities. Marine species, including birds and mammals, can become entangled with plastics and other solid waste and as a result are injured or killed. The amount of solid waste created by a large cruise ship can be as much as 8 tons in a week and it has been estimated that as much as 24 per cent of the solid waste in the oceans comes from cruise ships.

Although ships have tried increasingly to minimize solid forms of waste and as much as 75 per cent is incinerated on board and the rest is usually pulped or ground up, most of what is left after these processes, including ash from incineration, is still dumped in the sea. Some rubbish is taken off ships for recycling, including glass and aluminium, but the scale of this removal operation is well beyond the capacity of many ports in the world. Only those in North America and a few elsewhere can handle the volume of material.

Cruise ships also produce hazardous waste including batteries, light bulbs containing mercury, medical waste, paint, and cleaning chemicals. The amounts of these materials are relatively small but they are very toxic and harmful to marine organisms if dumped at sea.

A cruise ship with 6,000 passengers on board can produce 225,000 litres of human waste and 2 million litres of grey water per day. Although most cruise ships chemically treat sewage and they must log when and how much they discharge, they are allowed to discharge this treated sewage almost anywhere – but they are not then required to monitor the quality of the sea where they dump it. Untreated sewage can be stored on board ship and then discharged outside regulated areas which means it is legal for cruise ships to release this at more than 3 miles (5 km) from shore.

There have been a number of attempts to regulate the activities of ocean going vessels, probably the most significant being the 1973 MARPOL convention, although this was not actually implemented until 1983. MARPOL specifies what can be dumped and where this can occur, so that, for example, no plastics at all can be dumped from cruise ships under MARPOL. However, 'floatable' rubbish can be dumped more than 25 miles (40 km) from shore, unground-up rubbish more than 12 miles offshore and macerated (chopped-up) rubbish smaller than 2.5 cm, at locations only 3 miles (5 km) offshore.

The cruise ship industry had until very recently a poor record in terms of its responsibility towards the environment and its ability to self-regulate. Fines totalling tens of millions of dollars have been levied against some of the major cruise companies including Royal Caribbean, Carnival Corporation and the International Council of Cruise Lines. These have been for dumping oily wastewater, discharging bilge water and damaging coral reefs, with much of this taking place in US waters.

The industry also has the reputation of stopping the introduction and application of environmentally focused laws and regulations. In the US, the cruise ship industry has been very active in lobbying the US Congress, spending hundreds of millions of dollars in doing so, to prevent acts aimed at getting the industry to clean itself up from becoming law, or at least slowing down the passage of such laws. Although the industry has negotiated memoranda of understanding (MOU) with certain US states, this has been largely interpreted as a way for the industry to stave off external regulation, rather than an indication of an industry willing to accept responsibility for the environmental consequences of its activities, as the MOU are not legally binding, do not apply to all cruise ships and do not have penalties if broken.

Many cruise ships sail under what is known as a 'flag of convenience'. This means the ship is registered in a country, such as Liberia, Panama or the Bahamas, which does not have strong environmental laws, but has low taxes and weak labour laws. Some cruise ship companies have argued that as they are registered in a 'flag of convenience' country, they are not subject to the environmental laws of the sea areas, such as the US, where they sail. Royal Caribbean argued this in relation to its dumping activities in US waters, but lost its case in 2003 and was required to pay an $18 million fine.

In the past ten years or so, the cruise ship industry appears to be making a concerted action to clean up its act. In 2003, the Ocean Conservation and Tourism Alliance was established as an industry-sponsored initiative aimed at minimizing environmental impacts in the oceans and protecting marine biodiversity. More recently, in 2006, an industry-supported NGO 'Conservation International' produced a comprehensive publication 'From Ship to Shore – Sustainable Stewardship in Cruise Destinations', which outlines a range of sustainability initiatives by cruise lines, governments and shore operators.

(Based on Brown, 2013 and Copeland, 2008.)

Not all industry sectors have the poor reputation of the cruise ship industry in relation to sustainability issues. Some accommodation providers in a number of countries have been in the forefront of attempts at more environmentally friendly, better planned forms of tourism. The Chateau Whistler Hotel Group in Canada, for example, was one of the first hotel chains to develop a code of conduct for its staff members in relation to environmental issues. In the United Kingdom, a major chain, Travel Inn, part of the Whitbread Group, which owns and operates low-cost overnight hotel/motel-style accommodation is one of several organizations attempting to minimize resource consumption. They provide the following information in each hotel room:

> Going for Green. As you know, a huge amount of washing is done every day, using large amounts of water and washing powders, which can pollute our rivers and seas. If you are staying another night and don't mind using towels again, please leave them on the towel rail and help us help the environment. . . . Help Travel Inn to help the environment. By acting in this small way, we can safeguard clean, unpolluted water for the future.

Club Méditerranée is a large global hotel chain. It has operations in many countries worldwide, including Australia. The following case study focuses on one particular Club Méditerranée development that was established in the early 1990s on one of Australia's Whitsunday Islands.

Case study: Club Méditerranée Lindemann Island, Australia

The Club Méditerranée Group's core business is resort villages, of which it had 106 in 35 countries in 1995. Its Club Méditerranée Lindemann is one of the organization's more recent developments. Lindemann Island is part of the Whitsunday Islands, which are themselves within the Great Barrier Reef Marine Park. Most of the island is a national park, controlled by the Queensland Department of Environment and Heritage (DEH). Lindemann Island has coral sand beaches and parts of the interior eucalyptus forest and rainforest were modified by pastoral farming that continued into this century. The first resort was built here in 1936 and the Club Méditerranée resort in 1992.

Although Club Méditerranée no structured approach to environmental matters in the mid-1990s, there was significant awareness within the organization of the need to factor in environmental concerns at the development stage of the operation on Lindemann Island.

At the start of the development, Club Méditerranée established a close working relationship with DEH. A major initiative requested by Club Méditerranée was the establishment of a golf course. DEH eventually granted permission but with two major conditions. First, Club Méditerranée could only develop areas that had previously been for pastoral usage and that work was to be supervised by DEH staff. Second, an agreement was signed between DEH and Club Méditerranée providing compensation for land used during the golf course development. This agreement also led to the provision of a full-time park ranger position on Lindemann, the construction of a ranger station and an interpretation centre and the making available of a Club Méditerranée staff member to work half time for 1 year at a time with DEH.

Lindemann Island Resort has a number of features that are an attempt to create a more sustainable resort facility. The details are as follows:

- *Resort buildings*. The resort was built to blend with the natural environment in terms of visual appearance, building materials, colours and it has also used some recycled materials.

- *Power*. Power is generated by an on-site generator, which has several noise limiting features. The system is computer monitored to note demand peaks and troughs. This system also controls the resort's sewage and water delivery systems. Energy minimization systems operate in the guest rooms with lights/power automatically turned off when guests leave.
- *Water resources.* Water is stored in a dam built in the 1930s. On average, there is sufficient water for 2 years, but usage is carefully monitored. Dam water is used to irrigate the resort area. There is a physical limit on the amount used each day, as the day's rations are physically stored in a tank.
- *Waste management.* All waste that decomposes quickly is crushed. Glass, cardboard, plastics and metals are separated from other waste. All waste is shipped backed to the mainland on a weekly basis. Waste levels are monitored by Club Méditerranée staff.
- *Chemical usage.* All cleaning products are phosphate free. Fertilizer usage is limited. Only occasionally is herbicide used. Chlorine is currently added to pool and drinking water.
- *Staff.* Staff are told their environmental responsibilities during their induction. Each staff member is given a copy of the Environmental Charter issued by the company. This charter has detailed statements in the form of a code of conduct, with supporting guidelines under general headings including: the web of life; the living world; and specific headings concerned with their work, including 'in the kitchens', 'laundry', 'rooms', 'boutiques' and there is also reference to 'wildlife', 'marine and land based sports', 'special events' and the 'clubs organized for children'.
- *Guests.* Guests receive information upon their arrival and are advised during their orientation session of the need to adopt a responsible attitude to their activities within the national park area. They are also informed about the availability of printed brochures on the national park.

(Adapted from Harris and Walshaw, 1995.)

The example of Club Méditerranée on Lindemann Island is a resort scale development in which environmental aspects have been factored in at an early stage of development. From the discussion in earlier chapters it should be clear that the scale of tourism operations is particularly significant in relation to tourism impacts, and by implications the management response to these impacts. The following case study discusses a small-scale, private sector development in which environmental considerations have been utmost, but also indicates the importance of economic and socio-cultural factors.

Case study: Lisu Lodge, Thailand

Lisu Lodge is located 50 km north of the northern Thai town of Chang Mai. The land on which the Lodge is located is leased from the nearby village and the development is owned by the company East West. The Lodge has been made from largely local materials based on the design of a traditional hill top tribal home of the region. It has only six

(continued)

Case study: Lisu Lodge, Thailand (continued)

bedrooms and can accommodate a maximum of 12 guests at any one time. The rooms were built following advice from tribal members of the local village

The Lodge employed seven local tribal people in the early years of the twenty-first century. One of the seven is the lodge manager. A number of guides who lead treks with tourists are local tribal people. Excursions are available to other nearby tribal communities. Tourists can also make contact with local people and the local environment via treks, lasting from one to four days, white water rafting, mountain-biking and elephant safaris. Contact between villagers and tourists is encouraged and visits to local families can be made on request. The Lodge has established a handicraft centre to employ local people. Here villagers can show their ability in weaving, embroidery, jewellery and woodwork. They can also sell products to tourists.

A key component of the visitor experience at the Lodge is learning about the local environment, its wildlife and the culture and traditions of the hill tribe people of the region. The education process involves the use of fact sheets, but in addition, local people act as tourist guides on excursions from the Lodge. Presentations are made to tourists by locals with discussion of, for example, their attempts at environmental conservation. Visiting different tribal villages in the region is a part of this educational process.

The management team of the Lodge believe that by working closely with local hill tribes, this will help promote their distinctive culture. In turn, local people will feel pride in presenting their culture to visitors. This close link between the Lodge management and local village elders is in order to ensure as authentic a visitor experience as possible. This process is made easier by the fact that the manager is a Lisu tribe member. A key aim of the Lodge management is to conserve the land around the Lodge in its natural state, while providing opportunities for education and recreation. The Lodge is marketed as an ecotourism experience and initially word-of-mouth promotion was important. Increasingly marketing is being conducted via the Internet. However the marketing approach needs to be carefully monitored as with such a small-scale development, demand could very easily exceed supply.

Lisu Lodge has won a number of major awards. In 2000, it received the Conservation International – Ecotourism Excellence Award for its contribution to conservation and the safeguarding of society and culture. In 2001 the Lodge received the USA Condé Nast *Traveler* magazine Ecotourism Award. The *Traveler* magazine, on giving the award, reported that the Lodge was evidence that the natural world and business world can not only co-exist, but even work to mutual benefit.

(Based on Johanssen and Diamantis, 2004.)

Summary

The term tourism industry is rather a misnomer as there is not one industry, rather a collection of both linked and also unrelated activities that make up what is termed 'the industry'. Partly as a result of this, the tourism industry has until very recently not viewed the planning of tourism as its responsibility. Tour operators are one key component in the industry that could make an important contribution to tourism planning and management. In the past, tour operators have had a bad reputation in terms of the impacts of tourism. The case study of the cruise ship industry provides some evidence of this. However, as the research of Forsyth (1995) suggests, some tour operators are taking more responsibility for their actions. The case study of Club Méditerranée Lindemann Island development gives an indication of what can be done, particularly in relation to environmental management. The example of Lisu Lodge also indicates that small-scale private ecotourism style developments may also assist in environmental conservation, provide educational experiences for visitors as well allow local people to financially benefit from their culture and traditions.

Student activities

1   How do tourism operators cause problems and how can they assist in the better management of tourism?
2   Study Table 12.1 in the case study of 'business attitudes'. What factors, do you suggest, contribute to the responses given by the tourism industry?
3   Study Table 12.2 in the case study of 'business attitudes'. Give reasons why you think members of the tourism industry believe these are the major obstacles to achieving sustainable tourism.
4   Study Table 12.3 in the case study of 'business attitudes'. Suggest reasons why the responses given in Forsyth's research are in the top five priorities of the tourism industry.
5   In relation to the case study of the cruise ship industry, what factors have contributed to the poor reputation of the industry in relation to waste management? What actions has the industry taken recently to improve its behaviour in relation to waste management?
6   What are the advantages of Club Méditerranée pursuing its current policy on Lindemann Island? What could be the disadvantages?
7   Lisu Lodge in Thailand appears to be a very successful tourism venture. What factors have contributed to its success? Why is this form of tourism not necessarily a solution to the problems associated with tourism in general?

Chapter 13

Partnerships and collaboration in tourism

Learning objectives

At the end of this chapter you should be able to:

- understand the meanings of collaboration and partnerships in tourism;
- understand how collaboration and partnerships in tourism are important within tourism planning and management;
- understand the nature and significance of the processes involved in collaboration and partnerships in tourism.

Introduction

The importance of involving different stakeholders in tourism planning and management received growing recognition during the last decade of the twentieth century. As Bramwell and Lane (2000: 1) claimed, 'stakeholder collaboration and partnership has the potential to lead to dialogue, negotiation and consensus building of mutually acceptable proposals about how tourism should be developed'. Clements *et al.* (1993) suggested that it is vital partnerships are developed in tourism to ensure that a high quality of product is delivered, and because tourism experiences rely on all aspects of the community.

This chapter considers advantages and disadvantages of collaboration and partnerships. It presents two case studies of partnerships – one between a number of tourism industry representatives, government officers and a non-governmental organization (NGO) and the other a community based pro-poor tourism project

Key perspectives

A number of different terms are used to describe the variety of collaborative arrangements that exist in tourism. These include coalitions, forums, alliances, private–public partnerships and also task forces. The term collaboration is particularly common in academic literature, while in government and practitioner circles the term partnership is especially popular (Bramwell and Lane, 2000).

Tourism partnerships are now relatively common in the United States and United Kingdom. It has been suggested that a major reason for the development of such partnerships is to give destinations a competitive edge (Kotler *et al.*, 1993). Broadly based ownership of tourism policies can also bring 'empowerment and equity, operational advantages and an enhanced tourism product' (Bramwell and Lane, 2000: 2).

A partnership has been described as 'an on-going arrangement between two or more parties, based upon satisfying specifically identified mutually needs (and) such partnerships are characterised by durability over time, inclusiveness, co-operation and flexibility' (Uhlik, 1995: 14). Middleton and Hawkins (1998) discussed partnerships in relation to achieving sustainable tourism. They suggested that such partnerships should be jointly negotiated and agreed approaches to tourism management in which the goals are mutually defined and endorsed, and the techniques designed to achieve matching of demand and supply are jointly operated.

Collaboration occurs 'when a group of autonomous stakeholders of a problem domain engage in an interactive process, using shared rules, norms and structures, to act or decide on issues related to that domain' (Wood and Gray, 1991: 146). As Bramwell and Lane (2000) argued, this statement by Wood and Gray is particularly useful as it encompasses the diversity of partnership forms that are likely to be found in practice. It also makes no assumptions about who is involved, how much power they may have, how representative they may be, and even how many stakeholders are involved.

Collaborative relationships can have many forms and the processes involved in the partnerships can also vary greatly. It is possible to conceptualize the relationships along a continuum from very formal to very informal. It is also possible to view the relationships as a complex web between the various stakeholders. This complex web will be greatly dependent on the nature of social, economic and political forces, but may also vary according to the particular issue that is the focus of the collaborative relationship.

Collaboration and partnerships have been advocated in tourism because of the perceived benefits they can bring. One of the major benefits, it has been suggested, is that collaboration can avoid the adversarial conflicts between different interest groups (Bramwell and Lane, 2000). There are also a number of problems with collaboration. These include mistrust and misapprehension between the interest groups, embedded power relations which favour certain interests over others and perceived and real barriers that may restrict access by some groups to partnerships entirely. Figure 13.1 provides more detail on the potential benefits of collaboration, while Figure 13.2 provides a number of potential problems. As Figure 13.1 indicates, the potential benefits of collaboration can be a greater democratization of tourism decision-making, with the involvement of a range of players, the sharing of a range of views and the possibility of synergy and creative solutions to tourism problems. However, as Figure 13.2 suggests, collaboration may be costly, time consuming, not representative of some views and involve unbalanced power relationships.

- There may be involvement by a range of stakeholders, all of whom are affected by the multiple issues of tourism development and may be well placed to introduce change and improvement.
- Decision-making power and control may diffuse to the multiple stakeholders that are affected by the issues, which is favourable for democracy.
- The involvement of several stakeholders may increase the social acceptance of policies, so that implementation and enforcement may be easier to effect.
- More constructive and less adversarial attitudes might result in consequence of working together.
- The parties who are directly affected by the issues may bring their knowledge, attitudes and other capacities to the policy-making process.
- A creative synergy may result from working together, perhaps leading to greater innovation and effectiveness.
- Partnerships can promote learning about the work, skills and potential of the other partners, and also develop the group interaction and negotiating skills that help to make partnerships successful.
- Parties involved in policy-making may have a greater commitment to putting the resulting policies into practice.
- There may be improved coordination of the policies and related actions of the multiple stakeholders.
- There may be greater consideration of the diverse economic, environmental and social issues that affect the sustainable development of resources.
- There may be greater recognition of the importance of non-economic issues and interests if they are included in the collaborative framework, and this may strengthen the range of tourism products available.
- There may be a pooling of the resources of stakeholders, which might lead to their more effective use.
- When multiple stakeholders are engaged in decision-making the resulting policies may be more flexible and also more sensitive to local circumstances and to changing conditions.
- Non-tourism activities may be encouraged, leading to a broadening of the economic, employment and societal base of a given community or region.

Figure 13.1 Potential benefits of collaboration and partnerships in tourism planning
Source: Bramwell and Lane (2000)

- In some places and for some issues there may be only a limited tradition of stakeholders participating in policy-making.
- A partnership may be set up simply as 'window dressing' to avoid tackling real problems head on with all interests.
- Healthy conflict may be stifled.
- Collaborative efforts may be under-resourced in relation to requirements for additional staff time, leadership and administrative resources.
- Actors may not be disposed to reduce their own power or to work together with unfamiliar partners or previous adversaries.
- Those stakeholders with less power may be excluded from the process of collaborative working or may have less influence on the process.
- Power within collaborative arrangements could pass to groups or individuals with more effective political skills.
- Some key parties may be uninterested or inactive in working with others, sometimes because they decide to rely on others to produce the benefits resulting from a partnership.
- Some partners might coerce others by threatening to leave the partnership in order to press their own case.
- The involvement of democratically elected government in collaborative working and consensus building may compromise its ability to protect the 'public interest'.
- Accountability to various constituencies may become blurred as the greater institutional complexity of collaboration can obscure who is accountable to whom and for what.
- Collaboration may increase uncertainty about the future as the policies developed by multiple stakeholders are more difficult to predict than those developed by a central authority.
- The vested interests and established practices of the multiple stakeholders involved in collaborative working may block innovation.
- The need to develop consensus, and the need to disclose new ideas in advance of their introduction, might discourage entrepreneurial development.
- Involving a range of stakeholders in policy-making may be costly and time-consuming.
- The complexity of engaging diverse stakeholders in policy-making makes it difficult to involve them all equally.
- There may be fragmentation in decision-making and reduced control over implementation.
- The power of some partnerships may be too great, leading to the creation of cartels.
- Some collaborative arrangements may outlive their usefulness, with their bureaucracies seeking to extend their lives unreasonably.

Figure 13.2 Potential problems of collaboration and partnerships in tourism planning
Source: Bramwell and Lane (2000)

The following case study discusses the World Wide Fund for Nature (WWF) Arctic Tourism Project. This project involved a number of different players, including local government officials, tour operators, researchers /academics and environmental NGOs in developing a framework and guidelines for linking tourism and conservation in the Arctic region. The study indicates a number of the potential benefits and problems of tourism partnerships.

Case study: the WWF Arctic Tourism Project

The WWF Arctic Tourism Project was established by the WWF Arctic Programme in 1995 with the aim 'to make Arctic tourism more environmentally friendly and . . . to generate support for conservation projects' (Pedersen, 1998: 3). The specific goals of the project are:

- To identify common interests of tourism and conservation and use these to reduce environmental problems and maximize the advantages for the Arctic environment and the local people.
- To develop guidelines for Arctic tourism that not only educate tourists about conservation and appropriate behaviour, but that also generate political support from the tourism industry and tourists for WWF's conservation objectives.
- To develop competition among tour operators concerning compliance with the guidelines, which will require a form of evaluation/certification that can be used for marketing purposes, and that will be awarded to those tour operators who comply with the guidelines.
- To increase recognition of the global significance of the Arctic.
- To increase recognition of local needs in the Arctic and its cultural diversity.

Brief project history

The WWF project was established largely as a result of the polar tourism conference held in St Petersberg in 1994. The first meeting of the project took place in January 1996 in Longyearbyen, Svalbard, Norway. The chief aim of this meeting was the drafting of basic principles for Arctic tourism. The 43 participants, covering most, but not all, of the Arctic countries, included tour operators, members of conservation organizations, representatives of indigenous peoples' organizations, government representatives and scientists. Most of these had been specifically invited, by the WWF Arctic Programme Director, on the basis of their expertise.

The meeting produced a Memorandum of Understanding which made reference to minimizing negative impacts of tourism, optimizing benefits to local communities and promoting the conservation of nature. It suggested that cooperation between tour operators, as well as competition, could be in their interests. The memorandum recommended the creation of guidelines and codes of conduct for Arctic tourism. It indicated the need for local involvement in tourism and advocated the use of a contract between local communities and tour operators. It also contained suggestions for operators to reduce the use of resources, to recycle and to minimize damage. It recommended a wide dissemination of the guidelines/codes and suggested that financing for the development of these should be sought from Arctic tour operators.

The next phase of the project was held in September 1996 in Cambridge, UK. Those present here comprised a number of participants from the Svalbard conference and several new collaborators, and it transformed the Memorandum of Understanding into ten basic principles for Arctic tourism. Working group members also produced draft codes of conduct for both tour operators and tourists, and recommendations for communities involved in tourism. In March 1997, the WWF Arctic Programme, working jointly with the Norwegian Polar Institute and the Svalbard Tourism Board, held a second workshop on Svalbard. A number of those present at earlier meetings attended this meeting. Those who attended represented a variety of communities of interest and came from 12 different countries, including all the Arctic nations. The objective of the workshop was to develop a process to implement the principles and codes of conduct that had been developed at earlier meetings, and to refine those principles and codes of conduct.

To support implementation, the workshop participants decided to create an eight member Interim Steering Committee which would guide the project in the coming year. The Steering Committee members were elected by the meeting participants to represent indigenous peoples (2), destination tour operators (1), international operators (1), local tourism NGOs (1), conservation NGOs (2) and the research community (1). Individuals were also selected to ensure geographical representation among the Arctic countries. In order to enable participation of observers, such as members of the Arctic Council or the Nordic Council of Ministers, it was intended that an accreditation procedure be established.

It was decided that a number of pilot projects would be established to evaluate the usefulness of the various components of the guidelines project. Evaluation of the pilot projects was to take place a year later, at which point a new Steering Committee would be elected and the office of the permanent secretariat would be formalized.

In December 1997, the WWF Arctic Programme published Ten Principles for Arctic Tourism, A Code of Conduct for Tour Operators and A Code of Conduct for Arctic Tourists. These documents were the first to put this material into a widely available published form. Five thousand copies of this document were distributed to tour operators, tourist boards, environmental management organizations and government officials as well as to the general public. The intention was to promote awareness of the principles and codes and to encourage further discussion on their content.

In February 1998, a workshop was held in Iceland to bring together the Interim Steering Committee, interested tour operators and tourism researchers. The purposes of the meeting included: developing methods to measure compliance with codes; developing a structure for future implementation; examining funding sources; and identifying appropriate pilot projects to evaluate various aspects of the principles, codes and implementation.

The project used the processes of negotiation and consensus building in an attempt to achieve its aims. A key problem was the lack of continuity, as not all participants at early meetings could make follow-on meetings. English was not the first language of most participants but was the main language of the project. Although many views were represented, not all voices were heard and some were more powerful than others. Meeting structures were relatively informal, but gave a good deal of ownership to participants, although this may have contributed to a lack of direction at times. Despite these shortcomings, the project did build consensus and had notable achievements, not the least being the codes of conduct and the introduction of pilot projects to apply the codes and guidelines.

(Adapted from Mason *et al.*, 2000a.)

The case study of the WWF Arctic Tourism Project reveals a number of issues in relation to collaboration and partnerships in tourism planning and management. One of the major issues in the case study was the nature of the arrangements for collaboration. In the WWF study, it is clear that not all of the parties who wanted to play a part were able to do so consistently.

This problem of inclusion (or lack of it) is significant. As the WWF study indicated, some stakeholders were unable to make it to all meetings, partly because of a lack of travel funds; others had problems communicating between meetings because of technical difficulties and some may not have participated because of the politics of WWF.

Although the WWF project had overall aims and reasonably clear objectives for each of the meetings, the arrangements were relatively loose and ad hoc and did not have the highly institutionalized structure of a task force (see Hall, 2000b). This appeared to suit most participants in that they were to some extent empowered and given a degree of ownership of the agenda and products. However, the project arrangements contributed to a problem of a lack of direction and leadership at times. Hence, the WWF project was more 'networked' than 'centred around' a highly institutionalized structure (see Parker, 2000). There is the possibility that this 'loose' structure may have had negative effects in terms of the long-term viability of the project.

However, the WWF project appeared particularly good at building a consensus. Due to the nature of arrangements for the project, this process took the form of negotiated consensus building. Although not all participants agreed with everything that took place, their commitment to the idea that such a project was necessary took them beyond individual concerns to accept a majority view in order to keep the whole process moving.

The WWF project presented a major problem of coordination. As the focus was the Arctic region, it was by definition an international project. Participants came from many different countries as well as a variety of backgrounds and represented different views and stakeholders. On one level, this led to potential communication problems, although attempts to resolve this involved the use of English as the key language. On another level, the implementation stage was difficult to operationalize. Nevertheless, by the latter part of 1999, codes of conduct had been created and a number of pilot projects had been put into action. In July 2001, WWF Arctic produced a document that evaluated a number of these pilot projects and in this document was able to provide advice to communities and tourism businesses in the Arctic on better ways to achieve a stronger link between conservation and tourism.

The issues presented in relation to the WWF project are not unusual. In fact, as Bramwell and Lane (2000) argued, such issues are to be expected. Hence, these issues need to be taken very carefully into consideration when considering collaboration and partnerships as part of tourism planning and management.

In some parts of the world, particularly in developing countries, tourism is being actively used as a tool to overcome poverty. The British government office the Overseas Development Institute (ODI) has been involved in a number of development projects that have used tourism in an attempt to achieve the aim of reducing poverty (Ashley et al., 2005). Between 2002 and 2005, the ODI worked on pilot projects in Southern Africa. These, and other such projects, are part of what is now known as pro-poor tourism (PPT). The PPT projects involved businesses working in partnership with local communities. Five companies were involved in the Southern Africa PPT pilot projects: a safari tour operator, a music festival organizer, a safari camp and accommodation provider, a leisure company and an urban resort organization. Experiences from these pilot projects enabled the creation of a document that indicated the nature of linkages between tourism businesses, local communities and entrepreneurs (Ashley et al., 2005). These five types of linkage are shown in Figure 13.3.

These PPT pilot projects revealed that the ways in which the partnerships operate are not that straightforward and suggested a number of key challenges. These are shown in Figure 13.4.

However the PPT pilot projects also suggested that there are a number of important benefits for businesses that can be derived from the type of partnerships in the PPT pilot projects. These are shown in Figure 13.5.

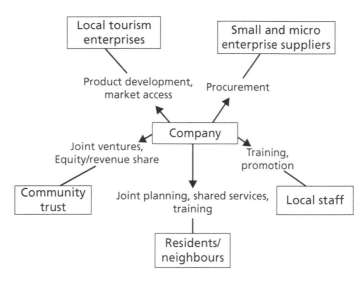

Figure 13.3 Five types of linkage between a tourism company and the local economy from the PPT pilot projects

- **A champion** and driver of the process is essential, as is top management leadership. Pro-poor approaches will always be just one of many actions on a company's agenda, and unless there is a champion they are likely to remain on the 'to do' list.
- Considerable amount of **time input** is needed, and therefore so is a staff member or facilitator who can do this. This person who does the legwork of implementing new procedures may well be a different person to the 'champion'.
- Beyond the champion, wider **buy-in across staff and management** is needed. While the champion can act as a catalyst for a process, s/he will have to engage other key operational staff to succeed in changing business practice. Stimulating interest or support among staff is a first step, but full implementation may require changes in job functions, expectations of staff, and Key Performance Indicators.
- **Learn by doing**: get practical and get going, and adapt from there. Garnering support from others in the company and community is only likely once they can see practical results.
- The process is not just about changing company practice, but also **changing attitudes** to communities and local entrepreneurs. This is particularly so where history has led to deeply entrenched paternalistic approaches to communities, or to assumptions that local entrepreneurs cannot deliver reliably.
- A **slow pace** must be accepted, and **expectations managed** – without dampening enthusiasm. Change is likely to be incremental – one thing leads to another.
- Finding the **right partners in the community** is key. However, it is also often a difficult first step.
- Success lies in finding local linkages that help address current drivers of change in the company and **complement core business concerns**. There is no point investing in linkages that conflict with core business. Where linkages are risky, they should be pursued as an add-on at first. Local linkages should fit into bigger strategic objectives.
- **Partnership with others** will be needed. Bring in expertise from others, whether it is in community development, small business support, or technical aspects of production such as cleaning or recycling.

Figure 13.4 Key challenges to a PPT partnership
Source: Adapted from Ashley *et al.* (2005).

- **'Social licence to operate'**. It is not just the legal or official licences that matter, but the acceptance of a company's legitimacy amongst local institutions that really matters.
- **Enhanced brand**. If each business within a partnership has a positive reputation, all organizations will benefit and achieve an enhanced brand.
- **Diversification of products for guests**. This type of partnership allows for the provision of a greater range of products than from just one of the organizations.
- **Government procurement, preferred partner, recognition**. If a partnership achieves a higher status through 'social licence to operate', enhanced brand and diversified products, it is more likely to be recognized and receive more work as a 'preferred partner' with e.g. a government body.
- **Awards, publicity and marketing**. A higher status partnership is likely to benefit more from greater, more positive publicity and may receive awards as a result, which in turn may generate more publicity.
- **Enhanced corporate governance and staff morale**. Staff morale can be enhanced through local linkages. Staff morale boosts customer service. Developing linkages can complement broader changes in corporate governance, by identifying wider needs for staff training, or revision of procedures relating to procurement, contractor payments or internal communication.

Figure 13.5 Benefits that can be derived by businesses from the type of partnerships in the PPT pilot projects

Source: Adapted from Ashley *et al.* (2005).

The case study below discusses a pro-poor community project in the Southern African country of Namibia and indicates some of the issues in connection with, and advantages of, such a collaborative project.

Case study: the Namibian Community Based Tourism Association

The Namibian Community Based Tourism Association (NACOBTA) has been created from a number of local community tourism enterprises in Namibia, and is a non-profit organization which strives to improve the living standards amongst the communities of rural Namibia. It also attempts to ensure that community based tourism enterprises are viable and to integrate community tourism into the Namibian tourism sector. Visitors to Namibia who support these enterprises will be making an important contribution to rural development in Namibia. Support by tourists for the enterprises allows communities to take part in the tourism sector and to develop businesses, which will provide employment opportunities and generate income in the region where they live. This in turn provides communities with another livelihood strategy and gives them more control and choice over their own development.

NACOBTA is recognized by government and consulted on many tourism related matters. One of NACOTBA's roles has been in relation to nature conservancies. Residents of Namibia have been forming conservancies which under the law give them conditional use rights over wildlife. Nearly all the four registered conservancies and more than a dozen emerging conservancies are actively developing tourism plans and have become key actors in rural tourism development. In one such example, residents of the Bergsig area have formed the Torra Conservancy, which became involved in a partnership with two different tourism investors. The investors were interested in setting up luxury lodges in the area. However, the residents selected a small camp-style proposal over a potentially more lucrative lodge development suggested by the investors, because of their community values. The proposed lodge would have impinged on current livestock management strategies, limited access to water sources that are vital during drought and required a 30-year lease. The community selected the camp because it was small-scale, required a lease for only 10 years and, importantly, the campground operator had established a high level of trust within the community.

(Source: Pantin and Francis, 2005)

Summary

Tourism partnerships are now relatively common in both the United States and United Kingdom and are growing in importance in other developed and developing areas of the world. Partnerships (or collaboration) are attempts to bring together different players in tourism. They may take a number of different forms, from loose, informal, ad hoc arrangements, to tightly structured, time-tabled, formalized groupings. Partnerships are important in relation to tourism planning and management as they have the potential to lead to dialogue and consensus building between potentially adversarial participants, around mutually acceptable proposals about how tourism should be developed. Information on the WWF Arctic Tourism Project has been presented and discussed and this has revealed some of the advantages of collaboration, as well as indicating the nature and impacts of obstacles. The PPT pilot projects in South Africa and the case study in Namibia reveal a number of challenges that can confront such partnerships, but also show the benefits that can be derived.

Student activities

1 What are the major advantages of tourism partnerships?
2 What are the major disadvantages of tourism partnerships?
3 Who was involved in the WWF Arctic Tourism Project?
4 What do you think each of the parties involved in the WWF partnership hoped to get out of their involvement?
5 What factors have contributed to the relative success of the WWF project?
6 What factors have acted as obstacles to the success of the WWF project?
7 What tourism proposals/developments in your area would benefit from a partnership approach?
8 Figure 13.6 provides greater detail on the processes that operated in the WWF Arctic Tourism Project. Please study Figure 13.6 and then answer the questions below:

   a) How was consensus building achieved?
   b) What part did group dynamics play in the project meetings?
   c) How did a lack of continuity of participant involvement affect the project?
   d) What were the advantageof WWF involvement and what problems did this cause?
   e) The project has been considered a success. By what criteria could it be viewed as successful and what reasons would you give for its success?

The main processes involved in the project meetings were consultation and negotiation. Although activities varied from meeting to meeting, common to all was a process in which participants were involved actively in preparing and presenting their own material and, in addition, commenting on and questioning the work of other participants. Hence, this was an interactive process of consultation, and as the Arctic Programme Director indicated at the first project meeting, the aim was to achieve a consensus of views. This process of consultation had the advantage that it gave ownership of the tasks to participants. At the early stages, an individual's interpretation of the direction of the project was important as it formed the foundation for the particular activity. A consultative approach can contribute to a general feeling of involvement and the belief that one's views are significant. Individuals had a substantial degree of involvement in the early stages of the project. This also worked to motivate participants and contributed to a generally high level of commitment. Allowing a high degree of control appears to have been a successful strategy as the meetings generally achieved the tasks suggested.

Group dynamics were important in the working groups. In these situations there were individuals with very different backgrounds, experiences, interests and concerns. Workshops were held in English, which was not the first language of many participants. This gave an advantage to some participants over others. A combination of factors contributed to varying levels of participation: some individuals expressed well-articulated views while others contributed little in formal discussions. At some meetings there was evidence of what has been reported elsewhere in similar circumstances, with 'strong voices' dominating and 'weaker voices' not being listened to, as well as there being unarticulated views. Despite this, it was evident that although there were differences of opinion on details, there was a general feeling that such an initiative was necessary and hence individuals gave way to a majority view to keep the project moving.

Attempting to develop consensus among a diverse and widely scattered group of individuals with varying levels of resources (such as computer access, translation services, funds for travel) has meant that some individuals' ideas were not incorporated until late in the process or were not incorporated at all. The direction taken by earlier participants formed the foundation and also informed subsequent revisions of project work. This continues to be a factor in the development of the initiative. An example of communication difficulties is the problems that develop in transferring information between computer network programmes. A more fundamental problem arises from the inability of some participants to return to later meetings, and the complete absence throughout the process of participants from various segments of the communities of interest. The latter problem means that some views were never heard while the former means that continuity was disrupted. Both are almost inevitable in such a project, but they have important implications for the process and the final product.

A number of tourism operators may have resented the possibility of the imposition of external evaluation and some may have disliked the inclusive focus on all Arctic tourism; others may have felt left out of the process, and yet others may have disagreed with the nature of the initiative. Some operators may also have taken issue with the politics of the lead organization, although the Project Director indicated that a number of operators were very willing to be linked with the WWF panda logo, presumably for the marketing advantage it would bring. At various points during the development stages comments were made that the very involvement of WWF could hinder operator and community participation in the project. The acceptance of WWF varies from place to place in the Arctic, and by interest group. However, local operators and community representatives will have at least a chance to hear the aims of the project and make their view known in the locations involved during the community consultation parts of the project. For example, a series of community meetings in Nunavut (the newly created Inuit territory in Canada) in 1999 brought the programme to local residents to seek their input into draft guidelines.

Nevertheless, in summary it is possible to state that during consultation and negotiation, despite some evidence of disagreements, dissatisfaction and delays, the major aims of

Figure 13.6 The processes involved in the WWF Artic Tourism Project
Source: Adapted from Mason *et al.* (2000a).

avoiding conflict and building consensus, were generally successful. The success reflects a number of related factors. These are as follows:

- having meetings open to whoever displayed an interest and attempting to advertise such meetings widely;
- encouraging discussion of presentations and position papers at meetings;
- using working sessions to focus participation and the development of 'products';
- seeking input via the Internet for versions of the guidelines and codes;
- giving feedback to participants in the form of summaries and documents.

The processes outlined above were used in an attempt to hear people and incorporate their ideas. While it is clear that not everyone agreed with everything, it would seem that most project participants agreed with the basic principle that a project like this was necessary. Therefore, they were willing to have their own interests subsumed in order to keep the project moving. Hence, this was a form of negotiated consensus building that required participants to accept a majority rule approach in the interest of moving forward. That this negotiated consensus happened should be viewed as a major accomplishment of WWF.

This project demonstrates an important role for environmental NGOs such as WWF in making a significant contribution to attempts at developing sustainable tourism. In this project, WWF provided its organizational skills in initiating the project, in seeking funding to continue the project and in conducting several international meetings to accomplish particular tasks. In bringing together individuals with differing perspectives who shared a willingness to listen and respond, and also the ability to usefully inform the debate. WWF staff indicated that the project required action, not only words, and that the organization was committed to acting quickly to facilitate the achievement of the project aims. The success to date of this project also suggests that, despite some opposition, WWF had an important advantage over an industry-based organization: a genuine and credible concern for the key resource for sustainable tourism, the environment.

Figure 13.6 (*continued*)

9 Study Figures 13.4 and 13.5. From the perspective of (a) local businesses and (b) local communities consider the advantages and disadvantages of the PPT pilot projects.
10 With reference to the case study of NACOBTA, what are the advantages and disadvantages of the community based tourism project for local communities involved?

Chapter 14

Destination management

Learning objectives

At the end of this chapter you should be able to:

- understand the nature of tourism impacts in a destination;
- understand the meaning of destination management;
- understand the meaning of the relationship between tourism planning and destination management;
- understand the nature and role of destination management organizations;
- understand the history, nature and characteristics of a variety of different types of tourism destination.

Introduction

The impacts of tourism take place in time and space. A major spatial element of tourism impacts is that, although they can take place almost anywhere, they tend to be concentrated in certain areas. Such areas may be referred to as tourism resorts, or tourism areas, or tourism zones. However, the concept that has been used increasingly to suggest the main focus of tourism impacts is that of the tourism destination.

'Tourism destination' is an important concept because not only is this the location where services and facilities, such as hotels restaurants, bars and entertainment centres, are located, but it is where the tourists are found and often they are there in large numbers. The destination is also the location where visitors will interact with the host, or local, population as well as be in contact with the local environment. Tourists are also likely to interact with other tourists in the destination area. As a result of the concentration of tourism facilities and the interaction of tourists with other tourists, with local people and the local environment, it is here that many of the impacts discussed in the first section of this book will occur. If tourism impacts are viewed as being concentrated spatially then the planning and management of the response to these impacts will also be focused spatially and, hence, in tourism destinations.

This chapter discusses tourism impacts in tourism destinations prior to a consideration of planning for and management in destinations. The nature of destination management organizations is discussed and a number of case studies are presented to highlight the range of destinations and details of the destination management process.

Key perspectives

It has been traditionally the case that tourism destinations are regarded as geographical areas. Such areas are usually considered to have well defined boundaries (Hall, 2000a). It is relatively easy to envisage this concept of a destination when applied to a geographical feature such as an island. However, it is also the case that the notion of a destination can apply to entire countries and here it is primarily a political definition that is being used. Destinations can also comprise towns and cities – these are both geographical and political concepts. In relation to cities and towns, the tourism element of the settlement may be of significance, but is likely to be found alongside other important functions, related to, for example, manufacturing industry, banking, trade or transport. In other words, tourism destinations often have other functions than those just linked to tourism. Nevertheless, some geographical locations owe their existence almost exclusively to tourism. Such locations would include coastal towns in Britain such as Blackpool, Scarborough and Brighton.

However, a problem with the use of the concept of a tourism destination, which should be apparent from the discussion above, is that it can be used at a range of different scales. So a part of a city can be a destination, a small coastal town can be a destination, but an entire country or even a continent (Antarctica would fit into this category) can be considered as a destination. What is considered to be a destination seems to depend largely on the researcher's focus of enquiry (Augustyn, 1998).

Applying the concept of scale to tourism destinations, Ritchie and Crouch (2003) provide a six-fold classification. This classification, which has an underlying formal political jurisdiction aspect, starting with the largest geographical area at the top, is as follows:

- A macro-region consisting of several countries (e.g. Europe) or a region that crosses several borders e.g. the Alps.

- A nation or state.
- A province or state within a country (e.g. Ontario in Canada).
- A localized region within a country (e.g. southwest England).
- A city or town.
- A unique locale, such as a national park, heritage site, memorial or monument that is significant enough to attract visitors.

A particularly useful definition of the destination which draws on the important geographical aspect is that of Murphy *et al.* (2000) who indicated that it is an amalgam of tourism products, available in certain geographic locations within a country, drawing tourists from beyond its boundaries.

However, there is an overlap between the concept of a tourism destination and other geographically based notions of the location or area where tourism is focused. So for example, there is a link between the concept of a destination and that of a resort. A resort can be narrowly defined as a localized self-contained tourism complex providing a variety of recreational activities in one location (Gunn, 1994). So, using this definition it is possible to put theme parks, some hotels that also provide significant entertainment activities, and even cruise ships into the category of resorts (see Laws, 1993; Buhalis, 2000).

It has been argued that a key element of a tourism destination is that it has a range of different tourism facilities (Smith, 1994; Kozak and Rimington, 2000). Indeed, some authors differentiate a destination from a resort when they indicate that a destination has a variety and range of different tourism facilities and activities, whilst a resort tends to be focused on one single tourism attraction, such as a resort hotel (Ekinci *et al.*, 1998). However, the terms resort and destination are often used as if synonymous and it should be clear how this is possible when a resort has been regarded by some researchers as a town or settlement, with a significant range of tourist activities and facilities, or a region or even country in which several holiday centres are located (see Medlik, 1993; Laws, 1993).

Before a discussion of the planning and management issues, it is important to consider the nature of tourism impacts in destinations, as these will influence the nature of the planning and management response.

Chapter 3 provides a number of questions in relation to factors affecting tourism impacts and these are presented again below:

- Where is tourism taking place?
- What is the scale of tourism?
- Who are the tourists?
- In what types of activity do tourists engage?
- What type of infrastructure exists for tourism?
- For how long has tourism been established?
- What is the tourist season?

In relation to a tourism destination, the most obviously important question from the list above is 'Where?' as this question clearly relates to geographical factors. However, several of the other factors are also very important. The scale and type of activity are both significant, who the tourists are will be important, the nature of the tourism infrastructure and length of time tourism has been established are likely to be influential and, depending on particular circumstances, seasonality may be another major issue in regard to tourism impacts in destinations.

As stated above, destinations can vary greatly in terms of their scale and also their type. Some destinations are almost exclusively devoted to tourism activities whilst others have a range of functions including tourism. Destinations which have tourism as the major activity are discussed later in this chapter and particularly in relation to tourism planning and management. However, initially two locations which are major world cities are presented, as they indicate how old industrial towns can become tourist attractions and hence destinations.

Case study: urban destinations – Birmingham, UK

Birmingham, with over one million residents in 2013, was for over 200 years considered to be England's second city. Its origins are very much linked to the UK Industrial Revolution. By the early part of the twentieth century it was known for making a range of iron and steel items including weapons and motor vehicles. However, after the Second World War and particularly after the 1960s, as its main industries fell into decline, it tended to be regarded as a provincial, unfashionable and unloved city usually referred to as 'Brum', with its local people derided for their accent – regarded by many English people as the worst accent in the country.

In the 1970s, attempts were made to improve Birmingham's image and put it on the visitor map. In 1976 the National Exhibition Centre (NEC) was opened on the outskirts of Birmingham, although there was still a feeling, both locally and nationally, that Birmingham was not the appropriate location for a national centre. These fears proved unfounded as the NEC has hosted many major national/international events since, including the International Motor Show, the Boat Show, the Confederation of British Industry National Conference, Crufts Dog Show and the Horse of the Year Show. In the 1990s, the largely unattractive city centre underwent large-scale redevelopment, following the 1990 City Centre Urban Design Study. This led to the building of the International Convention Centre, the National Indoor Arena and the Birmingham Symphony Hall. By the mid-1990s, Birmingham had over 40 per cent of the entire UK conference and exhibition trade. Supporting what had been achieved via public funding was the creation, largely via private investment, of over 3,000 hotel rooms and 250 licensed premises, located in what became known as the 'convention quarter'.

By the mid-1990s Birmingham was addressing its old 'declining industry/boring city' image issues with new marketing. This was the focus of the public–private partnership, Birmingham Marketing Partnership (BMP), which ambitiously used the strapline: 'Birmingham: Europe's Meeting Place'. Some evidence to support this claim can be seen in the Lions Club International decision to hold in Birmingham what was reputed at the time to be the biggest global meeting ever, and following this the Eurovision Song Contest was held there and, in 1997, a G8 Summit.

A new organization replacing the BMP, Marketing Birmingham (MB) – which was strongly supported by Birmingham City Council – was created and combined with the Council's Tourism Team in 2002. The financial support of the Council for MB remained strong during the first decade of the new millennium. Major events have taken place in this period including the European Gymnastics Championship and the Annual Rotary International Convention in June 2009, which had over 20,000 delegates.

(continued)

Case study: urban destinations – Birmingham, UK (continued)

By 2011, Birmingham could offer potential visitors not only a range of high quality traditional activities such as sporting venues, including several premiership/championship football grounds and an international test cricket ground at Edgbaston, but at the NEC and National Indoor Arena a number of one-off international sporting events. The city was also hosting a range of major national and international conventions at the NEC and, in the city centre, visitors could go to major art galleries, the Birmingham Symphony Hall and two new tourist centres at the Rotunda and Birmingham New Street. At this point the city was also realizing its potential as a multi-cultural tourism attraction, with the creation of the 'Balti Triangle'. This was in recognition of the post-war migrants, many of whom were Pakistanis from Kashmir and served 'Balti', a special type of curry dish and sold it originally to Birmingham residents in restaurants and takeaways. By 2011, these food sellers were known not just locally, but nationally and even internationally, adding to the attractions of what was once described by Jane Austen as 'not a place to promise much' but by Bill Clinton, following his G8 visit, as 'a jewel of a city . . . it is quite wonderful'.

(Based on Heely, 2011, with additions)

The case study of Birmingham indicates how an old, industrial city with a poor image can be re-invented to become a tourist destination. The key factors in this process were planning decisions taken that were concerned with Birmingham acting as a major event and exhibition centre, and what contributed to the success of this planning was a partnership between public and private sectors. Another European city, once important for industry and not until recently perceived as a tourist destination, is Barcelona. As the case study below reveals, there are other similarities between Birmingham's and Barcelona's rise to prominence as tourism destinations, not the least being the importance of the hosting of international events.

Case study: urban destinations – Barcelona, Spain

Barcelona is the second city of Spain after the capital Madrid. With a population today in excess of 1.5 million, Barcelona became important in the nineteenth century as Spain's leading manufacturing centre, focusing on the production of textile machinery and related products. Barcelona's potential for tourism was not recognized until the mid-1980s. This was very much the result of Spain's political history in the twentieth century. During the Spanish Civil War in the 1930s, as a largely left-wing city, Barcelona supported the Republican cause and as a result of Franco's victory its economic development was held back. This was compounded by the strong desire of the Spanish region Catalonia, of which Barcelona is the capital, to be independent of the rest of Spain, which put it in continual conflict with Franco's dictatorship based in Madrid.

After 1975, with the gradual transition to democracy in Spain, Barcelona began to develop its economy, including tourism, more rapidly. However, the real spur to Barcelona's tourism rise was its designation in 1986 as host for the 1992 Olympic Games. Having secured the right to host the Games, after 1986, Barcelona went through a period of re-assessing its role as a tourism destination. This resulted in the Barcelona Chamber of Commerce and Barcelona Municipal Council meeting regularly to systematically plan the exploitation of the city's tourism potential. This paved the way for the Barcelona Strategic Tourism Plan, which was eventually delivered in 1993. However, leading up to the Games there was a strong public–private sector partnership, particularly in the building of the facilities required for the Games. This partnership also managed to secure much more sponsorship than any previous Games, meaning that 75 per cent of the organizational costs were recouped from sponsorship and TV rights. The expenditure for the Games was primarily on venues and transport, but also used to improve run-down areas such as the harbour side Port Vell area and the decaying industrial area, Poble Nou.

The politicians and planners did their best to harness the spirit of the Olympics and attempted to create a new image for Barcelona, with an identity based on urbanism, culture and style and endeavoured to showcase the heritage, independence and regional identity of Catalonia. The Mediterranean climate and the distinctive cultural and architectural achievements of Picasso, Gaudi and Miro were emphasized as part of this process. The effectiveness of the process has been such that successful urban regeneration linked to major events has become known as the Barcelona model.

The success of the Barcelona model can be seen in the fact that following the Games, the tourism strategy became less generic 'destination' marketing and much more tactical marketing, focusing on a range of different market segments, namely: meetings, culture, shopping, cruises, sport, gastronomy, the LGBT community and health. However, hosting major events is still very important for Barcelona's tourism economy, with for example, regular festivals and conferences but also one-off events such as Gaudi Year (2002), the Universal Forum of Culture (2004), Picasso Barcelona (2006) and World Architectural Year (2009). The city also has a number of other pre- and post-Olympic attractions, including the Sagrada Familia (Gaudi's unfinished church), Gaudi's Parc Guel, the Opera House, the Picasso Museum, the Miro Foundation, the Museum of Catalan Art and FC Barcelona's Football Museum. There are also new conference centres, including the Barcelona International Convention Centre opened in 2004, and the city has continued to host major events, such as the International Rail Forum and the World Conference of the Association of Corporate Travel Executives and the World Mobile Phone Convention.

An indication of the rise of prominence of tourism in Barcelona can be seen in the following figures for the period 1990 to 2006:

- a 141 per cent increase in the number of hotels
- a 182 per cent increase in the number of bed spaces
- a 233 per cent increase in airport passengers
- a 318 per cent increase in staying tourists
- a 468 per cent increase in meetings delegates.

These statistics also indicate that in 2006 Barcelona received as many as 7.1 million tourists, there were 12.2 million bed nights and the city had a room occupancy rate of 78 per cent compared with 71 per cent in 1990.

(continued)

> ## Case study: urban destinations – Barcelona, Spain (continued)
>
> Despite a reputation for petty crime, particularly bag snatching and various theft-related scams, Barcelona no longer fits George Orwell's description from the time of the Spanish Civil War of a partially destroyed city with a 'gaunt, untidy look', but has become much more a global trademark of refined urban life, advanced design and Mediterranean hedonism and in 2009 was Spain's most popular tourist destination.
>
> (Adapted from Heely, 2011 with additions)

Destination management

The case studies of Birmingham and Barcelona include discussion of examples of various tourism plans and policies. The task of developing policies is the responsibility of different bodies in each of the destinations, but local government bodies such as Birmingham City Council and Barcelona Municipal Council have played major roles in creating the specific policy for tourism within each city.

The tasks of developing tourism policy and then implementing policy may appear to be part of the same process. However, as Ritchie and Crouch (2003) indicate, although there is an overlap between policy and planning processes and the processes of management of a destination, particularly when both processes focus on sustaining tourism and making the destination more competitive, they are in fact different activities.

Ritchie and Crouch (2003) indicate that policy and planning development is an intellectual process that uses information to create macro-level decision-making to develop the type of destination that is viewed as desirable. It will involve monitoring how well the destination is performing in relation to criteria established in the planning and policy formulation and also in comparison with other destinations. It is intended that the policy, planning and development process will provide the framework to implement the vision for the destination and enable the day-to-day management of the destination.

Destination management is more of a micro-level process, in which all industry stakeholders and many destination residents carry out organizational activities, on a day-to-day basis, in an attempt to achieve a macro-level vision contained within the destination policy and planning (Ritchie and Crouch, 2003). The implementation of the tourism policies is the responsibility of a destination management organization (DMO).

There are a number of key activities involved in the destination management process, in which a DMO will be involved. However, these processes are not separate but interdependent. Nevertheless, in an attempt to understand the processes, they are listed below and this is followed by a brief discussion of each. The processes are as follows:

- Organization
- Marketing
- Providing quality of service experience
- Gathering information/conducting research
- Human resource development
- Finance

- Visitor management
- Resource stewardship
- Crisis management.

Before any of the other processes can occur, some form of organization is essential as this will ensure that there is the leadership and coordination necessary to carry out the other processes. The structure of a particular organization will be linked closely to the different level or scale at which it operates. Hence, at national level the DMO will almost always be a government department with a tourism brief – usually a national tourism office. At the state or province level, the organization may also be a government office or possibly a joint public–private partnership. At the city or urban area level, there may be a city tourism department or the tourism role may be combined with another role, such as leisure or recreation. It is also possible, as evident in the case studies of Birmingham and Barcelona, that chambers of commerce (private sector business representatives) may have a significant role. It is also possible, particularly where events are a key element of a destination, that a convention bureau has a major role in the DMO.

With regard to the other DMO processes listed above, it is frequently marketing that is regarded as the key one (see Morgan *et al.*, 2010). Indeed for many authors marketing is the most important role of a DMO, and in fact so significant, that the 'M' in DMO has often been understood to stand for marketing and not management. The marketing role has traditionally been one of promotion and selling (Ritchie and Crouch, 2003). A key element of the marketing dimension is identifying the various visitor segments of the destinations. The DMO's role will then be to match the differing visitor segments to the potential visitor experience. In relation to the marketing aspect of the DMO, another key activity will be to gain an understanding of the level of awareness of the destination. The level of awareness of a destination is likely to be very important for the long term sustainability of a destination and has been the focus of much tourism research in the past 25 years or so (see e.g. Echtner and Ritchie, 1993).

Knowing the level of awareness can lead to a better understanding of the image of the destination, and image is important in relation to the various visitor segments. Hence, if those involved in the DMO know the level of awareness of the destination and understand its image amongst visitors, then it will be possible to plan promotional activity to attempt to sustain current visitor numbers and hopefully bring more visitors to the destination. Those working in the DMO also want to establish the destination's image in the mind of potential visitors and in this way, they will feel that they have created a brand. Creating a brand is important for the DMO as it is intended that visitors will link the brand with their experience in the destination and return to the same destination in the future. The DMO will also hope that visitors who are satisfied with their experience will tell their friends and family of the destination. This is referred to as 'word-of-mouth advertising' and is often considered the best form of advertising in tourism (see Morgan *et al.*, 2010).

The DMO also has the role to ensure that the visitor experience involves enjoyable encounters and interaction with those working in the tourism industry. Visitors want a pleasurable experience but also one in which they feel comfortable and secure and they want to be able to feel they have interacted well with service providers and to take away good memories of this encounter (Ritchie and Crouch, 2003).

If it is important for visitors to the destination to be offered an enjoyable experience, another major role of the DMO will be to ensure staff working in tourism are well prepared for this work. This means the DMO will be involved in training and certification programmes. This may not be direct involvement, but will be at least ensuring that tourism staff are suitably qualified and experienced.

A DMO should be actively involved in research and in particular gathering the information about, for example, visitor demographics, visitor experience of the destination and their satisfaction with their experience (Ritchie and Crouch, 2003). The information gathered will provide feedback on the current situation in the destination and also help to plan further promotional activity.

DMOs also have a role in relation to the financial aspects of a destination. A DMO has the possibility of gaining access to finance in a way that separate businesses will find very difficult to obtain. DMOs may also be able to gain venture capital (Ritchie and Crouch, 2003). If this is not possible then a DMO should be in a position to offer financial advice. The DMO may also be able to provide information to the financial community on the role and importance of tourism.

A key role that has assumed much more importance for a DMO recently is taking care of the tourism resource base. This stewardship role is important as there has been growing concern, as discussed in other chapters of this book, about negative impacts of tourism on the resource base in destinations and consequently calls for more sustainable forms of tourism activity. Related to both the stewardship role and that of providing a good service experience, a significant role of the DMO is visitor management. This role will attempt to ensure visitors have the best possible experience in their interaction with service providers and local residents, contribute financially to the destination economy, but also have minimum negative impacts on the local environment.

There are now so many examples of destinations being unexpectedly hit by human-induced problems such as diseases or war, or natural disasters, including tsunamis and volcanic eruptions, that a DMO must also be involved in crisis management. Crisis management is essential as a destination without a contingency plan may not survive even a small short-lived crisis.

The different roles of a DMO have been presented and discussed above. However, in the discussion, emphasis has been placed in particular on the significance of the marketing role and how DMOs try to create a destination image and establish a brand. The earlier case studies in this chapter, concerned with Birmingham and Barcelona, focused on cities that were previously important for traditional industries, but have recently attempted to rebrand themselves and create an image that can be used to promote each city as a tourism destination. There are, however, around the world a number of geographical locations which have been devoted to attracting tourists for long periods and in some cases tourism is their main economic activity. Such locations have particular images that have been developed over relatively long periods. Two such destinations are discussed below. In addition to the marketing activities in these destinations, the case study of Brighton and the discussion of Scarborough focus on the importance of information gathering and research and indicate how image and brand may change over time and the effects this can have on the destination.

Case study: coastal resorts – Brighton, UK

Brighton is a 'traditional' British seaside tourist destination. It has attracted visitors for over 250 years. It has benefited from being a destination that is relatively close to London, and has attracted aristocracy and members of the British royal family. In the

1780s, the future King George IV visited and subsequently built the Royal Pavilion. Brighton's popularity grew particularly rapidly during the age of steam trains. The first trains arrived in 1841 and by 1860 Brighton was receiving 250,000 annual visitors, with most of them coming by train.

During the British summer, Brighton has 'sun, sea and sand' (or at least shingle) providing swimming and sunbathing opportunities. From Victorian times (1837–1901), it developed traditional seaside facilities, including piers and a beach-side promenade, as well as hotels, bed and breakfast accommodation, restaurants, cafés, bars, public houses and entertainment venues.

However, as early as 1900 Brighton was being described as outdated and unattractive. It suffered during both World Wars because of its location on the south coast of Britain, developed a reputation for crime in the 1930s, made famous by Graham Greene in his novel *Brighton Rock*, and was the scene of mob violence in the 1960s when 'mods' and 'rockers' clashed, which became the subject of the film *Quadrophenia*. By the 1970s, British tourists were more likely to go to Benidorm than Brighton, and despite the traditional fish and chips and candyfloss, it began to decline as a tourism destination. The town's fortunes were somewhat improved by the building of the Brighton Centre in 1977, which put it on the international convention centre map. However, the decline in the importance of leisure activities continued until the mid-1990s.

In the early twenty-first century Brighton's fortunes began to improve. It became a city in 2000 (having had the status of a town before), and developed a trendy, cultural dimension, via an artists' quarter, with clubs, bars and restaurants. It has a three-week annual festival beginning in May, and its theatres often premiere major London West End productions. It has developed a laid-back, bohemian atmosphere and has become important for gay tourism, being frequently voted the best gay destination in the UK.

It is known by many as the 'city by the sea', or 'London by the sea'. Being only 1 hour from London by train and 30 minutes from Gatwick Airport it has also developed significant international tourism. By 2012, it had a reputation for culture, good food, good shopping and a range of accommodation including the traditional and contemporary. There were 8 million visitors, a combination of leisure tourists and conference attenders, to the city in 2012, and they spent over £400 million.

Despite the recent change in its fortunes, the City Council is aware of what has happened during the previous 250 years and does not want to see tourism decline in Brighton. In 2006–7 the Council began research in an attempt to rebrand Brighton so it can keep ahead of its competitors and create a recognized brand based on its own research. Nine focus groups, held in 2006–7, and a questionnaire survey of just over 1,000 visitors, were conducted. A major element of the research was asking respondents the strengths (S), weaknesses (W), opportunities (O) and threats (T) in relation to Brighton as a tourism destination. The SWOT analysis shown in Table 14.1 emerged from this research.

(Adapted from Mason, 2013b.)

(continued)

Case study: coastal resorts – Brighton, UK (continued)

Table 14.1 SWOT analysis of Brighton

Strengths	Weaknesses
Architecture/heritage (e.g. Royal Pavilion). A good UK profile.	Conflict between the night-time economy and the need to remain an attractive and safe destination for other visitors.
Access for visitors from London and overseas, via Gatwick and Heathrow.	Significant periods when supply of restaurants/hotels exceeds demand.
Good choice of accommodation, dining, shopping and attractions. A successful conference and business tourism market.	Weekend rail engineering works inhibit potential for Brighton to attract visitors at times when it really needs them. Hence, poor visitor experience, particularly as visitors unaware of the work before commencing their journey.
English language students and recent modern English language training centres. A young, tolerant and liberated culture.	Parking is an issue – cost and availability. Helping visitors locate and understand parking arrangements is the best way of responding to this weakness.
Easy to get around Brighton. Proximity to sea. Attractive hinterland (e.g. South Downs)	Despite an excellent collaborative community of local tourism businesses, not everyone that benefits from the destination marketing contributes to the work. Finding ways to get even greater cooperation and support is essential.

Opportunities	Threats
Plenty of available off-peak capacity to offer to visitors. Growing interest in the city from established and growing overseas markets.	Official Brighton website attracts tens of thousands to the web every month. However, competition from other destinations as well as local, competing sites can dilute the efforts of targeting prospective visitors.
A number of major developments locally that can and will bring visitors directly (e.g. Brighton Centre and Stadium) and indirectly (e.g. King Alfred Marina).	Some competitors have larger private sector investors, so can outspend Brighton in key markets. Brighton needs to be smarter than competitors regarding how and where to apply the marketing spend.
The city's growing 'sustainable' credentials are elements that are of increasing appeal to visitors.	Failing to address the absence of demand at certain times of the year will inhibit local businesses' ability to invest in and improve their businesses, as well as develop their staff.

Table 14.1 (*continued*)

Opportunities	Threats
The heritage of the city as a spa and health resort as well as proximity to the Downs (now a national park) are natural benefits that can be exploited further.	Wider economic conditions remain a major threat to an industry which is heavily reliant on economic conditions and discretionary spending habits of consumers.
While global climate change presents many challenges for a destination, there is a desire to exploit any opportunities that it presents.	Lack of local skilled labour is a threat to the continued development of the sector and for businesses. Need to promote the idea of hospitality and tourism as an industry offering a career path, especially for locals.
	As the Brighton Centre redevelopment comes forward, everything possible must be done to ensure Brighton maintains tourism business during the years of redevelopment.

The SWOT analysis in the case study of Brighton reveals the Council's use of research to gather information. This information obtained from the sample of visitors will have been used not just to reveal the views of visitors on tourism in Brighton, but also in attempts to find ways to overcome perceived weaknesses and also respond to potential opportunities. Dealing with the perceived threats may also be a part of the strategy to enable Brighton to compete with other destinations.

Brighton's use of the SWOT analysis responses is intended to create a better quality tourism destination. The term 'quality', when applied to a tourism destination, has become particularly important in the past 20 years or so, in the belief that a quality tourism destination will be more competitive and thus attract more visitors. However, although the term has been used frequently, there is no clear definition of what quality in relation to a destination actually means, but it is a theme that is being increasingly researched. For some researchers, it is the service encounter between the visitor and host in the destination that should form the basis for studies of quality, while for others it is the range and nature of tourism facilities. However, according to the results of research involving tourists (Seakhoa-King, 2007), it would appear that it is a combination of elements of the service encounter and the destination facilities, including aspects such as affordability, variety of facilities, authenticity, cleanliness, security, comfort, friendliness of the host community and the nature of weather conditions, that helps define a quality tourism destination.

The town of Scarborough, located on the Yorkshire coast in England, has a number of similarities, in terms of its tourism history, to that of Brighton. Scarborough developed as a spa tourism destination as early as the middle of the seventeenth century, following the discovery of a mineral water spring, with healing qualities, to the south of the town. Later in the seventeenth century, members of the local aristocracy began to come to the spa in significant numbers following the publication of a book by a doctor indicating the health-giving qualities of the water. By the middle of the eighteenth century sea bathing had also become popular, making Scarborough the very first UK seaside resort.

A major growth in visitor numbers to Scarborough occurred following the opening of the Scarborough to York railway in 1845. In the same year the Crown Hotel, the first purpose-built hotel in Scarborough, was opened. Other hotels quickly followed and in 1867 the Grand Hotel was opened. At the time this was the largest purpose-built hotel in Europe, with 12 floors and 365 bedrooms. Tourism continued to grow in importance until the early twentieth century, with the building of more hotels, other types of accommodation, as well as several entertainment attractions including theatres and cinemas.

However, by the late 1960s, tourism in Scarborough was in decline. Attempts were made to rejuvenate tourism in the town including the building of more indoor attractions, to offset the problem of unpredictable summer weather conditions, and the targeting of different visitor segments, particularly day visitors and short stay visitors, as well as those staying for the traditional week or two week period. In the early part of the twenty-first century, Scarborough Borough Council embarked on a scheme to bring about a renaissance in the town's tourism activity. However, this has been, at best, only partially successful, with a number of hotels closing and other hotels and visitor accommodation greatly in need of better maintenance and improved investment. This means Scarborough has not been able to rejuvenate itself to the extent that Brighton has (Mason, 2013b). The causes of this are various, but include the fact that unlike Brighton, Scarborough is not that close to London (although it does have several large urban areas including Leeds and Sheffield not far away). Partly because of its location, and distance from major airports, Scarborough does not attract significant numbers of international tourists in the way that Brighton has managed to. Scarborough also has been unable to throw off its image as a place largely for older, more conservative visitors compared with the 'young and liberal image' of Brighton.

Although tourism in Brighton recently has followed a different path compared with that in Scarborough, it is possible to apply Butler's (1980) theory (discussed in Chapter 2) to each location. Both destinations have a long history of tourism development and appear to have passed through all the stages of the theory and have reached the final stage – rejuvenation or stagnation. It would seem that Brighton has re-invented itself to a great extent and is therefore currently in the rejuvenation stage. However, Scarborough, despite recent efforts via its renaissance initiative, is at best in stagnation.

Nevertheless, by the end of the first decade of the twenty-first century tourism remained important in Scarborough, despite a continuing image problem of a dated resort, as well as a partially dilapidated infrastructure of old hotels and entertainment facilities. However, in 2010, tourism's contribution to the local economy was just under £300 million, it provided just over 8,000 jobs and Scarborough was identified as the third most important destination in England after London and Blackpool for domestic leisure tourism (Scarborough Borough Council, 2011).

Table 14.2 provides information on major events in Scarborough and the surrounding Yorkshire east coast area during the six weeks of the main summer period of 2013. As Table 14.2 indicates, there is a combination of different types of events, some clearly linked to the traditional image of Scarborough and the local area, such as SeaFest, Whitby Regatta and Scarborough Cricket Festival, whilst others, such as those featuring McFly, Status Quo and Katherine Jenkins, would seem to be targeted at a very different type of tourist market.

Summary

This chapter has indicated that tourism impacts are felt strongly in tourism destinations. These impacts will be particularly noticeable in destinations such as small towns and cities and coastal destinations. However, the concept of 'a destination' has been applied at a variety of scales

Table 14.2 Scarborough/East Yorkshire events 19 July–30 August 2013

Timetable of events in East Yorkshire and Scarborough during summer 2013

- Seafest Maritime Festival Scarborough, 19–21 July
- Cock of the North Bike Road Races, Oliver's Mount, Scarborough, 20–21 July
- Status Quo Live, Scarborough Open Air Theatre, 27 July
- Muston Scarecrow Festival, Muston, 27 July–4 August
- The Launch Event, National Parks Week, The Moors National Park Centre, Danby, 28 July
- National Parks Week 2013, Actively Yours, The Moors National Park Centre, Danby, 29 July–4 August
- Katherine Jenkins Live, Scarborough Open Air Theatre, 3 August
- Whitby Lifeboat Station Flag Weekend, Whitby, 3–4 August
- Whitby Regatta, Whitby, 10–12 August
- Home International Golf Championships, Ganton Golf Club, Ganton, 12–16 August
- National Hill Climb Championship, Oliver's Mount, Scarborough, 18 August
- Whitby Folk Week, Whitby, 17–23 August
- The Saturdays Live, Scarborough Open Air Theatre, 23 August
- Scarborough Cricket Festival, Scarborough Cricket Club, 28–31 August
- McFly Live, Scarborough Open Air Theatre, 30 August

ranging from the relatively small dedicated tourism locations, such as seaside resorts, through cities, up to geographical regions and even large countries. The term destination is also used rather loosely and often as if synonymous with 'tourism resort' and 'tourism zone'. Nevertheless the term is a useful one and particularly so in relation to the concept of destination management.

The fact that there are a large number and range of impacts in a destination means that the destination is a major location for tourism planning and management. Whilst there are some dedicated destinations, many old towns and cities have become tourism destinations, possibly because of their history or, as in the case of both Birmingham and Barcelona, they have been selected as the location for major events. Destination planning and policy in a destination are, however, not the same thing as destination management. Planning and policy are usually thoughtful, reflective, but proactive macro-level processes, whilst management is a much more immediate, hands-on, day-to-day, micro-level and probably reactive activity. The destination management process involves DMOs and these perform a range of activities, in which marketing and increasingly stewardship of tourism resources are very significant.

Some locations have been tourism destinations for a comparatively long period. Such locations are frequently in need of some form of rejuvenation. The examples of two British coastal destination have been discussed in this chapter. One destination, Brighton, has achieved a high degree of success in rebranding and re-inventing itself, whilst the town of Scarborough has been, to date, somewhat less successful in its attempts to change its image, despite a number of attempts to do this.

Student activities

1 Why is the concept of 'a destination' problematic? Why is the concept, nevertheless, a useful one?
2 Why do many tourism impacts occur in the destination?

3   Working in small groups of three or four, discuss the types of tourism impact you would expect in a tourism destination. Create a table similar to that below and complete the table by arranging the types of impact under the headings:

Economic impacts	Socio-cultural impacts	Environmental impacts
Positive impacts	Positive impacts	Positive impacts
Negative impacts	Negative impacts	Negative impacts

4   In terms of the historical development of Birmingham, why does it appear to be an unlikely place for tourism to be important? What factors have led to the growing importance of tourism in Birmingham in the past 40 years?

5   Explain why tourism has become a very significant activity in Barcelona in the past 30 years?

6   Working in small groups of three or four, discuss the various roles of a destination management organization. Put what you regard as the five most important roles in rank order and provide a rationale for your choice.

7   What factors have contributed to tourism enjoying a resurgence in Brighton in the past 20 years?

8   Explain what has contributed to the importance of tourism in Scarborough. What factors have led to Scarborough not having a significant recent growth in tourism?

PART III

Tools and techniques in tourism planning and management

Chapter 15

Education as a technique in tourism planning and management

Learning objectives

At the end of this chapter you should be:

- aware of the meaning of education in relation to tourism planning and management;
- aware of educational techniques that can be used in tourism planning and management;
- able to critically evaluate educational techniques in tourism planning and management.

Introduction

Education can be used in tourism planning and management in a variety of ways. It is used frequently in relation to providing information to visitors, hence education here is used as a technique in visitor management. There are many situations in which it is necessary to give visitors information. This educational process can take the form of a relatively formal lecture, for example, on board a cruise ship, about a specific destination, or a topic such as a particular wildlife species. A guide accompanying a coach tour telling those on board the likely time of arrival is providing information and is therefore engaging tourists in an educational process, although this will be less formal than a lecture. Education also takes place when a prospective tourist reads a guidebook or even reads signs in, for example, a museum or a zoo. It is possible to distinguish between different types of educational process by the media used (e.g. oral, written), the information content of the activity and the style of presentation, in terms of degrees of informality and interactivity. It is conventional to discuss the presentation of information to visitors in a tourism context using the term 'interpretation' (see Tilden, 1957; Stewart et al., 1998; Moscardo, 1999).

This chapter discusses and critically evaluates the concept of interpretation. It investigates how tour guides act as interpretation agents and presents a case study of zookeepers as interpreters as well as considering how guides need to be culturally sensitive to be effective communicators. It also discusses research concerning visitors as potential ambassadors for Antarctica.

Key perspectives

Interpretation

One of the earliest commentators on heritage interpretation, Tilden (1957) suggested that interpretation is an educational process that employs objects, illustrative media and the use of first-hand experience. The aim of interpretation, Tilden claimed, is to reveal meaning and relationships. A variety of 'objects', such as urban monuments, works of art and flora and fauna, as well as media such as print and photographs can be used to achieve this (see Photo 15.1). Prentice (1995: 55) defined interpretation in the following way:

> a process of communicating to people the significance of a place so that they can enjoy it more, understand its importance and develop a positive attitude to conservation. Interpretation is used to enhance the enjoyment of place, to convey symbolic meaning and to facilitate attitudinal or behavioural change.

Interpretation can therefore be seen as part of the process of making places accessible to a public audience and providing visitors with insights into places. The more specific aims of an interpretation programme are 'to stimulate, facilitate and extend people's understanding of place so that empathy towards conservation, heritage, culture and landscape is developed' (Stewart et al., 1998: 257).

As Stewart et al. (1998) indicated, a major aim of interpretation is to stimulate interest and develop understanding in visitors. It has been argued that visitors can respond to interpretation in two major ways. As Moscardo (1996) suggested, visitors have two modes of response for dealing with new social situations: 'mindless' or 'mindful'. A 'mindless' state is characterized by mental passivity, while 'mindful' means a state marked by active mental processing (Moscardo and Pearce, 1986; Moscardo, 1996). Moscardo (1996) argued the importance of promoting 'mindful' tourism through interpretation programmes.

Photo 15.1 Interpretation can take a variety of forms: here it is on a sign at the Citadel in Halifax, Nova Scotia in Canada

Only a limited amount of research has been conducted into the effectiveness of interpretation. Stewart *et al.* (1998) indicated that what evaluation studies of interpretation exist usually determine their effectiveness by how much factual information visitors can recall. Such studies, however, provide little idea of how people use interpretation to help them understand the places they are visiting, they argued.

Orams (1994, 1995) suggested that interpretation programmes are usually designed not just to inform, but to change visitors' behaviour. Orams (1995) indicated, however, that there is little evidence to suggest that interpretation programmes will necessarily lead to a change in the behaviour of visitors. He suggested the need to conduct evaluation to ascertain any changes in behaviour and advocated the use of 'cognitive dissonance' as a way to get visitors to modify their behaviour. Orams (1994) argued that cognitive dissonance can be used in interpretative programmes to challenge people's belief systems. Such programmes would be an attempt to throw people off balance and put questions in their minds. Orams suggested that the eliciting of emotional responses from visitors, as part of a strategy involving cognitive dissonance, may be the way to counter the problems inherent in educating tourists.

As suggested in the introduction to the chapter, interpretation can involve formal or informal educational processes as well as a variety of media and presentational forms. The following section discusses the use of tour guides in the process of interpretation.

The role of the tour guide and interpretation

Tour guides may be the most maligned people in the world of travel. They are blamed for the problems of travel such as bad weather and traffic jams. They are also called the shepherds of the industry, as they herd tourists around safely and try to ensure that they return with fond memories of their holiday (Ang, 1990). As Ang (1990: 171) indicated, 'they exist not merely as a mouthpiece, mindlessly rattling information or as a merciless shopping sales person . . . The job calls for commitment, enthusiasm and integrity as the entire experience of the tourist lies in their hands.'

Early tour guides were usually unpaid, but had a strong motivation and a desire to share the feelings and values they held with others (McArthur, 1996). They also wanted to promote a conservation ethic in order to ensure what they had first experienced was maintained in the same state.

Pond (1993: 76) suggested that a tour guide has five roles: leader, educator, public relations representative, host and conduit. Pond (1993: 78) indicated that these are, in practice, 'interwoven and synergistic'. Pond also suggested that the roles of tour guide and adult instructor are very similar. She suggested that an adult educator has four key roles: a programmer who sets up the conditions to facilitate learning, a guide, a content resource and an institutional representative. Pond argued, however, that the roles of teacher and guide, although similar, are not identical. Guides must focus on the diversity of an audience, be more flexible and be more aware of their other roles (leader, host, public relations and conduit) than teachers.

The main interaction involved in tour guiding is between the visitor and the guide. Hence, tour guiding, with its key role to inform and educate visitors, is a part of the process of interpretation (Pond, 1993; Knudson et al., 1995; Prentice, 1995). According to Howard (1997), the guide's role in relation to the visitor is as follows: telling (provision of information), selling (interactive communication that explains and clarifies), participating (being a part of activity) and delegating (giving responsibility to some future behaviour). The role of the tour guide in this situation can be viewed as assisting in the interpretation of the site for the visitor.

Those who participate in guided activities are doing so to meet certain of Maslow's hierarchy of needs (Howard, 1997). Maslow (1943) indicated that there is a five-tier hierarchy of needs. These needs are, at the lowest level, physiological, followed by safety then ascending to a feeling of belonging and being accepted as a friend, through status and self-respect needs at the fourth level, to the highest level of self-development, accomplishment and growth. Maslow suggested that a need creates a tension, pleasant or unpleasant, that has to be resolved. The goal of people's behaviour is therefore to reduce the tension.

The decision to participate in a guided tour may be based on the expectation that certain needs will be fulfilled and these are likely to be relatively high-level needs of seeking friendship, personal development and recognition. Many visitors find it necessary to satisfy their lower-level needs and the need for refreshment, relief and details on the length of stay are often uppermost in people's minds (Knudson et al., 1995). To maximize the experience of visitors and minimize discomfort, Howard (1997) suggested that three principles should be employed. These are as follows:

- minimize the threat to safety or to psychological needs;
- satisfy social esteem, self-actualization needs;
- avoid mixing groups with different needs.

However, it is through the interpretation process that tour guides can provide important educational experiences for tourists. A good tour guide should offer his or her clients not only information, but also the opportunity of seeing the world differently (Pond, 1993; Knudson et al., 1995), hence guide training must prepare guides for this role. Mason and Christie (2003) suggested that the great majority of tour guide training programmes have traditionally concentrated on the competencies required to be a tour guide rather than providing opportunities for guides to examine their own assumptions and values. They argued that what is required is for trainee tour guides to become critically reflective practitioners and they proposed a model of guide training which requires modifying the competency-based nature of most tourist guide training. In addition to studying a skills based curriculum, guides would learn a number of techniques that promote critical reflection of their own values and assumptions. As Mason and Christie (2003) argued, if tour guides can be convinced of the significance of values education, then there is chance that they will be better critics of their own practice and better interpreters of the sites they visit. Not only will they be more sensitive in relation to the site and culture for which they are providing interpretation, but also sensitive to the needs of their clients, the tourists (see Photos 15.2 and 15.3).

Photo 15.2 The Parthenon in Athens is one of the most visited attractions in the world

Photo 15.3 A tour guide at work on the steps leading to the Parthenon on the Acropolis in Athens

The need for guides who are culturally sensitive as well as skilled and knowledgeable about a specific destination is well expressed by Ridenour (1995). He relates the story of two friends visiting the Canyon de Chelly in the United States, an area once inhabited by significant numbers of Navajo people. One of the two friends makes an unguided walk and returns later with a broken piece of pottery. Her colleague, somewhat knowledgeable of Native American traditions, is annoyed and scolds her friend for picking up the sherd. This leads to the response: 'What is wrong with me taking it, since I value it?' The other friend counters with a question: 'Would you feel happy if somebody took a silver spoon that had belonged to your grandmother from your house, simply because they valued it?' This situation remains unresolved, but later in the day, the two friends take a walk led by a Navajo guide. During the walk the two learn about Native American spiritual beliefs and values. The one who took the sherd of pottery is so taken by this new perspective that she admits what she has done and asks if she should return the sherd. The guide responds: 'No, leave it with me. I will cleanse it and pray over it before returning it to the earth. You may pray that the spirits return to it' (Ridenour, 1995).

Zoos are an example of a particular type of visitor attraction that use guides. The guides do not usually accompany the visitors as they make their way around the zoo, but give presentations at particular locations in relation to specific animal attractions (Broad, 1996). The following case study examines the nature of this process of interpretation at a zoo and considers the role of interpretation in visitor management.

Case study: keeper talks at Wellington Zoo

The keepers at Wellington Zoo, New Zealand give talks on a number of the animal exhibits. Talks concerning the following were observed: chimpanzees, 'big cats', Malayan sun bears, giraffes and exhibits in the Nocturnal House. The results from these observations provide an insight into the issues of presenting and interpreting wildlife under zoo conditions.

- *Chimpanzees*: the keepers offered audience members the opportunity of feeding the chimpanzees. This enabled interaction between the audience and the animals. Audience members were offered the opportunity to feed the animals if they could answer questions. It appeared a successful strategy as many children put up their hands and wanted to become involved in feeding. The keeper questions in this talk were also useful as they helped point out differences between monkeys and other primates. The talk was predominantly specific to chimps, but also raised the bigger issues of conservation, habitat loss and ideas on endangered species.
- *Big cats*: the 'tiger talk' was very informative and engaging because the animals were fed and talked about at the same time. The keeper fed one tiger by hand, from outside the cage. Hence, the audience could get close, still feel safe and yet also be aware of the 'presence' of the animals. The behaviour of the different tigers in the zoo was discussed. This was linked to conditions for tigers there, and the animals' preference for different activities. Hence, this was a story of animals that have strong links with Wellington Zoo and New Zealand and was not just another talk concerned with 'animals in captivity'. However, the type of talk observed (part of the Zoo School activities) is not generally available to zoo visitors and during a subsequent visit it was reported by several visitors that the animals were generally rather docile and difficult

to see. This is of importance, as for many visitors the 'big cats' are their favourite zoo exhibit, hence they may feel cheated if they do not see 'cats' in action.

- *Nocturnal House*: talks observed here were detailed and informative, but tended to be very exhibit specific. However, the size and layout of the Nocturnal House makes it difficult to engage a large audience. In particular, this is a problem at the entrance and exit and means it is difficult to give a presentation. Problems of presentation here also relate to the dark. Some young children are frightened of the dark. Also, the darkness means it is less easy for the audience (or at least some) to concentrate. Some exhibits here are very static, for example, tuatara and bats. Hence, the time spent here is quite likely to be short.
- *The Malayan sun bears*: one talk observed lasted just over 20 minutes and amplification was used. This talk was given to an audience of approximately 60, about one-third of whom were parents with young children. However, it seemed that this tended to make the audience less attentive. A number of parents with younger children left after about 8–10 minutes, and by the end there were virtually no parents with young children left. On a later visit, it was revealed that two cubs had been born and these provoked a strong audience reaction and a number of questions at the end of the talk. The audience during this talk was smaller, had slightly fewer younger children and was generally more attentive.
- *Giraffes*: the audience on each occasion was made up of approximately one-third children (aged 3–13). This exhibit appeared particularly interesting for children as they could directly feed the animals. The arrangements at the zoo are good as visitors are at the same height as a giraffe's head. However, the physical area under cover, and where there is direct access to feed the giraffes, is rather small. A small number of people left during one of the talks observed as it appeared they could not get close enough to feed or see the giraffes adequately. The talks were focused on these giraffes and also links with other zoos in New Zealand. The comparison between giraffes and people appeared to provoke a high level of response from the audience, including questions.

The investigation of keeper talks at Wellington Zoo also revealed some general issues in relation to interpretation. All talks were very detailed in relation to the particular animal exhibit presented. A large proportion of the talks was about feeding and breeding and other bodily functions. In relation to particular animals, for example, the Malayan sun bears, much of the talk focused on the young. All talks made some reference to conservation issues, usually in relation to the specific animal in the talk. However, not all talks made more general comments, that is, going from the specific talk to larger issues.

Most of the talks observed were given by one keeper. However, one of the talks in relation to the sun bears and one of the chimpanzee talks involved, in each case, two keepers. For these talks, a microphone and loudspeaker system were used; all other talks were given without any audio aid. Some problems were caused by the amplification system.

The great majority of the talks were to audiences of mixed age groups. Young children (those under age 5) made up 10–30 per cent of such groups. Their attention span was very short. The audience usually contained the parents of these children, as well as

(continued)

Case study: keeper talks at Wellington Zoo (continued)

some unaccompanied children (usually older, 8–13). Other adults, not accompanied by children, made up 30–50 per cent of the audience. The audiences were predominantly female. The composition of the audience creates particular problems for the keeper in terms of the content of a talk and methods of presentation. Trying to keep the audience's attention is not always easy, but is clearly an important role of the zookeeper. In all talks observed, except those given in connection with the Zoo School, a proportion of the audience left during the talk. Those with young children tended to leave first.

(Adapted from Mason, 1999.)

As the previous discussion has indicated, it is frequently visitors who are the target for attempts to use education for tourism planning and management purposes. One particular location which has a unique role in relation to tourism is the continent of Antarctica. The following case study considers the importance of the visitor experience of Antarctica and how this may be harnessed to educate those who have not visited the continent.

Case study: visitors as Antarctic ambassadors?

Antarctica is probably the last terrestrial tourism frontier. It is a remote, unique environment. The terrestrial ecosystems on the continent are limited because of the almost permanent snow cover which accompanies the very low temperatures. Antarctica is one of the driest places on Earth as it has very little rainfall – its precipitation is mainly in the form of snow. However, the marine ecosystems are rich in wildlife. So, it is the very edge of this continent, around its coastline, that is relatively high in living organisms and relatively rich in biodiversity. The periphery of Antarctica is also the breeding ground for seabirds and in particularly a number of species of penguins. Killer whales are found around the edges of the continent, as well as seals and walruses. The landscape is mountainous in the interior with active volcanoes, but also ice sheets and glaciers. At the edge of the continent, glaciers break off into the sea creating huge icebergs. It is only the very edge of the continent that loses its snow cover during the brief Antarctic summer – the interior remaining permanently covered in a very deep ice sheet.

The continent is unique by global human standards in terms of historically never having any permanent inhabitants, and substantial human contact with the continent has only occurred since the early twentieth century. Its remoteness and inhospitable climate limited attempts to travel to it until only just over 100 years ago. This means that its geography until very recently was almost unknown. Its short period of contact with humans has given it a unique political status – it is the only continent that is one political entity, but does not belong to one nation. It is administered by a very unusual process using what is known as the Antarctic Treaty System (ATS). This unique form of government involves representatives from countries that have an interest in Antarctica, which includes the USA, the UK, France, Germany and Russia, but also China, Malaysia and India. These countries, which over the past 100 years have had major political differences and in some cases fought wars against each other, work together to administer the ATS and disputes over, for example, fishing are resolved through the ATS. This unusual status means that Antarctica is frequently viewed as a barometer of human use of the global environment and activities here are often compared with what goes on elsewhere on the planet. This reflection on activities here is often expressed in the following manner: 'if we cannot get it right in Antarctica, there is little chance of success anywhere else on Earth!'

In an attempt to prevent conflict and exploitation, it is the only continent devoted primarily to scientific activity and it is a neutral demilitarized zone. Scientists from many countries work together investigating, for example, glacial activity, ancient climate records stored in the ice, geology and marine biology. The scientists live on the continent for weeks, months, or in some case years, but there are still very few permanent inhabitants. Most commercial activity on the continent is banned, particularly mining and oil extraction. However, tourism has the very unusual status of being not only allowed but promoted.

Why would tourists come to, what at first glance appears to be, a very inhospitable place for visitors? The landscape is an important attraction, particularly when it is accompanied by the significant amount and variety of wildlife in the margins of Antarctica. There are also a small number of heritage attractions in the form of the huts of the early explorers such as Scott, Shackleton and Mawson. Unusually, scientists and the work that they do are a very significant draw-card for tourists. This is partly because the work in which many scientists are engaged has global importance, particularly that to do with climate change. As science is the major activity of Antarctica and the scientists are funded by taxpayers from the countries of many of the visitors, it also provides an opportunity for these people to see how their taxes are being spent! Some tourists want to see what they regard as a unique environment (perhaps before it is irrevocably changed?). Some may also come to experience the 'otherness' of the place.

The tourist season is short, lasting through the Antarctic summer from November to February. Tourism is also very concentrated in the coastal margins and particularly the area known as the Antarctic Peninsula, where many of the huts of the explorers are located. This area receives about 90 per cent of all visitors, with the South Pole itself also being significant for tourist visits. Almost all of the tourists arrive by cruise ship – they come from, for example, Chile, Australia and New Zealand and the ships anchor offshore from the landmass. Visitor numbers peaked at just over 30,000 per year in 2008, but have fluctuated since and have been generally lower than this at about 25,000 per year. Prior to arrival visitors are given lectures and provided with codes of conduct concerning, for example, behaviour in relation to wildlife and disposal of litter. Visitors are taken onto the continent by inflatable boats known as zodiacs and their activities/behaviour there monitored by tour guides. Upon return to the boat, tourists can also attend debriefing sessions about their experience.

The reaction of tourists to their experience of Antarctica was investigated by Maher (2011). Maher was particularly interested in whether the experience was such that visitors were so affected that they became 'ambassadors for Antarctica'. What he

(continued)

Case study: visitors as Antarctic ambassadors? (continued)

meant by this was that tourists would be so impressed/overawed by the Antarctic environment that they would have three reactions:

a) They would believe it themselves and tell their friends/family about Antarctica's attractions.
b) They would tell their friends and family about conserving the continent.
c) They would become much more aware, generally, about the importance of 'natural environments' and the need for their conservation.

Maher's approach involved reference to literature on tourism experience and environmental experience. This literature suggested that there are three phases of experience:

Phase 1 Travel to the site – this is the anticipation phase.
Phase 2 The on-site experience – which Maher considered was likely to be an 'extraordinary experience' for the visitors because of what Antarctica has to offer.
Phase 3 The travel back from Antarctica – which involves memory and recollection. This process involves the 'on-site' experience interacting with the pre-visit (anticipation) and post-visit (recollection/memory). Maher considered that this third stage (memory and recollection) would be most likely to contribute to the possible 'ambassador' role.

In the research process, Maher examined the phases of the experience and concentrated on the 'anticipation' and the 'recollection/memory phase'. He used a sample of 'ordinary' tourists to Antarctica, but also included 'VIPs to Antarctica' who comprised scientists, politicians, writers, artists and photographers. (Several countries, such as New Zealand and Australia, give awards to writers and artists to visit Antarctica and produce work, for example, poetry and paintings based on their experience.) Maher used questionnaire surveys, interviews and personal narratives. In total there were 87 respondents in part one of the field research (as indicated above as Phase 1 of the 'experience') and 75 of these in part two of the field research (Phase 3 of 'experience' above).

In terms of the results, as many as 95 per cent of respondents indicated their expectations had been met in the actual visit to Antarctica and 70 per cent indicated that they had enjoyed the experience 'more than expected'. In relation to the potential role as ambassadors for Antarctica, all the respondents indicated that they had shared the experience after the visit with friends and family and some respondents also shared this with other groups and all respondents regarded this as a very important activity. Respondents suggested that they had done this sharing mainly via discussion and/or photo/slide shows. However, some had also given formal speeches about their experience. Respondents suggested that the motivation for sharing their experience was to make Antarctica 'come alive', 'bring it closer to the listeners' and 'whet their appetite'. In terms of what they had learned during the visit, respondents indicated that they had found out more about the impacts of humans on Antarctica, the vulnerability of Antarctica, dealing with litter/pollution and specific wildlife information. Most of Maher's research questions were indirectly concerned with the role of ambassador for the Antarctic, and these did not make overt references to this role. However, Maher also asked a direct question about the role and just over 80 per cent of respondents indicated that they felt they had become ambassadors for the continent as a result of their experience. However, Maher also injected a note of caution in relation to his results, when he stated that they should be interpreted carefully, as Antarctic tour operators would be pleased to term tourists as 'ambassadors' as this would be a very good marketing device for them.

(Based on Mason and Legg, 1999; Maher, 2011.)

Summary

Education can be used as an important technique in tourism management. The use of education for tourism management is usually within the context of what is termed interpretation. Interpretation is an educational process, which involves not only the transfer of knowledge, but also the development of values to the environment and culture of the site visited and has been used extensively in visitor management. Interpretation can be via oral presentation, the printed word or even other media such as film, video or computer. Tour guides act as site interpreters and zookeepers are a specific form of interpreter used by zoos to help manage the educational experience for visitors.

Visitors to a site have particular needs and interpretation can be used to meet these. Interpretation can also be used to transform visitors' thinking and behaviour, with the intention that they become 'mindful' tourists. Although there is a lack of sufficient evidence, to date, that interpretation will necessarily lead to changes in behaviour, programmes that provoke an emotional response may lead visitors to modify both their attitudes and behaviour. In the case study of Antarctica, it is suggested that visitors can experience such a strong reaction to their visit that they may even become ambassadors for the continent. In this way, not only do they tell others about Antarctica and the need to conserve it, but may apply their newly acquired environmental awareness, knowledge and concern to other global contexts.

Student activities

1   What do you understand by the term 'interpretation'?
2   How can interpretation be used in tourism management?
3   What is the role of the tour guide in interpretation?
4   Produce a matrix with four boxes, in the format shown below, to compare the activity of a tour guide in comparison with that of a printed guide book:

Advantages of a tour guide	Disadvantages of a tour guide
Advantages of a printed guide	Disadvantages of a printed guide

5   What is the role of a zookeeper?
6   What are the advantages of a zookeeper over a printed zoo guide?
7   Summarize the response of visitors to their experience of interpretation by zookeepers at Wellington Zoo under the headings: positive responses and negative responses.
8   In relation to the study of Wellington Zoo discussed above, a number of recommendations relating to ways to improve the keeper talk were made. These recommendations are presented below.

- The keeper talk should be viewed as a performance in front of, and potentially involving, an audience. It should not be viewed solely as presenting information. Therefore, thought should be given to issues such as how to maintain audience attention, as well as ways to get the audience involved and/or to respond.
- Presenting some form of 'story' about the animals would seem an appropriate way to keep audience attention. This could involve reference to the animal's life at the zoo, or a discussion of similarities between the animal and other animals/humans.
- The process of the keeper asking questions and offering rewards (such as feeding the chimpanzees) appears a successful way of keeping the audience's attention, particularly children, and could be used in a variety of different talks.
- If the zoo's chief role is to educate, then the 'bigger picture' issues about the need for conservation, in general, need to be given in addition to discussion of matters relating to the individual species.
- If animals can be taken from cages or brought close to the audience (e.g. through feeding) this will help maintain audience interest. However, consideration should also be given to the stress that this puts on the exhibit.
- If amplification is required, then hand-held microphones are probably not a good idea, as they limit the overall 'performance'. It would be better to use small clip-on microphones.
- Using two keepers to present a talk would appear more successful than using just one in certain circumstances. This worked well with the Malayan sun bears and the chimpanzees. In this context, one person does 'the talk', the other interacts with the audience and the animals. An announcement, via a tannoy system, a few minutes prior to a keeper talk would probably increase the audience size, although this could disturb animals. Alternatively, an announcement by loudhailer in the area in which the talk will be given 5–10 minutes beforehand could help.

a) Suggest possible constraints to the application of these recommendations.
b) Do you agree with the recommendations?
c) Suggest what else could be done to improve keeper talks at the zoo.

9 In relation to the case study of Antarctica, working in small groups of 3–4, answer the following questions:

a) What are the attractions of Antarctica for tourists?
b) What type of tourist will be attracted to visit Antarctica?
c) Why do relatively few tourists visit Antarctica annually?
d) Why does Antarctica provoke such strong reactions from tourists, as indicated in the case study?
e) What do you understand by the term 'Antarctic ambassador'?
f) If you were to visit Antarctica, how would you react?

Chapter 16

Self-regulation as a technique in tourism planning and management

Learning objectives

At the end of this chapter you should:

- be aware of the meanings of regulations, self-regulation, guidelines and codes of conduct in relation to tourism;
- understand what tourism codes of conduct are;
- be aware of the different authors and target audiences for codes of conduct;
- be aware of critical perspectives on the use of tourism codes of conduct in tourism planning and management.

Introduction

This chapter discusses regulations, self-regulation, guidelines and codes of conduct in tourism planning and management. Although often linked, there are important differences between these three terms. As Stonehouse (1990) indicated, regulations usually have some form of legal status while codes of conduct, codes of practice and guidelines, although attempting to regulate tourism, do not have this status. Guidelines, however, are usually based on well-considered precepts, indicating a course of action to be followed with the reasoning behind it, while codes of conduct provide sets of rules for behaving in certain circumstances (Stonehouse, 1996). Codes of conduct are usually voluntary, tend to be self-imposed and are designed to act as a form of self-regulation (Mason and Mowforth, 1996). There are few examples of legally backed regulations pertaining specifically to tourism but a variety of tourism codes of conduct have been existence for at least 30 years. This chapter therefore focuses on codes of conduct in tourism and the guidelines that often accompany them. The chapter begins by setting codes within the wider context of ethics and morals.

Key perspectives

Codes, ethics and morals

Tourism codes involve not just the provision of information, but are concerned with the behaviour of tourists. As they frequently advocate desired behaviour and/or advise against undesirable conduct, they have an ethical dimension (Malloy and Fennell, 1998). Ethics is concerned with people making choices and acting in a reasonable manner (Fennell and Przeclawski, 2003) and is closely linked to morality where morality is taken to mean moral judgements, standards and rules of conduct (Taylor, 1975).

Many well-known philosophers and philosophies have made important contributions to ethics. Modern Western philosophy has provided significant ideas on ethics, including the arguments of Kant who referred to 'moral duty', meaning that the knowledge of one's duty is a major motivational factor in behaviour (Fennell and Przeclawski, 2003). The twentieth-century philosophy of existentialism was very much concerned with the actions of individuals and placed ethics at the centre, when suggesting that any human act is 'right or wrong' depending on the actor's free will and responsibility (Guignon, 1986).

Ethics has a number of key applications in the modern world. One of these relates to the behaviour of companies and commercial organizations. Much of this concern with 'corporate' ethical values and behaviour is directed at marketing (Fennell and Przeclawski, 2003). Underlying these corporate values are corporate ethical values (Hunt et al., 1989) which help establish and maintain standards and influence courses of action. Hence, there is a close link between values, ethics and the moral judgements that people make.

Historically, tourism and ethics have not been closely linked (Fennell and Malloy, 2007). However, tourism appears to be a very appropriate candidate for ethical scrutiny (Fennell and Przeclawski, 2003). Tourism involves many different players representing different viewpoints; it has social, economic, political and environmental dimensions and has been noted for its ability to create a range of important impacts (Fennell and Przeclawski, 2003). As the major players in tourism have different value positions, there is the likelihood of conflict and the interaction between the players is likely to create a number of ethical dilemmas (Fennell, 2000). These ethical dilemmas and conflicts are generally the result of the interaction of the main players in tourism, that is the tourists themselves, inhabitants of visited local areas and what

Fennell and Przeclawski (2003) refer to as the 'tourism brokers'; by this they mean, for example, members of the tourism industry such as tour operators and hotel staff. Tourism codes of conduct have been created, largely, as a response to these ethical dilemmas and the perceived negative consequences of tourism, and have usually been an attempt to generate more desirable and beneficial behaviour amongst the key players which minimizes conflict and helps reduce negative effects of tourism (Fennell and Malloy, 2007).

Aims, authorship and audiences of tourism codes

A number of earlier chapters have made reference to codes of conduct. The use of codes of conduct in tourism is a relatively recent phenomenon, although there are examples, such as the English Countryside Commission's Country Code, which date back to the 1960s (Mason and Mowforth, 1996). In the past few years, codes have been developed by governments, the private sector, concerned individuals as well as non-governmental organizations (NGOs).

The main aim of codes is to influence attitudes and modify behaviour (Mason and Mowforth, 1996). Codes are usually designed to improve environmental quality and minimize negative impacts of tourism. Hence, codes of conduct are used in an attempt to regulate behaviour. Codes of conduct are usually part of a process involving attempts to regulate tourism and are often used in conjunction with guidelines.

A number of discrete target groups for tourism codes of conduct have been identified. These groups are as follows: visitors, the tourism industry and members of host communities (UNEP, 1995; Mason and Mowforth, 1996). The most significant target audience in terms of sheer number of codes is the visitor; the WTTRC (1995), for example, listed almost 80 visitor codes in use around the world in 1994 and this has risen to several hundred by the early part of the twenty-first century. A number of codes have also been prepared for use by those directly involved in the tourist industry and more recently codes have been prepared for the use of host populations.

In addition to a variety of target audiences for codes of conduct, there are a range of different authors. A significant number of codes have been written by concerned individuals and NGOs while government bodies and the tourism industry itself have not been until recently very active in producing codes (Mason and Mowforth, 1996; Mason et al., 2000a).

However, codes of conduct frequently fail to specify either their broad aims or more specific objectives (Mason, 1994). Nevertheless, UNEP, having conducted a survey of voluntary environmental tourism codes in 1992 and received information on 30 codes used by countries and international associations, was able to deduce a number of specific objectives (UNEP, 1995). UNEP (1995: 8) produced, in summary form, five objectives of such codes, which are as follows:

- to serve as a catalyst for dialogue between government and other bodies involved in tourism;
- to create an awareness in government and industry of the need for sound environmental management;
- to heighten awareness amongst tourists of the need for appropriate behaviour;
- to make host populations aware of the need for environmental protection;
- to encourage cooperation between government agencies, host communities, industry and NGOs.

In that they provide information, advice and frequently instructions, it should be clear that in their attempt to regulate, codes of conduct also aim to educate.

It would appear from the UNEP summary of the aims of tourism codes above that they are primarily concerned with environmental impacts and improving environment management. However, the message of tourism codes is not just confined to environmental issues. A number of visitor codes, for example, make reference to socio-cultural matters, such as respect for local religious beliefs. Codes with industry as the audience frequently refer to the need for appropriate training and honest marketing of tourism products (Mason and Mowforth, 1996).

It is possible to categorize and group codes not just according to their message and audience, but also by whether they are deontological or teleological (Malloy and Fennell, 1998; Garrod and Fennell, 2004). As Garrod and Fennell (2004) indicated, deontological codes include ethical perspectives that are based on rules and assess 'rightness' and 'wrongness' according to certain actions and duties. Teleological codes, in contrast, are those that advocate the type of good behaviour 'which produces the best consequences for the greatest number of people' (Garrod and Fennell, 2004: 342). It is possible to illustrate the differences between deontological and teleological codes through the use of an example. A deontological code might contain an instruction such as 'Please do not feed the wildlife' while a teleological code would contain the statement 'Please do not feed the wildlife, as this may lead to behavioural changes and growing dependency on humans as food providers.' In simple terms, unlike deontological codes, teleological codes provide an explanatory guideline to support the instruction in the code.

Examples of codes of conduct in tourism are shown below. Figure 16.1 (the Countryside Commission's Code) is a visitor code. Figure 16.2, Tourismus mit Einsicht, is a code for the tourism

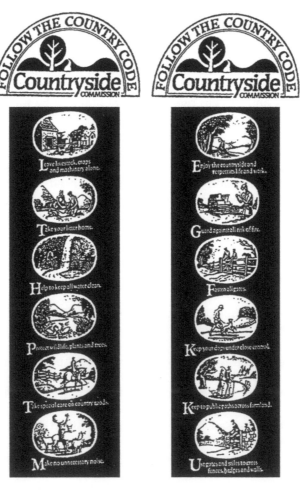

Figure 16.1 The English Country Code

We, the travel business

(1) We act as a business organized on commercial principles, which tries to meet the travel needs of its clients while acheving reasonable economic results. We can reach this goal in the long run only if we succeed in making better use of the opportunities of travel and simultaneously reducing its dangers. We shall therefore promote such forms of tourism which are economically productive, socially responsible and environment-friendly.

(2) We see our clients as people who enjoy life and who want their holidays to be the 'most pleasurable weeks of the year'. We also know that there is an increasing number of interested, considerate and environment-conscious tourists. We shall try to respond to and encourage this trend without preaching to our guests.

(3) We shall bear in mind the interests, independence and rights of the local population. We shall respect local laws, customs, traditions and cultural characteristics. We shall always remember that we as travel agents and as tourists are guests of the local population.

(4) We want to collaborate as partners with the service industry and the host population in the tourist areas. We advocate fair business conditions, which will bring the greatest possible benefit to all partners. We shall encourage active participation of the host population wherever possible.

(5) Our efforts to improve travel should include a careful selection and continuous training of our staff at all levels, as well as development and supervision of our services.

(6) We want to provide our clients with expert and comprehensive information about all aspects of the country they want to visit through catalogues, travel information and guides. Our advertising must be not only attractive but honest and responsible. We shall try to avoid the usual superlatives and cliched texts and pictures. Special emphasis will be placed on a respectful description of the population in the host areas. We shall desist from any advertising with erotic enticements.

(7) Our guides and social directors will have a particular responsibility in promoting tourism with insight and understanding. We shall provide special, and continuous, training for personnel working in these areas.

(8) We shall not organize travel, trips or expeditions to ethnic groups who live apart from our Western civilization. We shall not promise our clients 'Contact with untouched peoples' because we know that they are vulnerable and must be protected.

(9) All our activities and those of our business partners will have to meet the same strict quality standard. We want to make our business partners aware of the fact that they too should contribute to an environment-conscious and socially responsible tourism.

(10) We are prepared to formulate within our professional associations a set of principles encompassing the ethics of the tourist trade – which shall be binding for all members.

Figure 16.2 Tourismus mit Einsicht: code for the travel business

industry and Figure 16.3 a form of code for the Ministry of Tourism. Figure 16.4 provides a summary of key elements of codes of conduct.

Issues with tourism codes

Although many codes are impressive in terms of the range of issues that they cover and in their depth of discussion and information, there are a number of significant problems with them. Mason and Mowforth (1996) suggested four major problem areas.

First, codes must be put into action as intended, but as UNEP (1995) indicated most codes tend to be poorly implemented. An indication of whether codes are well implemented can be derived from monitoring. However, until very recently, the great majority of codes were not

Include aspects of nature tourism in national tourism policy.

Carry out marketing programme for nature tourism, including product identification, inventory of nature tourism attractions and visitor surveys to determine demand.

Design a mechanism, with the park service, for collecting entrance fees.

Change tourism laws as needed to include environmental protection clauses for natural areas.

Develop mechanisms to record statistical information about nature tourists.

Work with private sector and international funding agencies to develop adequate tourism infrastructure at each site not only to accommodate tourists but also to provide opportunities for tourists to spend money.

Create training programmes, with the park service and tour operators, for all park personnel and tour guides. Training should include natural resource education and tourism management skills.

Develop mechanisms to channel a portion of tourism revenue back into maintenance and protection of the park.

Monitor the quality of nature tourism services and facilities.

Figure 16.3 Checklist for the Ministry of Tourism
Source: Boo (1990).

Type of codes	Authorship	Audience	Message
Visitor codes	Predominantly NGOs and concerned individuals, but also some government bodies such as Ministry of the Environment.	Domestic visitors and international visitors, especially overseas visitors to developing countries.	Minimize environmental and socio-cultural damage to area visited. Maximize economic benefit to host community. Encourage more equality in relationships between visitors and hosts. Promote more responsible and sustainable forms of tourism.
Industry codes	Predominantly co-ordinating bodies such as WTO and IATA; also governments and to a lesser extent NGOs and concerned individuals; and exceptionally tourism companies (e.g.Chateau Whistler Hotel Group).	Tourism industry in general, and some codes for specific sectors such as the hotel industry	Appropriate training/education for staff. Honest marketing of product. Develop awareness of environmental and socio-cultural impact of tourism. Promote more responsible and sustainable forms of tourism. Promote recycling.
Host codes	Predominantly NGOs and concerned individuals; some host communities in both developed and developing countries; and a small number of host governments.	Mainly host communities, especially in developing countries.	Information and advice about visitors. Minimize environmental and socio-cultural damage. Maximize economic benefits to host community. Encourage more equality in relationship between host and visitors. Advocate more democratic and participatory forms of tourism development.

Figure 16.4 Key elements of codes of conduct in tourism
Source: Mason and Mowforth (1996).

monitored, so it is very difficult to evaluate their effects (UNEP, 1995). Nevertheless, in relation to the use of codes in the management of whale watching in the internationally important destination of Kaikoura, New Zealand, Curtin (2005) indicated that occasional 'spot checks' and consumer power in the form of complaints can offset the problems of the inability to constantly monitor the use of codes. In this New Zealand context, the fact that the licensing body providing a permit for whale-watching operators, the government Department of Conservation, is the same body involved in 'spot checks', may assist with effectiveness of the codes. Nevertheless, this is a relatively unusual situation and it would seem obvious that unless a code is implemented, there is little chance of it achieving its desired impact.

Second, several codes may be found operating in the same location but they may be written by different authors and aimed at targets existing at different scales, from local to national or even international. This suggests a much greater need to coordinate codes and there is perhaps a related need to reduce variability between codes. This is particularly the case when there is concern about the accuracy of the message of the code, or the rationale or guideline underlying the message. This is not so much to do with ethical choices, i.e. whether certain behaviour is 'right' or 'wrong', but with whether the code has been created with accurate scientific knowledge. For example, in relation to whale-watching codes, Garrod and Fennell (2004) indicated that there is a large variation in the content of various codes, which appears to be the result of a lack of precise knowledge. In relation to minimum approach distance to whales, there is no widespread agreement and while some codes make recommendations on swimming with cetaceans, others indicate that it should be prohibited altogether (Garrod and Fennell, 2004). This variability may not only cause confusion, but also provide users with an excuse to flout the suggested instructions.

As Valentine (1992) suggested, most codes are targeted at visitors, hence he argued that in any given situation it is necessary to employ simultaneously a number of codes of conduct with different target audiences. For example, a code aimed at visitors should be used in conjunction with another aimed at operators, as a code for one group on its own would not be as effective. However, this may lead to a proliferation of codes that could appear to contradict the argument for less variability in codes, but would nevertheless appear to further support the need for greater coordination between code authors.

Third, and of particular importance, is that codes may be little more than clever marketing devices, rather than genuine attempts to promote more sustainable forms of tourism. Under such conditions, a code can be used in an attempt to persuade potential customers that, for example, an ecotour operator adheres to a set of environmental and/or socio-cultural principles. The reality may be that the principles are not adhered to, and that this is little more than a cynical attempt to get customers to part with their cash, believing they are buying an ethical/green tourism product – a process that the media has termed 'greenwashing'. In this way, codes can give a tourism company a level of credibility in the eye of the consumer that is entirely fallacious.

It is likely, nevertheless, to be extremely tempting for a company to claim that they adhere to some form of environmental or socio-cultural code. As Smith and Duffy (2003: 89) claimed, 'Put simply, codes of ethics improve a company's image, allow it to avoid scandal and improve its sales.' Hence, monitoring will be essential to ascertain if an ecotourism company does indeed follow the code that it claims to espouse. However, as has been stated above very little monitoring of the implementation and effectiveness of codes has taken place.

Fourth, in terms of problems with codes is that they are voluntary – they are a form of self-regulation (Mason and Mowforth, 1996). As such, they can do little more than exhort the target audience to respond to the requests/instructions contained within the code. There are almost no codes backed up by actual legally binding documents, which, of course, limits their effectiveness. Evidence from a number of locations suggests that external regulation may be far more effective than self-regulation (Mason et al., 2000a). However, as Garrod and Fennell (2004) reported, there are variations in the attitudes to whether codes should be backed up by external regulation or not. They found that in relation to whale watching there were far more non-voluntary than voluntary codes developed in North America, while Europe developed far more voluntary than non-voluntary codes. This may be due to the fact that government was particularly active in creating codes in North America, while in Europe NGOs were more active in this area (Garrod and Fennell, 2004).

There is increasing evidence that the tourism industry will adopt voluntary codes, but as Mason and Mowforth (1996) argued, the motivation for self-regulation by the industry is that either it wishes to appear to be acting responsibly in advance of imposed regulation, to weaken the force of this regulation, or it is attempting to stave off external regulation entirely.

The case study below of codes used by cruise ships in the Arctic highlights some of the issues raised in the discussion above.

Case study: cruise ship codes of conduct in the Arctic

The Association of Arctic Expedition Cruise Operators (AECO) was set up in 2003 and in 2014 had 16 members. It has developed guidelines and codes of conduct for expedition and cruise operators in the Arctic. AECO covers an area that includes Greenland, Jan Mayen Island, Arctic Canada, parts of the Russian Arctic coast and one of the most visited Arctic destinations, the archipelago of Svalbard (Spitsbergen). Its guidelines are targeted at vessels from small yachts up to large cruise ships that carry hundreds of passengers and AECO has produced guidelines for both its members and non-members who are visiting the Arctic.

The guidelines and codes are mainly concerned with environmental factors. Although the guidelines refer to different legislations being applicable in different sea areas, they state that AECO members should recognize all sea areas as being of equal importance and each should be regarded as having protected status. Specific instructions in the codes of conduct for AECO members in relation to this protected status include the following statements:

- Do not remove anything – except rubbish. There are complex regulations about what can actually be taken, when and where. AECO staff should know the regulations.
- Do not allow physical disturbance to the environment, such as graffiti and the building of cairns.
- Ensure that visitors, crew and staff do not leave anything behind on land or in the sea.
- Make every effort to remove any rubbish found on the shore.
- Be considerate to other people or activities. Do not land near camps, trappers or others unless this has previously been agreed on.

These statements are directed at the ships' operational staff and the ships' crews and they also indicate that the preparation for visits to the Arctic must include the communication of relevant AECO policy to visitors, travel agents, authorities, research communities and the general public.

There are also specific guidelines and codes of conduct for visitors which include statements about leaving no lasting sign of your visit, taking no souvenirs, taking no natural material, such as plants, and not disturbing birds and animals.

There are several major issues in relation to the AECO guidelines. First, like almost all guidelines and codes of conduct of this type, those of AECO are voluntary so have no legal standing. Second, not all countries whose ships are using the Arctic for cruising are members of AECO. In fact, in 2010 only just under a half of the ships using the Artic cruising area were AECO members. Third, the sea area covered by AECO is not the whole of the Arctic sea area. Fourth, it is not possible to monitor the activities of all cruise/expedition ships at all times, whether the ships are in areas covered by AECO or not. Hence, there has to be a reliance on the honesty and integrity of members, but both AECO members and non-members will be very aware that their activities at sea are unlikely to be closely watched.

(Based on Hall and Page, 2014 and AECO, 2014.)

Despite the issues raised in the case study, in contrast to the activities of some cruise ships discussed in the case study in Chapter 12, AECO would appear to have policies, evident in their guidelines and codes of conduct, that are attempting to prevent environmental damage to the Arctic sea areas and land masses.

Summary

Codes of conduct and guidelines are part of the attempt to regulate tourism. However, codes of conduct and guidelines are not the same as regulations as these usually have legal status, while codes and guidelines are voluntary and a form of self-regulation. Codes of conduct have a range of authors, including governments, NGOs, industry representatives and concerned individuals.

Codes are targeted at tourists, industry, government and host communities. The message of most codes involves statements, or more usually instructions, about environmental matters and increasingly cultural factors. Some codes are deontological, merely providing a set of instructions, while others are teleological, having explanatory guidelines in connection with the advice/instructions provided. However, codes are not without problems. Few codes are monitored (as is discussed in the case study of Arctic cruise ship codes and guidelines), there is a great variability among codes and a general lack of coordination. Codes can also be misused. For example, an unscrupulous operator can claim that it meets certain requirements of a code written by say, an environmental group (with no evidence to support this) in an attempt to sell more holidays. Codes of conduct also suffer from the fact that they are largely voluntary. This has led to the conclusion amongst some commentators that external regulation is required.

Student activities

1 What are the main differences between codes of conduct, regulations and guidelines?
2 Take the examples of codes of conduct supplied, in Figures 16.1–16.3, and say how well you think they meet the objectives produced by UNEP.
3 Study each of the examples of codes of conduct (Figures 16.1–16.3). Classify the codes as either deontological or teleological and give your reasoning behind the classification.
4 Study each of the examples of codes of conduct (Figures 16.1–16.3) and also the summary shown in Figure 16.4, then read the following:

The scenario:

A new resort hotel with 120 beds, an indoor and outdoor swimming pool, restaurant and gift shops is about to be built in a developing area for tourism on the coast of a Mediterranean island. The main customers, it is hoped, will be from overseas, but significant numbers of domestic tourists will be attracted. The hotel will appeal to a broad cross-section of visitors including business travellers, families with and without children, but will be tending to aim slightly upmarket. In your study groups, create a code of conduct in relation to the hotel development for each of the following target audiences: visitors; the industry (hotel owners); the local and regional government.

Compare the completed codes for each sector and examine and comment on both similarities between them and possible points of conflict.

5   What has this activity (Question 4) taught you about tourism development?
6   Repeat the activity but this time set the hotel in Eastern Europe and once again compare and contrast the codes of conduct you have created.
7   In relation to the case study of Arctic cruise ships, in small groups of 3–4 discuss:

   a) the reasons you believe AECO was established
   b) the likelihood of the instructions in its code of conduct, as indicated above, being achieved.

Chapter 17

Information technology and tourism planning and management

Introduction

Tourism is a complex, global industry and information is its lifeblood. Information about the tourism product is vital to assist the consumer in making choices. This is particularly so given that the tourism product is intangible. Selling the product requires representations and descriptions by the travel trade. Electronic forms of messages about tourism products have certain advantages over printed sources. Electronic forms can be more up-to-date and hence topical, they can be more visual and colourful, and in relation to computerized systems such as the Internet, can provide tour operators and tourism providers with access to large numbers of potential customers simultaneously. Since at least the beginning of the millennium, consumers have been using Internet sites for planning, searching, reserving and purchasing tourism products and this trend appears set to continue.

There is increasing use of IT in tourism. Various types of IT are being used by industry, government departments, operators and even potential and actual customers to seek out data on holidays and tourist destinations. IT is also being used to display data in a tourism context. IT has been defined as follows:

> The collective term given to the most recent developments in the mode (electronic) and the mechanisms (computers and communication technologies) used for the acquisition, processing, analysis, storage, retrieval, dissemination and application of information.
>
> (Poon, 1993)

It is a common assumption that IT equates with computers. However, IT covers a large range of electronic devices including videotext, teletext, faxes, telephones, teleconferencing, satellites, mobile (cell) phones, computer networks and the Internet (Cooper *et al.*, 1998). IT can be used in tourism planning and management and one particularly significant use is with a GIS. This chapter discusses GISs in detail as it has been used extensively in the planning and management of tourism.

Key perspectives

Until about 20 years ago, IT and, in particular, computerized systems were not being used extensively in relation to tourism planning and management. However, in the early 1990s, destination management systems (DMS) were applied to tourism destinations and this involved the coordination of the activities of all partners (discussed in more detail in Chapter 14) involved in the production and delivery of the destination tourism product (Cooper *et al.*, 1998). Now being used increasingly, advanced forms of DMS:

> can rationalise destination management and marketing by supporting promotion, distribution and operation, while also offering innovative tools for strategic management, product differentiation and amelioration of tourism impacts by better balancing the needs and expectations of tourists and locals.
>
> (Cooper *et al.*, 1998: 441)

A particularly useful type of IT that can assist in the planning and management of the resources for tourism is the GIS. GISs are basically computerized systems for handling and processing data. They deal with geographical and other types of data, processing them to produce maps, graphs, tables and statistics. GISs can deal with information on the natural resources, human settlement and cultural resources for tourism (Doswell, 1997). GISs can either print maps as overlays or generate computer images as virtual overlays. Sophisticated GISs can also perform statistical and complex computational tasks. GISs can show clearly spatial relationships and other forms of relationship. In this way, they can show how activities, both tourism and non-tourism, are able to co-exist or may be in conflict. GISs can be used at a variety of scales and are particularly useful in integrating data from local, regional and national sources. They can also simulate a number of possible future scenarios that can assist in the planning and management process (Doswell, 1997).

GISs can be used for many tasks, and have been used by a number of government departments in many countries since the mid-1980s. GISs are particularly useful when a large amount of data needs to be manipulated. GISs are being used and reported on in an increasing number of tourism contexts, including locations as diverse as the Central American state of Belize, in the United Kingdom and in New Zealand.

In Belize, which is a small developing country, there was a need to map areas that could be established for a number of different uses, both tourism and non-tourism (BBC, 1991). The coastal area was considered suitable for tourism development, but also had a number of important wildlife habitats. GISs were used as a planning tool to create areas in the form of zones for the development of ecotourism. The planned ecotourism areas were in locations that were not likely to be damaged easily by visitors.

In New Zealand, GISs have been used in connection with the Resource Management Act (RMA), which was introduced in 1991 (Watkins *et al.*, 1997). In relation to planning and management, GISs have been found to be particularly useful in New Zealand in the following areas:

- making a contribution to environmental monitoring and the state of the environment;
- assisting with the assessment of the effectiveness of regional policy statements;
- helping with decisions on resource consents (planning permission).

MacAdam (1999) investigated the use of GISs by consultants in tourism in the context of the United Kingdom. In summary, MacAdam indicated that a GIS is particularly useful for data analysis, modelling and forecasting. More specifically MacAdam indicated that GISs had an important tourism planning and management role in terms of:

- the production of environmental statements;
- qualitative/quantitative data collection (particularly in terms of community involvement);
- the use of system analysis techniques/audit trails;
- the interviewing of local representatives and local people;
- the interpreting of sites using the result of visitor surveys;
- feasibility studies for a tourist facility;
- strategy programmes, including an action plan;
- traffic modelling from highway engineers' data;
- wildlife data given by English Nature for the management of ecology in local areas;
- infrastructure audit in the context of hotels, restaurants;
- policy studies.

Hasse and Milne (1999) investigated the use of GISs in relation to tourism in New Zealand. The particular focus of their study was on the potential use of a GIS for community involvement in tourism. Their findings are summarized in the case study below.

Case study: GISs and community aspects of tourism in New Zealand

Hasse and Milne (1999) investigated the uses of GISs in a tourism context and its potential for community involvement. In summary, they indicated that GISs could be used to:

- compare different sources of data/information;
- identify gaps and shortcomings in data;
- link different systems of understanding;
- analyse spatial patterns;
- highlight choices/preferences.

The particular community aspects of their findings were as follows:

- Data collected from the community using GISs (maps and diagrams) were used in a questionnaire survey and interviews.
- Data were presented visually to the community using GISs (particularly maps and diagrams). The rationale for this was that the community was likely to find it easier to understand maps/diagrams than figures/numbers.
- GISs can become a means for community participation in tourism decision-making.
- GISs can aid in analysing data, explaining key concepts and presenting findings and information.
- GISs can therefore contribute to the stronger possibility of more sustainable tourism, as the community is more involved.

(Adapted from Hasse and Milne (1999) and MacAdam (1999).)

GISs have also proved particularly useful in landscape areas that are important resources for tourism, but have the potential to be damaged by tourism and other activities. In certain locations damage to the landscape will require a long period of recovery, so GISs can be used to identify the fragile areas and then the information used to prevent, or at least limit, the damage. The following case study discusses just such a landscape in Iceland and how a GIS has been used to help manage this area.

Case study: landscape sensitivity and tourism zoning in Iceland

The northern periphery of the northern hemisphere is characterized by particularly fragile ecosystems. In Iceland, the vegetation and soil cover are susceptible to pressure, both natural and human induced. The major landscape problems of soil erosion and land degradation are a product of Iceland's climate and centuries of agricultural practice, but they can be easily triggered by unsuitable forms of tourism. However, as in many parts of the world, there has been relatively little research into the environmental impacts of tourism on the landscape of Iceland.

Over the past 1,000 years, the landscape of Iceland has been greatly affected by the natural climatic conditions: frequent rain, and seasonal frost, ice and snow. Overgrazing of this fragile landscape, throughout this period, has made conditions worse. Soil erosion has affected almost three quarters of the land area, of which nearly 20 per cent has suffered from severe or extremely severe erosion.

The landscape is made up of several vegetation systems of which the major types are river and glacial systems, wetlands, grasslands and heathlands. These different vegetation types have varying levels of sensitivity to human activities, including tourism. Moss heath is the dominant plant in many of the most popular tourist sites in Iceland and this has been identified as the most susceptible to trampling. Trampling has contributed to major soil erosion problems. In addition to vegetation type, soil type and slope angle can contribute significantly to soil erosion and land degradation.

The study area that forms the basis for this case study borders the largest glacier in Iceland, Vatnajökull. As a result of global warming, the Vatnajökull ice cap and its outlet glaciers have retreated a great deal during the course of the twentieth century. It seems very likely that the ice cap will continue to retreat over the coming decades. The result of glacial melting is the gradual exposing of land along the glacial margins. As newly exposed, this land is lacking in vegetation and is ultra-sensitive to physical and human impacts. Therefore the location of land in relation to glacial margins is another important factor in indicating sensitivity.

The sensitivity of the landscape to tourism pressure can be estimated by analysing vegetation type in a given region in combination with soil type, slope angle and proximity to glacial margins. Combinations of these physical variables can provide a sensitivity range that can be categorized into several classes of sensitivity.

Using geographical information system (GISs) – electronic tools that are able to handle multiple spatial criteria and manipulate these, making them powerful tools to aid decision-makers in planning tourism – these categories can be mapped and zones of sensitivity created. A typical GIS works by overlaying mapped information, which is usually in digital form, in this case derived from the variables of vegetation, soil type, slope angle and proximity to glacial margins. Through the GIS overlay, which combines the information from these physical variables, a new information layer is created, which consists of accumulated sensitivity values from the individual sensitivity classes. The layers of information build up a digital map that combines the variables. In this way a map of sensitivity to tourism impacts can be created, manipulated, modified and interrogated. This enables the creation of a digital map in which all the physical variables are accumulated and levels of sensitivity can be shown. The map is divided into four zones: 'no sensitivity', 'low sensitivity', 'medium sensitivity' and 'high sensitivity'

The research for this case study revealed that river and glacial systems have the least sensitivity to tourism impacts, wetlands with gravel soils on low angle slopes away from glacial margins have relatively low sensitivity to tourism impacts, whilst sandy soils on steep slopes with moss heath vegetation within 200 metres of a glacial margin have very high sensitivity to tourism impacts.

(Adapted from Olafsdottir and Rannstrom, 2009.)

The case study of Iceland indicates how GISs can be used to identify fragile, sensitive landscapes to help manage them for tourism and non-tourism purposes. The following case study in Sri Lanka suggests how this landscape identification process can be taken further by using GIS data to first identify, then direct tourists into specific areas and keep them away from others.

In a broader sense, the case study indicates the potential for the use of GISs in the planning of sustainable tourism.

Case study: sustainable tourism infrastructure planning in Sri Lanka

The key aim of this project was to incorporate sustainability criteria in an attempt to achieve development objectives. The context for the use of GISs in planning was the Sinharaja Forest Reserve, a protected area in Sri Lanka. The intention was to try to match different types of visitors to different land use zones and more specifically to 'direct visitors through preferred zones to undertake preferred activities at preferred facility locations' (Boers and Cotterell, 2007: 7). The specific infrastructure dimensions were the natural and built attractions, tourism services (including e.g. accommodation, restaurants, tourist information centres) and transport facilities which included route-ways and the transport services. A major objective was to achieve 'sustainable trails'. A sustainable trail refers here to a non-motorized path linking attractions and/or facilities with the intention that the trail would:

- contribute to protected area development objectives;
- enable visitors to realize their desired and expected experiences;
- safeguard resource-carrying capacity standards of the Forest Reserve; and
- limit resource impacts.

The implementation of this attempt to create sustainable trails occurred in three phases, two of which involved the use of a GIS. The first stage, which did not involve a GIS, was the segmentation of visitors. Ten survey items were measured using a five point Likert-type scale with visitors, and statistical analysis was conducted on the results of the survey. Phase 2 was an attempt to zone the Forest Reserve and involved the use of a GIS. Using two major criteria, 'forest cover' and 'slope gradient', the carrying capacity of the reserve was mapped using GIS 'overlay' techniques. Here the whole area of the forest was divided into small cells (30 x 30 m) and a value for each of the criteria, forest cover and slope gradient, was entered in each cell. In addition in this second phase, visitor preferences (see the second bullet point above) were mapped using a GIS, in relation to attractions, facilities and services. This was achieved by considering the particular attractions, facility and service attributes desired by visitors and giving them a weighting. Values for individual grid cells could then be calculated within the GIS. Once the visitor segments (Phase 1) and the zones produced (Phase 2) were complete, it was possible to move to Phase 3, which again made use of a GIS. This phase involved the creation of a visitor transportation network. Although it would have been possible, theoretically, to create route-ways anywhere in the forest, management choices needed to be made which would create a coherent network in terms of satisfying visitor needs by linking preferred attractions, services and facilities spatially and temporally, and at the same time minimize visitor impacts on the forest. In summary, the result of these three phases was the creation of a number of 'sustainable' trails which formed part of a visitor transport network in the Forest Reserve.

(Based on Boers and Cotterell, 2007.)

The case study of the Sinharaja Forest Reserve gives an indication of how GISs can be used to assist in the development of sustainable tourism. However, it should be noted that that the sustainable trails as part of a visitor transport network are set within a dynamic context. The forest itself is a living ecosystem which is gradually changing. In addition, although the trails are intended to be sustainable, inevitably visitors using them will have some impacts and over time visitor preferences may change, partly as a result of their experiences of the forest, but also because of factors external to the reserve. Nevertheless sustainable tourism has been discussed in this case study and referred to in other case studies in this chapter and in previous chapters. In the next chapter, sustainable tourism is the focus and it is examined in much greater detail than previously.

Summary

IT is being used increasingly in tourism planning and management and of particular importance is the use of computers. Destination management systems are one such use of computers. A particularly useful computerized tool in tourism planning and management is a GIS. Geographical information systems are computerized systems that handle and process geographical data. GISs can also handle other forms of data. GISs can be used for a wide variety of tasks in tourism planning and management, including the production of environmental statements, data collection, the interviewing of local people, site interpretation, feasibility studies, policy studies, landscape sensitivity studies and the creation of sustainable tourism trails.

Student activities

1 What do you understand by GIS?
2 How can a GIS be used in relation to resource evaluation?
3 How can a GIS be used in a tourism management context.
4 In small groups of 3–4 discuss how a GIS can contribute to attempts at sustainable tourism.

PART IV

The future of tourism planning and management

Chapter 18

Tourism planning and management and sustainability

Introduction

Sustainability is a concept used with increasing frequency in tourism development, planning and management circles. It is often linked to terms such as 'green' tourism and/or 'ecotourism'. Despite being used for over a quarter of a century, the term is not well defined, and tends to be used as a 'buzz' word by commentators, researchers and those in marketing. To a certain extent, sustainability is now an overused term and is open to abuse, particularly from those operators who wish to indicate that their product is worthier than another's, and even by academics who see that their careers could be advanced through work in this area of tourism!

Key perspectives

The modern usage of the term 'sustainability' would appear to date from the Brundtland Report of 1987 (Holden, 2000). In this report, the term sustainable development was used. The Brundtland Report focused on the Earth's environment and was concerned about unsustainable resource use associated with what was seen as too rapid development. This report also made the link between environment and development very clear.

At what was known as the Earth Summit, held in 1992 in Rio de Janeiro, the concerns that were expressed in the Brundtland Report were once again present. This conference set forward a programme for promoting sustainable development throughout the world. This came to be known as Agenda 21. Agenda 21 is an 'action plan laying out the basic principles required to progress towards sustainability' (Holden, 2000: 164). The particular approach of Agenda 21 is to involve local communities in a 'bottom-up' approach to their own development.

However, the concept of sustainable development was not fully defined either in the Brundtland Report or at the Rio Summit. This means that, for example, private organizations, governments, non-governmental organizations (NGOs) and academics may have very different views on its meaning. Nevertheless, the Brundtland Report stressed that sustainable development does not mean preservation of the environment, but sustainable development of it (Holden, 2000) and the focus is thus on conservation and not preservation.

Holden (2000) suggested that although there is a diverse range of views on sustainable development, they can be classified generally into two camps; there are 'technocentric' views and 'ecocentric' views. The technocentric view insists that problems can be quantified and solved largely through the application of technology. The ecocentric view places great emphasis on 'quality of life' rather than 'standard of living' and the measurement of economic growth in quantitative terms has little value. The opposite ends of the spectrum of the technocentric and ecocentric are shown in Figure 18.1. Here the ecocentric view is represented under the 'deep ecology' heading which follows from the ideas of Doyle and McEachern (1998). The technocratic view is recognized by most commentators as being the dominant one globally (see Bartelmus, 1994), hence is represented as such in Figure 18.1. However, it should be remembered that this is a spectrum and there are many views lying between the extremes.

Sustainable tourism

Mirroring the range of views on sustainable development there is also a number of different views on sustainable tourism. One perspective on the meaning of sustainable tourism is that of a sustainable industry of tourism (Coccossis and Parpairis, 1996). In this view of sustainable tourism, the development of tourism is one alternative and seen as more acceptable than

Dominant world-view	Deep ecology
• Strong belief in technology for progress and solutions	• Favours low-scale technology that is self-reliant
• Natural world is valued as a resource rather than possessing intrinsic value	• Sense of wonder, reverence and moral obligation to the natural world
• Believes in ample resource reserves	• Recognizes the 'rights' of nature are independent of humans
• Favours the objective and quantitative	• Recognizes the subjective such as feelings and ethics
• Centralization of power	• Favours local communities and localized decision-making
• Encourages consumerism	• Encourages the use of appropriate technology
	• Recognizes that the Earth's resources are limited

Figure 18.1 Differences in views of development between the 'dominant world-view' and 'deep ecology'

Source: Adapted from Bartelmus (1994).

other more environmentally damaging activities such as logging or mining (Holden, 2000). However, little allowance is made in this view for the cumulative impacts of tourism on the environment (Hunter, 1996).

Hunter (1996) suggested a number of other perspectives in which the environment is more or less central in concepts of sustainable tourism. There is another position in which the environment is given more consideration than in the previously discussed perspective. However, even in this position the environment comes second to attempts to develop tourism. Hunter stated this position may be defensible in communities that are heavily dependent on tourism and where changes would lead to significant threats to the community. Hunter suggested a third form of sustainable tourism that he termed 'environmentally-led tourism'. In this form, a quality tourism experience is equated with a high-quality environment. In this scenario, there would be a strong link between the success of the tourism industry and environmental conservation. Unlike the former example of product-led tourism, here the environment is prioritized and forms of tourism are developed that are not damaging to it (Holden, 2000). Hunter suggested a fourth scenario, which he termed 'neotenous' tourism, in which very little or actually no tourism is permitted. This would be in relation to particularly environmentally sensitive areas.

Much of the preceding discussion has not made explicit that statements on sustainable tourism need to be linked to value judgements. Hence, the interpretation of the term sustainable tourism is very closely related to the political context in which the term is being applied. Butler and Hall (1998) argued strongly that it is actually impossible to separate concepts of sustainable tourism from the value system and political context in which these are being used.

If in early definitions of sustainable tourism the environment was central, then during the late 1980s and early 1990s socio-cultural factors were linked closely to the concept. By the last decade of the twentieth century, sustainability was usually assumed to refer to the specifically environmental and cultural aspects of the visitor destination area. However, it is possible to suggest that it is rather artificial to consider only these aspects from the total of all elements that make up the tourism experience. Hence, 'tourism sustainability' has an economic and organizational dimension as well as socio-cultural and environmental aspects.

One of the early thinkers who set concepts of tourism sustainability within the context of tourism planning and management was Innskeep. His views give an indication of how sustainable tourism was conceived at the beginning of the last decade of the twentieth century. The case study of leisure and tourism planning later in the chapter gives an indication of some of Innskeep's ideas in action.

Innskeep (1991) suggested that, in relation to practical applications of concepts of sustainable tourism, there are a number of assumptions that underpin these concepts. These assumptions and further comments are presented in the case study below.

Case study: Innskeep's concept of sustainable tourism

Innskeep's (1991) assumptions underlying the concept of sustainable tourism include the belief that:

- It is possible to actually define and achieve the type of tourism you want.
- It is possible to establish and sustain appropriate levels of visitor flow.
- It is possible to define and promote equity in development and to reconcile any conflicts arising between the stakeholders involved – the tourist, the resident, the industry agent and the government – and that an appropriate balance of interests can be achieved between host and guest and between private interest and public good.
- Sustainability is maintainable over the long term.

A number of comments can be made in relation to Innskeep's claims:

1 In relation to the statement about equity, this implies equal rights and equal gains, or certainly a balance of interests and benefits that sustains all parties to the relationship. Such equity is established through a mix of formal rules and implicit understanding of the limits, directions and the boundaries of the development game. Development decisions, however, often involve more than just specifically tourism issues, but extend into wider physical resource issues and culture relationships that bring whole communities of interest together.

2 It is possible to sustain integrity/authenticity in the host tourism product. This has to do with keeping the original 'indigenous values' intact without any appreciable modification to accommodate its 'touristic' values. Product modification to suit tourism use, it is usually claimed, is to be avoided except where it accords with a natural restoration or compatible extension of the original function or purpose. This is not always easy. For example, controversy currently surrounds the degree of legitimate restoration allowable for historic places, monuments, buildings such as the ruins of Pompeii, the Sphinx in Egypt, the frescoes of Venice and the art and ruins of Ankhor Wat.

3 It is possible to ask the question: Does sustainable tourism actually work to improve the quality of life of the host community? It is possible that the outcome of contact between the host and the guest may be positive, both gain and negative aspects are minimal in the long term. However, the host community is generally poorly represented as a direct voice in tourism industry policy groups. It is usually non-existent at the national level of government and forms only part of the rate-payers' perspective at the local and regional levels. The surveys by Getz (1994) and Haralambopolous and

> Pizam (1996) in Chapter 5 and the study of the Pohangina Valley in Chapter 11 give an indication of local communities' stake in tourism development, and awareness of the costs and benefits of tourism.
>
> (Adapted from Innskeep 1991.)

Drawing on the work of Innskeep, a model of sustainable tourism can be created. This model can be represented as being: non-intrusive, non-depleting and renewable, scaled to the particular environment, natural in material make-up and presentation and well integrated into the local physical, social, cultural and economic environments. The characteristics of Innskeep's (1991) model are as follows:

- Non-depleting in its use of local resources.
- Non-intrusive in the way it fits with the local physical, social, cultural and economic environments.
- A user of natural resources that are minimally transposed or re-configured.
- Integrated with the local physical, social, cultural and economic environment rather than being shut in on itself.
- More focused on the high-quality–high-yield end of the commercial product spectrum in contrast to the high-profit rapid turnover model.
- More centred on the qualitative aspects of individual experience than a quantitative 'been there done that' model of many group-centred options.
- One in which the balance of market power lies with the host community and in which the resident has a recognized voice in the definition and management of the tourism product and its context.
- One in which the industry is managed by an appropriate blend of public sector good and enlightened private sector self-interest.

At approximately the same time as Innskeep was producing his ideas on tourism and sustainability, the UK Department of Environment/ETB in the report referred to in a number of earlier chapters (it produced the 'triangle' of environment, visitor and host, see Figure 7.3) developed some guiding principles for sustainable tourism. These are as follows (ETB, 1991):

- The environment has an intrinsic value that outweighs its value as a tourism asset. Its enjoyment by future generations and its long-term survival must not be prejudiced by short-term considerations.
- Tourism should be recognized as a positive factor with the potential to benefit the community and the place as well as the visitor.
- The relationship between tourism and the environment must be managed so that the environment is sustainable in the long term. Tourism must not be allowed to damage the resource, prejudice its future enjoyment or bring unacceptable impacts.
- Tourism activities and development should respect the scale, nature and character of the place in which they are sited.
- In any location, harmony must be sought between the needs of the visitor, place and the host community.
- In a dynamic world, some change is inevitable and change can often be beneficial. Adaptation to change, however, should not be at the expense of any of these principles.

- The tourism industry, local authorities and environmental agencies all have a duty to respect the above principles and to work together to achieve their practical realization in achieving sustainable tourism.

These guidelines stressed the need for a balance between the place, the visitor and the host community. However, as Holden (2000) suggested, the ETB Report is somewhat simplistic in that it implies tourists are one homogeneous group. Nevertheless, the report does emphasize the important role of the local community in sustainable tourism and the role of communities has been discussed in a number of earlier chapters.

By the middle of the first decade of the twenty-first century it was possible to discern three 'traditions' in sustainable tourism (Saarinen, 2006). The first, the 'resource-based' tradition, according to Saarinen, links tourism with conservation and focuses on restricting, or indeed preventing, the damaging effects of tourism on the environment. The second tradition is termed the 'activity-based' tradition (Saarinen, 2006). This tradition suggests that tourism can actually make a significant contribution to sustainability. In this tradition, it is the demand for tourism experiences that leads to attempts to conserve, for example, certain landscapes and heritage attractions that tourists want to visit. Perhaps, not surprisingly, this is the tradition particularly supported by the tourism industry (Holden, 2008). The third tradition is the 'community-based' one, and suggests that the local community or host population has a vital role in bringing about sustainability. Holden (2008) further distinguishes between these three traditions by indicating that the first (resource-based) may make use of 'real' measurements of sustainability (such as those acquired from Environmental Impacts Assessments), whilst the second and third traditions usually involve social constructs of sustainability. These two latter traditions involve judgements made about 'acceptable levels of trade-off between economic and social gains against natural resource losses' (Holden 2008: 161).

The ETB guidelines echo the resource-based tradition highlighted by Saarinen, clearly indicating the central importance of the environment. The ETB guidelines also refer to the local community's role in sustainable tourism. Increasingly it is being argued, particularly by those who advocate greater democracy in tourism decision-making, that the local community should not just be involved in attempts to make tourism more sustainable, but should have control over tourism development. However, even with tourism decision-making under local control there is no guarantee that sustainable forms of development will be selected. Indeed, Holden (2000) reported two examples in which local communities in Scotland and South Africa, respectively, supported development that was actually damaging to the environment. The rationale for the choice of the particular development in each case was the perceived economic and social benefits. It appears, therefore, that these two examples fit more closely with the 'activity-based' and 'community-based' tourism sustainability traditions, than the 'resource-based' one.

The ETB guidelines discussed above are an example of the involvement of government in tourism planning for sustainability in one country. However, international organizations have also produced guides for policy makers who are attempting to achieve sustainable tourism. The United Nations Environment Programme, working in conjunction with the World Tourism Organization, produced a major document, 'Making Tourism More Sustainable: a Guide for Policy Makers' in 2005 (UNEP/WTO, 2005). This document is important because not only does it provide advice on the process of developing a sustainable tourism strategy (which is very similar to the tourism planning process described in Chapter 7), but it also gives advice on the actual tools, or instruments, that governments can use to help bring about sustainable tourism. These instruments are presented in Figure 18.2.

As Figure 18.2 shows there are five main types of instrument. Under each of these five headings there are a number of sub-categories leading to a total of 13 instruments. As the

(1) *Measuring instruments.*
    (a) Sustainable indicators and monitoring: benchmarking
    (b) Identifying the limits of tourism: carrying capacity, limits of acceptable change

(2) *Command and control instruments*
    (a) Legislation, regulation and licensing
    (b) Land use planning and development control

(3) *Economic instruments*
    (a) Taxes and charges
    (b) Financial incentives and agreements

(4) *Voluntary instruments*
    (a) Guidelines and codes of conduct
    (b) Auditing and reporting
    (c) Voluntary certification
    (d) Voluntary contributions

(5) *Supporting instruments*
    (a) Infrastructure provision and management
    (b) Capacity building
    (c) Marketing and information services

Figure 18.2 Instruments for more sustainable tourism
Source: Adapted from UNEP/WTO (2005).

UNEP/WTO document indicates, however, these 13 instruments are interlinked. In terms of the five main categories of instrument, UNEP/WTO (2005) indicate that *measuring instruments* should be used to determine current levels of tourism and the impacts of current tourism. Processes involved here include benchmarking and identifying the limits of tourism, via assessments of carrying capacity and limits of acceptable change. The *command and control instruments* are largely regulatory and involve various forms of legislation, regulation and licensing. The *economic instruments* involve the use of taxes and charges which are intended to influence the behaviour of tourists. The *voluntary instruments* include codes of conduct and guidelines as well as voluntary certification. The *supporting instruments* involve infrastructure provision and management, capacity building, which involves increasing the knowledge, understanding, confidence and skills of stakeholders, and marketing initiatives.

A key instrument in the UNEP/WTO guide for policy makers is building capacity amongst stakeholders. The following case study of local planning in New Zealand discusses local community stakeholder participation and indicates the contribution that such groups and individuals can make to more sustainable forms of tourism. The initial stage in the UNEP/WTO guide involves measuring current levels of tourism and this study stresses the importance of gathering and using relevant data, in making planning decisions.

Case study: leisure and tourism planning in the Manawatu region of New Zealand

This case study is based on research that involved two projects investigating recreation and tourism issues. One study involved mountain biking in the Manawatu region and the other the use of an urban walkway in Palmerston North, both in New Zealand.

(continued)

Case study: leisure and tourism planning in the Manawatu region of New Zealand (continued)

The first stage of the mountain biking research consisted of a postal questionnaire, which was sent to all current members of the Manawatu Mountain Bike Club. One important recommendation made by respondents was the establishment of a mountain biking forum, to provide an opportunity for ongoing discussion of mountain biking issues. The first meeting of this mountain biking forum, hosted by the Palmerston North City Council (PNCC), and chaired by staff from the Recreation and Community Development Unit, was held in September 1998. A number of stakeholders were invited to the meeting, including the two Recreation and Community Development Unit staff, two members of the Manawatu Mountain Biking Club, a member of a local tramping (hill walking) club (also a mountain biker), a representative from the environmental organization Forest and Bird, and a couple who owned and ran one of the four bicycle shops in Palmerston North. A particular focus at the meeting was on whether there should be a dedicated mountain bike area or multiple-use tracks in the Palmerston North area. It was decided to investigate the possibility of sites within Palmerston North for a dedicated mountain biking area.

Resulting from this research, the authors were asked to comment on the PNCC's Recreation Plan for the Manawatu Region 1998–2003. It was noted in this report that only a limited amount of research had been conducted on user groups, different types of activities and potential management issues associated with a key recreational resource, the Manawatu Riverside Walkway and Bridle Track (MRWBT). The MRWBT research involved a questionnaire survey of a sample of the 'walkway' users, conducted on the MRWBT itself via face to face contact between researchers and respondents. The high-response rate would indicate a strong interest in the community concerning the recreational and tourism use of the MRWBT.

Figure 18.3 is an attempt to summarize the approach used in the mountain biking and the MRWBT research projects, set against the apparent PNCC response to planning decisions in the recreation/tourism area prior to this. Column A, in Figure 18.3, shows the PNCC (Council) approach. It is suggested in Figure 18.3 that such a policy is unsatisfactory for the following reasons:

- This approach appears to lack an explicitly stated rationale for the management of recreation/tourism issues.
- The actions of the council can be seen as reactive, not proactive, and decisions have been made without the necessary data to support them.
- The consequences in terms of views not being heard, needs not being met and the potential for user group conflict are indicated. The Manawatu-based research suggested the importance of acquiring the views of stakeholders.

The only perceived advantage of such an approach is that, as it does not involve detailed consultation, it is relatively inexpensive. However, the political process often requires the compilation of strategies within tightly defined time frames, which is not necessarily accommodating of the suggested 'research approach' shown in columns B and C of Figure 18.3.

	A	B	C
	Council approach	Mountain Bike Research approach	Walkway Research approach
	Need for policy		
Initial planning response	Create policy without data	Independent research: questionnaire and focus groups (one user group involved)	Independent research: questionnaire and focus groups (a number of user groups involved)
Initial consequence	Policy inaccurate?	Recommendations based on research findings	Recommendations based on research findings from a larger sample of user groups
Long-term consequences	(a) User group conflict (b) Needs not met (c) Lack of consultation (d) Lack of involvement	(a) Establishment of a forum (b) Informed discussion (c) Views heard (d) Ongoing involvement	(a) Establishment of a forum? (b) Informed discussion? (c) Greater variety of views heard? (d) Ongoing involvement
Time dimension	Quick? (quick fix)	Slow? (continuous monitoring)	Potentially slower? (continuous monitoring)
Cost dimension	Cheap?	Expensive?	More expensive
Local political dimension	Satisfies elected council	Satisfies user group	Potentially satisfies more user groups

Figure 18.3 Recreation and tourism planning approaches in Manawatu

In contrast to column A, column B in Figure 18.3 summarizes the approach used in the mountain bike research. This 'research approach' is viewed as a more desirable approach to planning for the following reasons:

- The decision-making was based on the gathering of data relevant to the issue.
- Informed discussion took place. The views of one user group, the Manawatu Mountain Biking Club, were stated via the questionnaire survey and the focus groups. The views of the club were also reiterated at the mountain biking forum meetings. Additionally, some indication of the views of other users groups, stakeholders and interested parties was heard at the mountain biking forum meetings.

Such an approach, as indicated in column B of Figure 18.3, suffers the disadvantage, however, of being slow and hence perceived as expensive. Column C exemplifies the evolutionary stage of an applied recreation and tourism planning model, and it is possible to indicate the following:

- The research approach adopted has generated responses from a number of user groups, which it is hoped will provide detailed data to inform the planning and management decision-making process.
- The research approach involving personal contact on the MRWBT during the questionnaire survey has enabled users to express their preferences and concerns. Traditionally, on issues such as this, consultation with the public has taken place via public submissions and interactive public. These place the onus on the participant.

(continued)

Case study: leisure and tourism planning in the Manawatu region of New Zealand (continued)

- A significant number of respondents indicated their willingness to participate in follow-up focus groups, providing further opportunities for opinions to be expressed.

However, a disadvantage of the process shown in column C is that it is likely to be more time consuming and more costly. Nevertheless, as the research has sought to involve the community in the planning process, it is suggested that a variety of views will have been heard. Hence, it is hoped that any decision relating to the future recreation and tourism use of the MRWBT will reflect a number of community values. Ideally, the process outlined in column C will ensure that recreation and tourism planning does not occur in isolation from its social context. It is hoped that the planning process adopted in column B and, to a greater extent, in column C of Figure 18.3 may lead to more sustainable forms of recreation and tourism, as the views of user groups are heard and heeded, rather than these groups having decisions forced on them.

(Adapted from Mason and Leberman, 1998 and Leberman and Mason, 2002.)

Although, as stated above, there is a lack of agreement on precisely what constitutes sustainability in relation to tourism, it is becoming increasingly possible to discern what can be termed ideal types of sustainable tourism. These types can be represented by the extremes, which are at opposite ends of a spectrum (Weaver, 2006). At one end is 'minimalist sustainable tourism' and at the other 'comprehensive sustainable tourism' (Weaver, 2006). These ideal types are shown in Figure 18.4. As Figure 18.4 indicates, minimalist sustainable tourism is concerned largely with environmental, socio-cultural and economic impacts of tourism. It is generally site or product specific, focuses on the short term, tries to largely maintain the status quo and does not link tourism to wider societal issues.

Minimalist sustainable tourism	Comprehensive sustainable tourism
• Environmental, socio-cultural or economic impacts	• Environmental, socio-cultural and economic impacts
• Site specific or local focus	• Regional or global focus
• Short-term effects of actions	• Long-term effects of actions
• Tourism sector only	• Tourism in the context of other sectors
• Direct impacts only	• Direct, indirect and induced impacts
• Intergenerational equity	• Intergenerational and intragenerational equity
• Status quo sustainability	• Enhancement sustainability
↓	↓

- Weak or strong sustainability approach, depending on context
- Financial sustainability

Figure 18.4 Minimalist and comprehensive tourism ideal types
Source: Adapted from Weaver (2006).

However, comprehensive sustainable tourism involves a holistic approach, setting economic, environmental and socio-cultural impacts of tourism within a wider societal and global context. It is therefore concerned with not just tourism but other major human activities, and also involves a long-term approach in an attempt to achieve intergenerational equity (see the Brundtland Report of 1987). It is not necessarily destination or product specific, but starts from the premise that the environment is already degraded and that some areas are economically impoverished, and is therefore enhancement-based (Weaver, 2006). As Weaver indicated, it is important to recognize that these are ideal types and this means that real examples can be compared with them.

This reference to comprehensive sustainable tourism and holistic perspectives indicates that discussion on sustainable tourism in this chapter so far has concentrated largely on the impacts of tourism itself, and how tourism can become more sustainable in terms of, for example, the environment or local communities. However, this ignores the fact that tourism like many other human activities is affected by events beyond the control of those directly involved in it (such as tourists, host communities and even members of the tourism industry). In other words, tourism is subject to important external forces, both natural and man-made.

However, much thinking in tourism planning and management has ignored external factors. If these are ignored, then it is relatively easy to believe that tourism activities are the result of known factors and are generally predictable. The assumption that causal relationships can be discerned easily and hence that events are predictable is based on a view of the world that is often described as reductionist (Capra, 1982). In this view, which is largely influenced by the ideas of scientists such as Galileo and Newton, objects and events can be understood in terms of their constituent parts and these parts fit together like cogs in a machine and hence every event is determined by initial conditions that are, in principle, predictable (Faulkner and Russell, 1997). This view has held sway in the natural sciences until the early part of the twentieth century and has also been greatly influential in the social sciences, including tourism studies until very recently.

However, particularly in the second half of the twentieth century, the ideas of Einstein on relativity and Heisenberg's uncertainty principle meant a revolution in scientific thinking in which it was accepted that the universe is more complex and chaotic than originally conceived. Faulkner and Russell (1997) have applied the idea of chaos to the social sciences and specifically to tourism studies. They suggested that in science, the language used, involving linear concepts and machine analogies, is now being replaced by a world of non-linearity, spontaneity and surprise and these concepts are being set alongside attributes normally associated with living organisms, such as adaptation, coherence and organization (Faulkner and Russell, 1997).

In terms of tourism, Faulkner and Russell put forward a number of key ideas based on the application of the notions of chaos and complexity and these are shown in Figure 18.5. In Figure 18.5, a number of examples are provided, and several of these, such as changing of gambling laws in Nevada and the development of new forms of transport, indicate that there are changes from outside that have influenced tourism.

Figure 18.5 does not, however, indicate that natural events can greatly influence tourism. For example the eruption of a dormant volcano on the Caribbean island of Montserrat in 1997 severely disrupted the tourism economy, not only because of the perception created, that the island was a dangerous place to visit, but because it permanently covered some of the island's tourism resources in lava and ash. Storms, floods and tsunamis are other natural events that can cause major disruptions to tourism activities. Although it is generally known when such events might occur and even where, the specifics of the force of individual events, precisely when and exactly where they will occur, are still not possible to accurately predict. The tsunami

Concept	Tourism elements/examples
Bottom-up synthesis: individual agents driven by simple rules of transaction give rise to complex, dynamic systems.	• Host–guest relationship between visitors and residents. • Client–service provider relationship between tourist and tourism industry. • Competitive relationships between providers of similar services/product. • Cooperative relationships between vertically integrated providers or coalitions of providers at a single destination. • Regulator–regulatee relationship between public and private sector agents.
Butterfly effect: initial small random change or perturbation induces a chain reaction that precipitates a dramatic event or shift of considerable magnitude.	• Relaxation of legal restrictions on gambling in Nevada initiates development of Las Vegas as major tourist destination. • Terrorist activities in Europe in the 1980s boost international arrivals in safe destinations such as Australia (Faulkner, 1990).
Lock-in effect: where accidents of history have a lasting effect long after the conditions that influenced their initial impact have subsided or where innovations have a lasting effect despite being superseded by new technology.	• The Las Vegas example (i.e. in the sense that this destination has maintained and enhanced its position in spite of Nevada no longer being the only state in the US to have legalized gambling).
Edge of chaos (phase shift): a state of tenuous equilibrium whereby small changes ('mutations') involving individual agents may be enough to precipitate evolutionary change in the system through mutual adaptation of its constituents.	• Displacement of railway-based system of tourist services by car-based network. • Phase shifts in the life-cycle of destinations.

Figure 18.5 Basic concepts of chaos and complexity and corresponding examples in tourism
Source: adapted from Faulkner and Russell (1997).

that hit Southeast Asia and particularly Indonesia, Thailand, India and Sri Lanka on Boxing Day 2004 was not predicted and its impact was far more significant than any other such event in the recent history of tourism. Hence, such events do not fit neatly into the scientific 'linear conceptualization' of tourism activities.

It has been argued that if we accept that we live in an increasingly complex world, then the type of natural or man-made disasters referred to above will become more common (Faulkner, 2001). However, the impacts of disasters on tourism activities (and hence by implication their relevance for tourism planning and management) have been little researched. Faulkner, in attempting to create an agenda for this type of research, tried to distinguish between disasters and crises. He indicated that it is commonly accepted that crises tend to be associated with ongoing change that an organization has failed to respond to and not adapted, while a disaster is the result of a sudden event (or events) that an organization has failed to respond to at all.

Nevertheless, both crises and disasters may have very similar features and, in particular, generate similar impacts (Faulkner, 2001). Fink (1986) attempted to distil the main ingredients of disasters and crises and came up with the following aspects:

- There is usually a triggering event, which is so major that it challenges existing structures, routines and even survival of an organization.
- They are characterized by fluid dynamic situations.
- There is an element of surprise with a high threat and short decision time.
- For at least part of the event, a feeling of an inability to cope.
- A turning point, when a decisive change will happen which may have both negative and positive dimensions, to the extent that even if the event is well managed, the organization will experience great change that may be irreversible.

In the early part of the twenty-first century, despite the general belief that life on Earth is becoming more complex, there is as yet insufficient evidence to indicate whether crises and disasters are becoming more common than in earlier epochs. Neither is it clear, yet, the effect that such events may have on tourism and the various attempts to make the activity more sustainable. Nevertheless, chaos theory provides important perspectives on tourism planning and management. In the final chapter of the book, a number of important events that have occurred in the early part of the twenty-first century, and in particular, global terrorism are discussed in relation to global complexity and chaos.

Although it may not be fully understood how important external factors, such as extreme weather conditions, earthquakes and volcanoes, are in relation to attempts to create sustainable tourism, it is clear such factors need to be built into discussions on the subject.

The earlier parts of this chapter have indicated that despite at least a quarter of a century of attempts to create sustainable tourism, it has yet to be fully realized. The case study below considers why achieving sustainable tourism continues to be problematic.

Case study: problems in achieving sustainable tourism

Although the concept of tourism sustainability emerged at least 25 years ago and has evolved since then, a key problem is that there is still no agreed definition of what sustainable tourism actually is. This issue is not solely a dry, theoretical topic for discussion by academics, as it has important practical ramifications – without agreement on what the concept actually means, then there is little chance that it will be achieved!

For the tourism industry, sustainable tourism may be regarded as little more than the creation and marketing of a specific product. A product which will be targeted at a small section of consumers, as it may well be regarded as a form of 'alternative' or 'responsible' tourism, possibly analogous to ecotourism. Its appeal will therefore be mainly to a small number of wealthy, elite tourists.

However, a product termed 'sustainable tourism' misses the point of sustainability. To counter the notion of sustainability as only being for 'those who can afford it' is the

(continued)

Case study: problems in achieving sustainable tourism (continued)

argument that true sustainability will only be achieved when mass tourism is the target. So to achieve really sustainable tourism, mass tourism, and indeed all types of tourism, will need to be addressed to indicate what can be done to make them more sustainable, rather than create something called 'sustainable tourism'.

Nevertheless, a dilemma for tourism planners in specific destinations is that mass tourism has traditionally catered for large numbers of low-spending consumers and this volume of visitors has contributed to damaging effects on the environment. So the solution, to protect the environment and still have a profitable industry, it would seem, is that tourism will need to be targeted at a smaller number of wealthy tourists!

However, perversely, if sustainable tourism is believed to be the best approach to conserving the environment and the policy is to strongly promote it, there is a danger that as it grows, sustainable tourism begins to demonstrate the characteristics and have the effects of current mass tourism (see McKercher, 1993; Wheeler, 1993; Page and O'Connell, 2009). As Page and O'Connell argue, green tourism policies often advocate lengthening the tourism season and 'spreading the load' spatially. If these policies are implemented at the same time as there are rapidly increasing numbers of tourists, then they would very likely contribute to tourism having more damaging impacts on the environment!

Another key issue is that even after a quarter of a century of tourism projects with sustainability as a key component, not enough is known of the impacts of such projects. Hence, more monitoring of projects is very important, particularly in terms of revealing the reality that lays behind the rhetoric of some supposedly sustainable projects. But also, such monitoring should provide the opportunity to create a database of good practice.

The relationship between the tourism industry and other stakeholders in tourism has frequently been a difficult one with much misunderstanding on each side. With reference to the concept of sustainability, the failure to agree on what it means contributes to the 'industry' and 'environmentalists' appearing not to speak the same language. Even if they do speak the same language, it seems that neither group is really listening to what the other is saying! A common language and a shared understanding of the issues and problems will therefore be necessary.

As long ago as the mid-1990s, Muller (1994) observed that:

● There are too many experts offering advice on sustainable tourism and this has created several different theories.
● Despite growing environmental awareness, most tourists still have a view of their holiday as a primarily hedonistic experience, so acting responsibility does not feature high on the tourists' lists of probable behaviour.
● Tourist numbers continue to rise.
● There needs to be a change in social attitudes, particularly to the environment and leisure, to ensure greater social and environmentally compatible lifestyles.

More than 20 years on from the mid-1990s, when Muller put forward these four points, there do not seem to have been many significant changes to the claims!

(Based on Page and O'Connell, 2009 and Mason, 2013a.)

Reflecting on the discussion in the case study, perhaps it may be better, as Holden (2008) argues, to think of sustainability not as a desired 'end point', but rather as a process, a guiding philosophy that incorporates certain principles about the way we interact with the environment.

Summary

Sustainability is a term that is used often in relation to tourism planning and management. Concepts of sustainable tourism have been derived from concerns with sustainable development. A number of statements on sustainable development appeared in the 1980s, whilst the first major statement on sustainable tourism appeared in 1990. Since then the concept of sustainable tourism has developed and changed. Early ideas on sustainable tourism usually focused on environmental sustainability. More recent statements have been concerned with socio-cultural and economic factors. The role of host communities has also featured significantly in recent comments on sustainable tourism. It is possible to sub-divide comments on sustainable tourism into groupings such as 'technocentric' or 'ecocentric'. It is also possible to discern three traditions, 'resource-based', 'activity-based' and 'community-based', in the relationship between tourism and sustainability and also recognize ideal types of sustainable tourism which range from the minimalist to the comprehensive. However, achieving sustainable tourism has proved to be a very difficult task. Nevertheless, it is very likely that concepts of sustainable tourism will continue to evolve over the next decade, and that tourism planning and management will reflect these changing notions.

Student activities

1 What do you understand by the term sustainability?
2 What is sustainable development?
3 What is sustainable tourism?
4 Why could it be difficult to achieve sustainable tourism?
5 How have views on sustainability and sustainable tourism developed since the early 1990s?
6 Study Figure 18.2. Assume the role of a journalist preparing to interview the chief tourism planner in a region just starting to develop more sustainable tourism. How would you make use of the instruments shown in Figure 18.2 to create the questions you would ask at interview?
7 With reference to the case study of planning in the Manawatu area of New Zealand, how can the involvement of the local community contribute to more sustainable tourism? What problems may arise as the result of greater involvement of local communities in tourism development?
8 In relation to the case study of 'Problems in achieving sustainable tourism', which of the problems presented do you believe are the major difficulties to achieving sustainable tourism? In addition to the problems presented in the case study, what else may prevent sustainable tourism being achieved?
9 What do you think will be the chief components of sustainable tourism in the year 2025?

Chapter 19

Conclusions and the future of tourism planning and management

This book has discussed social and economic factors that have contributed to the rise of modern mass tourism. It has considered a variety of tourism effects under the headings of economic, socio-cultural and environmental impacts. It has also tried to show that although it is conventional to sub-divide these impacts in any given situation under a number of headings, it is most likely that the impacts will be multi-faceted and not that easily separable.

The fact that tourism impacts are multi-faceted contributes to them being difficult to plan for and manage. There are a number of different organizations, groups and individuals that have an important role to play in tourism planning and management. These key players, in the form of tourists, host community members, industry members, government representatives, and to a lesser extent the media and voluntary organizations, are involved in the day-to-day problems of tourism. In most democratic countries, at least, these individuals, groups and organizations are in a position to play an active part in tourism planning and management.

The book has considered a number of different approaches and techniques for managing tourism. Managing visitors is clearly an important part of managing tourism. The natural resources for tourism, the environment and landscape require particular approaches and techniques. The use of both education, through interpretation, and regulation, particularly in the form of guidelines, eco-labels and codes of conduct, are assuming greater importance as tools in tourism management. Information technology, particularly the use of various forms of geographical information system (GIS), is also becoming a significant factor in tourism management.

The different sectors and players in tourism have tended, traditionally, not to work together. In the last 10–15 years of the twentieth century, this situation was changing as partnerships between the public and private sector and collaboration between individuals, groups and organizations became not only more common but also perceived as generally desirable. A major reason for this desire for collaboration has been the wish to achieve more sustainable forms of tourism. Despite a lack of full agreement on their meanings, sustainability and tourism were almost inextricably linked concepts by the early twenty-first century.

Influences on the future of tourism

A number of issues are pertinent to the future direction of tourism and there are various influences on these possible future directions. As Chapter 18 indicated, there are several factors which are external to tourism, some of which are natural in their origin and others very much the result of human activity, which will affect the future of tourism and the ways it can be planned and managed.

Probably the major challenge to the expansion of tourism over the next 50 years will be the effects of global warming. Over the past two decades, there have been major arguments about whether global warming, induced by human activity, is actually occurring. In 2015, it is generally accepted by the great majority of scientists that global warming is occurring. However, there is still argument about the degree to which human activity is responsible for this warming of the Earth's atmosphere and how much it is the product of natural cycles. If it is accepted that global warming is occurring, and is largely the result of human activity, then unless major changes in current trends occur, there will be significant impacts on tourism. There has been discussion in previous sections about the increase in extreme weather conditions over the past 15 years or so and the effects on tourism. These unusual conditions have been attributed to global warming, but have tended to be localized in the impact they have had on tourism. An important predicted consequence of global warming that will have major global consequences is the melting of both polar ice caps. As well as the localized environmental changes in the polar regions, the global effect will be a rise in sea level. If this occurs, then it is likely that low-lying countries, such as Bangladesh, and very large regions of countries such as the Netherlands and the United Kingdom will be flooded, as will many small island nations that act as tourism destinations, such as the Maldives. Clearly this will mean the disappearance of coastal tourism in current destination regions of these, and other low-lying, parts of the world.

Mountain areas will also be affected by global warming, as there will be less snow in areas where it currently falls in significant amounts, meaning the decline or disappearance of snow-based tourism pursuits. Tourism is also likely to be affected as migration occurs from flooded areas to locations currently important for tourism and the loss of farmland resulting from flooding will not only reduce food producing capacity, but protected landscapes, at present important for tourism, are likely to come under pressure to be used for intensive agriculture or the building of settlements.

However, the effects of global warming on tourism are still viewed as being some way off. In the immediate future, consumer choices and preferences will be a key factor in this future direction of tourism. In the past, the 'pile 'em high sell 'em cheap' approach secured a market made up of the great majority of tourists. By the early twenty-first century, there was a grow-ing number of tourists who appeared to be willing to pay a premium for a high quality tourist experience. For some, ecotourism is the chosen option when seeking out what they regard as a high quality holiday. However, confusion still surrounds the exact nature of ecotourism and it has been suggested that, over time, it will become merely a variant of mass tourism, rather than a true alternative to it.

It is clear that the resources for tourism, particularly the natural and semi-natural environ-mental features, but also man-made components of the environment that have become attractions, are actually finite. This has led to calls to make these resources in particular, but also the field of tourism generally, more sustainable. With reference to specific destinations, a complete halt to tourism development may be considered desirable by some members of the community, and in a number of cases this may be a majority view, but it is unlikely that tourism growth will be stopped. In fact, the reverse of this looks more likely as all types of tourist travel continue to grow. Virtual tourism using electronic media such as the Internet is becoming increasingly popular. This is not necessarily a substitute for real journeys but is being use for marketing purposes and as a foretaste of the real experience. In early 2001, the first space tourist orbited the Earth on a Russian rocket. Several others have followed, and it may soon be possible for significant numbers of travellers (albeit a small elite group of the very wealthy) to leave this planet and take holidays in space on a more regular basis.

Evidence from the previous century, particularly the last 40 years of it, would seem to sug-gest that neither virtual tourism, nor space tourism, is likely to off-set longer-term growth trends for tourism on planet Earth. However, a number of critical incidents in the early part of the twenty-first century have called into question whether this growth will continue as rapidly as previously, or may indeed even fall away.

In the United Kingdom, the outbreak of foot and mouth disease in early 2001 led to almost complete closure of large parts of the UK countryside until late summer 2001. This not only caused major disruption to the farming community, but also more importantly, in terms of the focus of this book, led to significant impacts on tourism in the UK countryside. Lack of access during the outbreak of foot and mouth disease, for both domestic and international visitors, was the key effect on UK rural tourism and visitor numbers were down throughout most of 2001.

However, impacts in terms of visitor numbers were geographically patchy, as UK coastal and urban areas appear to have been far less affected during the summer of 2001 than rural areas, and may even have benefited from the restrictions on access to rural areas. Nevertheless, when foot and mouth disease returned again to the United Kingdom in 2007, the government made reassuring promises that it would not close down the countryside and therefore negatively affect leisure and tourism pursuits.

In the early part of the twenty-first century, other global tourism destinations also suffered from localized problems affecting visitor numbers, including the effects of natural phenomenon such as volcanic eruptions, storms and flooding. But these were not particularly unusual in terms of the history of global tourism development. However, the events of 11 September 2001 in the United States and other related terrorist attacks appear more unusual and may have long-term effects on the global tourism industry. The terrorist attacks are seen as different, as they are being viewed as part of a global, not local threat. In terms of tourism, in the United States particularly, the terrorist attacks have had a significant impact on potential and real travellers. The impacts of the events of 11 September 2001 have also continued well after the event. In terms of consequences for the tourism industry, for example, the bankruptcy of the large carrier American Airlines in 2002 was linked closely to the drop in passenger numbers following the terrorist attack. The failure of tourist numbers in the United Kingdom in the autumn of 2001 to recover from the foot and mouth disease outbreak was attributed at least in part to the relatively small number of US visitors compared to previous years coming to Britain then. The effect of events in the United States on tourism in the United Kingdom also indicates the global nature of this problem.

Although the terrorist attacks of 11 September 2001 had effects on tourism at a global scale, in the immediate aftermath of the attacks they were seen as having only indirect effects. However, in October 2002 this perspective changed radically when tourists became the major target of terrorists. On the Indonesian island of Bali, two night-clubs, containing mainly international tourists, became the target of terrorists who were linked by the media to the groups that had perpetrated the attacks in the United States in September 2001. Almost 3 years later bombings occurred again on Bali. The nature and consequences of these direct terrorist attacks on tourists are discussed in the following case study.

Case study: the Bali terrorist bombings

On 12 October 2002, the bombing of two night-clubs at Kuta Beach on the coast of the island of Bali, Indonesia, killed more than 180 people and was the worst terrorist attack in Indonesian history. By 18 October, 183 people were known to have died and more than 300 were injured. The largest group of dead and injured came from Australia, but British, Americans, New Zealanders, Germans and French were among the casualties, as well as local Indonesians.

In the immediate aftermath of the bombing no one claimed responsibility. But the apparent sophistication of the operation and the known existence of active groups of supporters of Osama bin Laden led both the Indonesian authorities and President Bush to blame the terrorism on Al-Qaeda and its extremist allies.

This attack followed on from recent attacks on a French tanker and American soldiers in Yemen. One consequence of this action in Bali is that Indonesia will need to re-evaluate its relaxed policy towards terrorism. It is likely that the Indonesian people will, however, not be spared the long-term consequences of the attack or the failure of the government

(continued)

Case study: the Bali terrorist bombings (continued)

to deal effectively with terrorists. Approximately 1.5 million foreigners visited Bali in 2001, almost one-third of the 5 million international visitors to Indonesia. Visitors to Bali contributed almost US $2 million to the Indonesian economy in 2001.

Indonesia is predominantly a Muslim country, but Bali is an island where the Hindu religion has been practised for several hundred years. The island's relaxed attitudes to sex and dress codes, as well as general expectations of tourist behaviour, compared with many other parts of Indonesia, have encouraged foreign tourists and particularly young Western backpackers to visit. It is probably the relatively unrestrained nature of life on an island surrounded by a country with generally stricter Islamic beliefs, coupled with the presence of large numbers of foreign visitors, that has made Bali a suitable – and now it is recognized, a too easy – target for militant Muslim terrorists.

As early as 2 days after the bombings, several tour operators from the United Kingdom, United States and Australia were flying clients out of the island. A large number of Western tourists in Bali were on round-the-world tickets and many of these were expected to be leaving earlier than planned. A senior spokesperson for the Association for British Travel Agents suggested that it would probably be a couple of years before the island recovered. He insisted that it would recover, arguing that it was unlikely tourists would be put off visiting Muslim countries.

The Luxor Massacre in Egypt in 1997 was the worst terrorist attack on holidaymakers before the Bali outrage. Numbers there were severely depressed for 2 years but were back to pre-attack figures by 2000.

At the end of December 2002, a somewhat confusing picture of tourism in Bali following the attack was emerging. The UK-based *Guardian* newspaper showed photographs of empty beaches and suggested that tourists had abandoned the island, while the Australian newspaper *The Sydney Morning Herald* published a story that Qantas Airlines had reported almost full flights to Bali over the Christmas 2002 period.

Almost 3 years after the 2002 bombings, there was a second series of bombings on Bali in October 2005. Although far fewer people were killed (20), the majority (15) were Indonesian, with 4 Australian and a Japanese tourist also killed; over 100 people were injured, the majority of these being Indonesians. The bombs exploded in two locations, Kuta, close to the site of the 2002 bombings, and Jimbaran, and both were areas popular with international tourists. The bombs were detonated by three suicide bombers who also died in the incidents. The suicide bomber suspects were part of an active terrorist network, Jemmah Islamiah, an organization linked to Al-Qaeda. This terrorist network allegedly carried out the 2002 bombings. After the 2002 bombings, the Indonesian authorities had warned that there was likely to be another attack and the US and Australian authorities had issued warnings, in early 2005, to nationals who were contemplating visiting Bali that they should avoid going there on non-essential travel.

International reaction to the 2005 bombings was swift and condemned the bombers and expressed much sympathy with the victims and their families. However, many countries also issued travel warnings against visiting Bali. By November 2005, the Indonesian authorities had made a number of arrests, and a key suspect for the 2002 bombings, who was also probably involved in planning the 2005 bombings, had been killed in a shoot out with police. However, the reaction of tourists on Bali was not the same as in the aftermath of the 2002 bombings. Relatively few people left the island, although a large number cancelled or postponed their visit. The reasons for the cancellations were the continued travel warnings issued by the Australian government, the televised confessions of the suicide bombers and the ongoing hunt for terrorists in Indonesia. Hence, during the Christmas/New Year Period of 2005–6 hotel occupancy in Indonesia as whole fell by 40 per cent. By late November 2006, the Bali based airline Air Paradise International had closed its service completely and laid off 350 employees. The Indonesian airline Garuda reduced its flights between Australian cities and Indonesia/Bali from 32 to 25 services and between Japan and Indonesia/Bali from 22 to 16 flights per week by mid-2006. A year on from the 2005 bombings the effects were as bad if not slightly worse in terms of international tourist numbers reaching Bali. However, amongst the Balinese there seemed to be far more resolve than in 2002. Local people, were angry and blamed non-locals for the bombings and were more intent on trying to kick-start their ailing tourism industry and welcome back tourists than previously – which was probably not the reaction sought by the bombers.

(Based on reports in the following newspapers and their respective websites: *The Guardian*, *The Sydney Morning Herald*, *The Age* and the *Milwaukee Journal Sentinel* for the 2002 bombings and *The Washington Post*, CNN and the *New Zealand Herald* and the Lonely Planet Guide: Tales from the Road website for the 2005 bombings.)

The case study of Bali makes reference to the terrorist bombings in Luxor, Egypt and the fact that it took at least 2 years after the attacks for tourism to recover. In relation to Bali, Weiping (2010) conducted research into the image of Bali amongst UK tourists and their reaction to the bombings. This research revealed that tourism numbers were almost back to the pre-2005 level by 2008. It also indicated that tourists who had actually visited Bali in the aftermath of the bombings were less likely to be concerned about security issues than other tourists who had not visited Bali at all. The effect of the media on the perception of the UK tourists who had not actually visited the island was suggested as the main reason for this finding (Weiping, 2010).

However, the Bali terrorist attacks on tourists call into question whether tourism will continue to expand in terms of visitor numbers, as well as spread relentlessly to all parts of the globe. In the period after 2008, global economic conditions have deteriorated, with one of the longest recessions for many years, and even in early 2015, the global economy had not recovered. Some significant areas for both inbound and outbound tourism, particularly continental Europe were still enduring difficult economic conditions.

Nevertheless, it is probably appropriate to assume that tourism numbers will increase on a global scale, although at a slower rate than prior to 2008 and despite possible significant setbacks at specific locations, for the foreseeable future. Under such circumstances, if tourism reaches almost all parts of the Earth, it will be vital that careful planning and management policies are adopted and applied. In the past, tourism planning and management has been viewed largely as the responsibility of government. In the future, it is likely that the private sector, in terms of representatives of the tourism industry, will be more actively involved in planning and managing tourism. This may occur in the form of partnerships with sectors of government. Such partnerships are also likely to involve other interested parties including non-governmental organizations (NGOs). It is a strong possibility that representatives of host communities will also be more involved in decision-making about future tourism developments in their immediate area.

The success of tourism planning and management in the early part of the twenty-first century in avoiding the worst excesses of uncontrolled tourism growth and in promoting more beneficial consequences of tourism, will depend not only on structures, organizations and individuals, but also on the political will that accepts that it is possible and desirable to plan and manage tourism.

Data in Chapter 1 indicated that one of the relatively unexploited areas for tourism in the early part of the twenty-first century is Africa. The final case study in the book considers the future of tourism in a relatively new country in Southern Africa. This country, Namibia, which has significant tourist attractions, has only a fledgling tourism industry. The case study presents information on the obstacles to and opportunities for successfully planned, developed and managed tourism in Namibia.

Case study: development of tourism in Namibia

Background

Namibia is an independent country located in southwest Africa. It gained independence from South Africa in 1990, having once been a German colony. Hence, Namibia is a very new country. Prior to independence, there was much political turbulence, but since there has been generally a high level of stability.

Tourist attractions

Namibia has many potential tourist attractions including an unusual landscape, an abundance of wildlife, unique flora and diverse cultures. The landscape features of importance include the Namib Desert, which has the world's highest sand dunes, Fish Creek Canyon (the only deeper canyon is the Grand Canyon) and Etosha National Park where there is a large range of wildlife. There is also interesting heritage from the German colonial period, particularly in the capital, Windhoek. The country has indigenous tribes, although there are only about 2 million people in total living there.

Tourism was the country's fourth major economic sector in the early 1990s, with about 300,000 visitors (approximately 60 per cent from South Africa and 11 per cent from Germany, reflecting the close traditional ties with these countries). The remaining visitors come from mainly Europe (United Kingdom, Italy and France) and North America. Earnings from international visitor spend totalled N$4.2 billion in 2006. Within the economy these earnings are represented as exports and accounted for 20 per cent of total export earnings in 2006. The growth in tourism was between 6.5 and 10 per cent per year in the mid-1990s. The forecast for the period 2007–16 was 6.9 per cent per annum (in 2007, Namibia actually increased the number of tourists from Europe by 17 per cent) which would make Namibia the thirteenth fastest growing country in terms of tourism total demand. The direct contribution of tourism to the Namibian economy was just under 4 per cent of GDP in 2006. Almost 5 per cent of the Namibian workforce was employed directly in tourism in 2006 and it was estimated that the combined direct and indirect impact of tourism was 16 per cent of the economy.

As a new country, Namibia has a great opportunity to ensure its tourism development is cautious, well planned and managed. It has the advantage of a large land area and a relatively small population. By the mid-1990s, as much as 15 per cent of the land had been designated as national park area. In 1992, the country created its first tourism master plan. This involved a 5-year strategy for the tourism industry. The plan contains statements on product development, organizational structure, the establishment of a tourism management information system, training and educating staff, marketing and financing. There is also a 'Green Plan' study, which is an attempt to control negative impacts of tourism. All tourism developers will need to conduct an Environmental Assessment Study. This study will be judged on how it contributes to sustainable development and minimizes damage to the environment.

A hotel school has been constructed near the capital, Windhoek. Consultants from South Africa have been brought in to assist with the initial establishment of the school. Trainers come from a Namibian hotel chain, Namib-Sun. Short courses are organized (2–3 weeks) for front of house staff, reception staff, chefs and waiters. The school also plans to train managers. A Namibian Academy for Tourism and Hospitality has also been created and this offers training in tour guiding. This began offering diploma and degree courses in the late 1990s.

The tourism industry is fairly well organized in Namibia. There are associations for tour operators, hotels, travel agencies and car rental companies. An organization, the Federation of Namibian Tourism Associations (FENATA), has been established to act as a link between public and private sector. The organization has representatives from the private sector and also government ministries. FENATA is used as a sounding board for new tourism developments in Namibia.

Unlike many other southern African countries, Namibia's tourism infrastructure is relatively good. There is a well-maintained road system that reaches most parts of the country, as well as off-road areas that are accessible by four wheel drive vehicles. Utilities such as electricity, water and telecommunications are generally dependable. The country is also relatively safe for tourists, unlike several other southern African countries, although as Theroux (2013) indicates, petty crime directed at tourists is not uncommon.

The accommodation sector is well organized and also well regulated. The South African 1–5 star system was used in the past, but a new system is currently being established which is better suited to Namibian conditions. There is a licensing system with over 4,500 accommodation providers and approximately 10,500 beds. About two-thirds of the accommodation providers are privately owned. The government runs the other third, most of which are situated in national parks. Accommodation varies from tented safari to air-conditioned bungalows. However, there has been a shortage of up-market facilities and there are plans to upgrade existing accommodation as well as build new accommodation.

In 2006 the World Travel and Tourism Council made a number of policy suggestions on ways for Namibia to realize its potential in tourism. Several of these related to increasing the political prominence of tourism within Namibia. Other suggestions included the gathering of accurate data and statistics on tourism and appropriate funding to support data gathering and analysis, as well as marketing activities and regulatory roles. Specific policy recommendations were concerned with the establishment of a pro-poor community-based tourism strategy, increased investment in education and training, the need to develop domestic tourism and the establishment of Namibia's credentials in terms of sustainable tourism. These policy suggestions also made reference to the need for the whole country, as well as tourists, to benefit from natural and cultural resources.

(continued)

Case study: development of tourism in Namibia (continued)

Tourism in Namibia since independence has been hailed, generally, as a success story. Based on research with tourism industry members, other stakeholders and tourists, as well as those who had never visited Namibia, Buncle (2011) argues that a significant reason for this success is a close match between the image/brand of Namibia developed by the industry and the actual perceptions of Namibia by the different groups in the research. Hence, the key strengths of Namibia agreed on by both the industry and tourists were: a very attractive 'natural' landscape, tranquillity, uncongested space, the ability to get close to wildlife, an absence of mass tourism, a good standard of personal safety and security, and the ability to self-drive rather than needing to go on an accompanied tour. The only major disagreement was that the industry presented a strong cultural aspect to the country's image, which was not recognized as particularly important by the tourists. Nevertheless, Namibia as a tourism brand is well known by people in the country, by the industry, by visitors from other parts of Africa and, increasingly, by tourists from other parts of the world.

(Adapted from Echtner, 1999; WTTC, 2007; Buncle, 2011.)

The case study suggests that Namibia has established a tourism brand and has the potential to create a successful long-term tourism industry. It also indicates that there is the likelihood of well-planned and managed tourism, in which environmental factors and socio-cultural aspects are well integrated, which could act as a model for other countries that are developing tourism. However, whether Namibia, like many other developing countries, can develop sustainable tourism successfully may depend not just on factors internal to the tourism industry, but also on external aspects that are beyond its control.

Student activities

1   In relation to your own region, consider the likely impacts of global warming on tourism there.
2   Why was Bali a particularly 'easy target' for a terrorist attack in 2002? Why was Bali the target of terrorist attacks again in 2005? Why might actual visitors to Bali have a different view, on safety and security, to other tourists who have not visited the island?
3   What factors both local and on a global scale would (a) deter potential visitors from going to Bali and (b) encourage visitor numbers to increase?
4   New York was a major target for the 11 September 2001 terrorist attacks and it is also a tourist attraction. Compare and contrast the ways in which New York and Bali responded to their respective terrorist attacks. What do you think is the long-term prognosis for tourism in each location?
5   Compare and contrast the tourism infrastructures of Namibia with those of a developed country/region with which you are familiar. Why are there differences?
6   What other factors (particularly external) than those presented in this case study are important for tourism development in Namibia?

7   Namibia is at a very early stage in its tourism development. Use tourism theories (particularly those of Butler and Doxey and also chaos theory) to prepare a number of different scenarios for tourism development in Namibia in the next 15–20 years.

8   Working in groups of three or four, conduct a SWOT analysis of tourism in Namibia. SWOT stands for Strengths, Weaknesses, Opportunities and Threats. When preparing the SWOT analysis in your groups use the following headings:

- Current location of tourism activity.
- Current level of tourism development.
- Nature of tourism infrastructure.
- Number of tourists.
- Types of tourism activity.
- Resource implications – both human and natural.
- Management strategies in relation to tourism.

Also consider the following:

- Economic impacts of tourism.
- Likely involvement of host population.
- Changing attitudes of host population to tourism.
- Environmental impacts of tourism.
- Degree of each type of impact.

It is best to think of the SWOT activity in two parts:

a) The strengths and weaknesses relate to the current situation (what exists at present).
b) The opportunities and threats are related to the future. The work of applying tourism theories to Namibia in Question 6 will be useful here. Consider any other factors, such as political change, competition from elsewhere, economic change both locally and internationally and also environmental pressures.

References

AECO (2014). Arctic Expedition Cruise Operators. Available online at www.aeco.no/ [accessed 28 November 2014].

Agarwhal, S. (1997). The resort life cycle and seaside tourism. *Tourism Management*, 18 (2), 65–73.

Ang, E. (1990). Upgrading the professionalism of tourist guides. *Proceedings from the Travel Educators Forum*, PATA Conference Singapore, 11–14 July, PATA, Singapore, pp. 167–72.

Ashley, C., Poultney, C. and Haysom, G. (2005). *Pro-Poor Tourism in Southern Africa: Practical Implementation of Pro-poor Linkages by Tourism Companies*. London: Overseas Development Institute.

Augustyn, M. (1998). The road to quality enhancement in tourism. *International Journal of Contemporary Hospitality Management* 10 (4), 145–58.

Bartelmus, P. (1994). *Environment, Growth and Development: The Concepts and Strategies of Sustainability*. London: Routledge.

BBC (1991). *Ecotourism in Belize*. BBC London: Videotape.

Bernerman, C. and Petit, D. (2007). *Festivals and the Product Life Cycle: An Exploratory Study of the Rhone Alpes Region*. Groupe ESC, Saint-Etienne, France.

Blamey, R. (1995). *The Nature of Ecotourism*. Occasional Paper 21, Canberra, Bureau of Tourism Research.

Boers, B. and Cotterell, S. (2007). Sustainable tourism infrastructure planning: a GIS supported approach. *Tourism Geographies*, 9 (1), 1–21.

Bonzon-Liu, B. (1999). An Accreditation Scheme for Ecotourism in New Zealand. Wellington: Masters Dissertation, Victoria University (unpublished).

Boo, E. (1990). Ecotourism: *The Potential and Pitfalls*. Washington: WWF.

Bramwell, B. and Lane, B. (2000). Introduction. In B. Bramwell and B. Lane (eds), *Tourism Collaboration and Partnerships: Policy Practice and Sustainability*. Clevedon: Channel View Publications, pp. 1–23.

Broad, G. (1996). Visitor profile and evaluation of informal education at Jersey Zoo. *The Dodo: The Journal of the Wildlife Preservation Trusts*, 32, 166–92.

Brown, D. T. (2013). Tourism's wasteful ways. In A. Holden and D. Fennell (eds), *Handbook of Tourism and the Environment*. London: Routledge, pp. 460–93.

Buckley, R. (2002). Minimal impact guidelines for mountain ecotours. *Tourism Recreation Research*, 27, 35–40.

Buhalis, D. (2000). Marketing the competitive destination of the future. *Tourism Management*, 21 (1), 97–116.

Buncle, N. (2011). Branding, stakeholders and integration: Namibia. In N. Morgan, A. Pritchard and R. Pride (eds), *Destination Brands*. Oxford: Butterworth-Heinemann, pp. 251–68.

Burns, P. and Holden, A. (1995). *Tourism: A New Perspective*. London: Prentice Hall.

Burton, R. (1992). *Travel Geography*. London: Pitman.

Butler, R. (1980). The concept of a tourism area cycle of evolution. *Canadian Geographer*, 24, 5–12.

Butler, R. (1998). Still Pedalling Along: The Resort Life Cycle Two Decades On. Paper presented at the CAUTHE Conference, Gold Coast, Australia 1998.

Butler, R. W. (1991). Tourism, environment and sustainable development. *Environmental Conservation*, 18, 201–9.

Butler, R. W. and Hall, C. M. (1998). Tourism and recreation in rural areas: myth and reality. In D. Hall, and J. O'Hanlon (eds), *Rural Tourism Management: Sustainable Options*. Conference Proceedings, Ayr: Scottish Agricultural College, pp. 97–108.

Capra, F. (1982). *The Turning Point: Science, Society and the Rising Culture*. London: Flamingo.

Cater, E. (1994). Introduction. In E. Cater and G. Lowman (eds), *Ecotourism: A Sustainable Option?* London: John Wiley and Sons.

Chadwick, G. (1971). *A Systems View of Planning*. Oxford: Pergamon.

Chadwick, R. (1987). Concepts, definitions, and measures used in travel and tourism research. In J. R. B. Richie and C. Goeldner (eds), *Travel, Tourism and Hospitality Research: A Handbook for Managers and Researchers.* New York: Wiley.

Chavez, D. J. (1997). Mountain bike management: resource protection and social conflicts. *Trends*, 34, 36–40.

Christaller, W. (1963). Some considerations of tourism locations in Europe: the peripheral regions–under developed countries–recreation areas. *Papers of the Regional Science Association*, 12, 168–78.

Clements, C., Schultz, J. and Lime, D. (1993). Recreation, tourism and the local residents: partnership or co-existence? *Journal of Park and Recreation Administration*, 11, 78–91.

Coccossis, H. (1996). Tourism and sustainability: perspectives and implications. In G. K. Priestley, J. A. Edwards and H. Coccossis (eds), *Sustainable Tourism? European Experiences.* Wallingford, UK: CAB International, pp. 1–21.

Coccossis, H. and Parpairis, A. (1996). Tourism and carrying capacity in coastal areas: Mykonos Greece. In G. K. Priestley, J. A. Edwards and H. Coccossis (eds), *Sustainable Tourism? European Experiences*, Wallingford, UK: CAB International, pp. 153–75.

Cohen, I. (1972). Towards a sociology of international tourism. *Social Research*, 39, 164–82.

Cooper, C., Fletcher, J., Gilbert, D. and Wanhill, S. (1998). *Tourism: Principles and Practice*. London: Longman.

Cooper, C., Fletcher, J., Gilbert, D., Fyall, A. and Wanhill, S. (2005). *Tourism: Principles and Practice*, 3rd edn. London: Longman.

Copeland, C. (2008). 'Cruise Ship Pollution, Background, Laws, and Regulations and Key Issues', *Congress Research Series, Order Code RL32450*, National Council for Science and the Environment, Washington. Available online at www.cep.unep.org/publications-and-resources/databases/document-database/other/cruise-ship-pollution-background-laws-and-regulations-and-key-issues.pdf/view [accessed 10 January 2013].

Crompton, J. (1979). Motivations for pleasure vacations. *Annals of Tourism Research*, 6, 408–24.

Crompton, J. and McKay, J. (1997). Motives of visitors attending festival events. *Annals of Tourism Research*, 24, 425–39.

Cukier, J. and Wall, G. (1994). Tourism and employment perspectives from Bali. *Tourism Management*, 14, 195–201.

Cullingsworth, B. (1997). *Planning in the USA: Policies, Issues and Processes*. London: Routledge.

Curtin, S. (2005). Whale watching in Kaikoura. *Journal of Ecotourism*, 2 (3), 173–95.

Davis, P. (1996). *Museums and the Natural Environment*. London: Leicester University Press.

Davison, R. (1996). The impacts of tourism. In R. Davison and R. Maitland (eds), *Tourism Destinations.* London: Hodder and Stoughton, pp. 18–45.

De Kadt, T. (1979). *Tourism: Passport to Development?* Oxford: Oxford University Press.

De Kadt, T. (1988). *Tourism: Passport to Development?* 2nd edn. Oxford: Oxford University Press.

Department of Tourism (1990). *Tourism Statistics 1988–9*. Kathmandu, Nepal: Department of Tourism.

Department of Tourism, Sport and Racing (1994). *Getting It Right: A Guide to Planning and Developing Sport and Recreation Facilities*. New Zealand: Brisbane, State of Queensland, Australia and Hillary Commission.

Dervis, D. and Harriot, V. (1996). Sustainable tourism development or the case of loving a place to death. In L. Harrison and W. Husbands (eds), *Practising Responsible Tourism*. New York: John Wiley & Sons, pp. 422–44.

Doorne, S. (2000). Caves, culture and crowds: carrying capacity meets consumer sovereignty. *Journal of Sustainable Tourism*, 8 (4), 34–42.

Doswell, R. (1997). *Tourism: How Effective Management Makes the Difference*. London: Butterworth-Heinemann.

Doxey, G. V. (1975). A causation theory of resident visitor irritants. In *The Sixth Annual Conference Proceedings of the Travel Research Association*. San Diego, California: Travel Research Association, pp. 195–8.

Doyle, T. and McEachern, D. (1998). *Environment and Politics*. London: Routledge.

Drake, S. (1991). Local participation in ecotourism projects. In T. Whelan (ed.), *Nature Tourism*. Washington, DC: Island Press.

Dunn-Ross, E. and Iso-Aloha, S. (1991). Sightseeing tourists' motivation and satisfaction. *Annals of Tourism Research*, 12, 256–62.

Dye, T. (1992). *Understanding Public Policy*, 7th edn. Englewood Cliffs: Prentice Hall.

Dymond, S. J. (1997). Indicators of sustainable tourism in New Zealand: a local government perspective. *Journal of Sustainable Tourism*, 5, 279–93.

Echtner, C. (1999). Three African success stories. In T. Singh and S. Singh (eds), *Tourism Development in Critical Environments*. New York: Cognizant Communications, pp. 159–69.

Echtner, C. M. and Ritchie, J. R. B. (1993). The measurement of destination image: an empirical assessment. *Journal of Travel Research*, 31, 3–13.

Ekinci, Y., Riley, M. and Fife-Shaw, C., (1998). What school of thought? The dimensions of the resort hotel quality. *International Journal of Contemporary Hospitality Management*, 10 (2), 63–7.

Elliot, J. (1997). *Tourism Politics and Public Sector Management*. London: Routledge.

ETB (1991). *Tourism and the Environment: Maintaining the Balance*. London: English Tourism Board/Ministry of the Environment.

Faulkner, B. (2001). Towards a framework for tourism disaster management. *Tourism Management*, 22, 135–47.

Faulkner, B. and Russell, R. (1997). Chaos and complexity in tourism: in search of a new perspective. *Pacific Tourism Review*, 1, 93–102.

Faulkner, H. W. (1990). Swings and roundabouts In Australian tourism. *Tourism Management*, 11 (1) 29–37.

FEEE (2012*). The Blue Flag Award,* Foundation for European Environmental Education. Available online at www.fee-international.org/ [accessed 3 July 2012].

Fennell, D. (1999). *Ecotourism: An Introduction*. London: Routledge.

Fennell, D. (2000). Tourism and applied ethics. *Tourism Recreation Research*, 25, 56–69.

Fennell, D. and Przeclawski, K. (2003). Generating goodwill in tourism through effective stakeholder interactions. In S. Singh, D. Timothy and R. Dowling (eds), *Tourism in Destination Communities*. Wallingford, UK: CABI, pp. 135–51.

Fennell, D. and Malloy, D. (2007). *Codes of Ethics in Tourism*. Clevedon, UK: Channel View.

Fink, S. (1986). *Crisis Management*. New York: American Association of Management.

Finnish Tourist Board (2007). Tourist Attractions in Finland, Finnish Tourist Board. Available online at www.mek.fi/web.MekEng/publish.nsf [accessed 10 July 2007].

Forsyth, T. (1995). Business attitudes to sustainable tourism: self-regulation in the UK outgoing tourism industry. *Journal of Sustainable Tourism*, 3 (4), 210–31.

Funkyluke2009 (2012). Kecak dance/Uluwatu, Bali. Available online at www.youtube.com/watch?v=t0HY0oD84OM [accessed 30 October 2014].

Garrod, B. and Fennell, D. (2004). An analysis of whale watching codes of conduct. *Annals of Tourism Research*, 31 (2), 334–52.

Getz, D. (1978). Tourism and population change: long term impacts of tourism in the Baden-och and Strathspey District of the Scottish Highlands. *Scottish Geographical Magazine*, 102, 113–26.

Getz, D. (1994). Residents' attitudes to tourism. *Tourism Management*, 15, 247–58.

Gilbert, J., Jones, G., Vitalis, T., Walker, R. and Gilbertson, D. (1995). *Introduction to Management in New Zealand*. Sydney: Harcourt Brace.

Glyptis, S. (1994). *Countryside Recreation*. Harlow: Longman/ILAM.

Gningue, A. M. (1993). Integrated rural tourism lower Casamance. In S. Eber (ed.), *Beyond the Green Horizon: Discussion Paper on Sustainable Tourism*. Godalming, UK: World Wide Fund for Nature/Tourism Concern.

Goodwin, H. (1996). In pursuit of ecotourism. *Biodiversity and Conservation*, 5, 277–91.

Gow, L. J. A. (1995). Implementing sustainability: New Zealand's experience with its Resource Management Act. Address to World Resources Institute/New Zealand Embassy Seminar, Washington, DC, 6 June 1995. Unpublished manuscript.

Guignon, C. (1986). Existential ethics. In J. Demarco and R. Fox (eds), *New Directions in Ethics*. New York: Routledge and Kegan Paul, pp. 73–91.

Gunn, C. A. (1988). *Tourism Planning*, 2nd edn. New York: Taylor and Francis.

Gunn, C. A. (1994).*Tourism Planning*, 3rd edn. London: Taylor and Francis.

Hall, C. M. (1992). Sex tourism in South East Asia. In D. Harrison (ed.), *Tourism in the Developing World.* Chichester: John Wiley and Sons.

Hall, C. M. (1995). *An Introduction to Tourism in Australia*, 2nd edn. Melbourne: Longman.

Hall, C. M. (2000a). *Tourism Planning*. London: Prentice Hall.

Hall, C. M. (2000b). Rethinking collaboration and partnership: a public policy perspective. In B. Bramwell and B. Lane (eds), *Tourism Collaboration and Partnerships: Policy Practice and Sustainability.* Clevedon: Channel View Publications, pp. 143–58.

Hall, C. M. and Jenkins, J. (1995). *Tourism and Public Policy*. London: Routledge.

Hall, C. M. and Page, S. (1999). *The Geography of Tourism*. London: Routledge.

Hall, C. M. and Kearsley, G. (2001). *Tourism in New Zealand: An Introduction*. Melbourne: Oxford University Press.

Hall, C. M. and Lew, A. (2009). *Understanding and Managing Tourism Impacts: An Integrated Approach.* London: Routledge.

Hall, C. M. and Page, S. (2014). *The Geography of Tourism* and Recreation, 4th edn. London: Routledge.

Hall, P. (1992). *Urban and Regional Planning*, 3rd edn. Penguin: Harmondsworth.

Hammitt, W. E. and Cole, D. N. (1998). *Wildland Recreation: Ecology and Management*, 2nd edn. New York: John Wiley & Sons.

Haralambopolous, N. and Pizam, A. (1996). Perceived impacts of tourism: the case of Samos. *Annals of Tourism Research*, 23 (3), 503–26.

Harrill, R. and Potts, T. (2002). Social psychological theories of tourist motivation: exploration, debate and transition. *Tourism Analysis*, 7, 105–14.

Harris, R. and Walshaw, A. (1995). Club Mediterranee Lindeman Island. In R. Harris and N. Leiper (eds), *Sustainable Tourism: An Australian Perspective*. Chatswood, Australia: Butterworth-Heinemann.

Hasse, J. C. and Milne, S. (1999). Tourism and community development: stakeholder participation and GIS. Paper presented at the Tourism Policy and Planning Conference, 12 September 1999. Oamaru, University of Otago, New Zealand.

Healey, P. (1997). *Collaborative Planning: Shaping Places in Fragmented Societies*. Basingstoke: Macmillan.

Heely, J. (2011). *Inside City Tourism: A European Perspective*. Clevedon, UK: Channel View.

Henderson, J. (2006). Tourism in Dubai: overcoming barriers to destination development. *International Journal of Tourism Research*, 8 (2), 87–100.

Hendricks, W. W. (1995). A resurgence in recreation conflict research: introduction to the special issue. *Leisure Sciences*, 17, 157–8.

Hirschmann, A. (1976). Policy making and policy analysis in Latin America: a return journey. *Policy Sciences*, 6, 385–402.

Holden, A. (2000). *Environment and Tourism*. London: Routledge.

Holden, A. (2008). *Environment and Tourism,* 2nd edn. London: Routledge.

Holden, A. (2013). Introduction. In A. Holden and D. Fennell (eds), *The Routledge Handbook of Tourism and the Environment.* London: Routledge, pp. 3–5.

Holden, A. and Ewen, M. (2002). Understanding the motivations of ecotourists. *International Journal of Tourism Research*, 4, 435–46.

Hopkins, D. and Maclean, K. (2014). Climate change responses and perceptions in Scotland's ski industry. *Tourism Geographies*, 16 (3), 400–14.

Horn, C. (1994). Conflict in Recreation: The Case of Mountain-bikers and Trampers. Lincoln: MA thesis, Lincoln University (unpublished).

Howard, J. (1997). Towards best practice in interpretive guided activities. *Australian Parks and Recreation*, Summer, 1997–8, pp. 28–31.

Hunt, S., Woods, V. and Chonko, L. (1989). Corporate ethical values and organizational commitment in marketing. *Journal of Marketing*, 53, 79–90.

Hunter, C. (1996). Sustainable tourism as an adaptive paradigm. *Annals of Tourism Research*, 24, 850–67.

Hunter, C. and Green, H. (1995). *Tourism and the Environment: A Sustainable Relationship?* London: Routledge.

Hunziker, R. (1961). *Revue de Tourisme*. Bern, Switzerland.

Indian and Northern Affairs (2004). Developing a Tourism Action Plan, Indian and Northern Affairs, Canada. Available online at www.ainc-inac.gc.ca [accessed 2 October 2007].

Innskeep, E. (1991). *Tourism Planning*. New York: Van Nostrand.

IRIN (2007). Humanitarian News and Analysis, UN Office for the Co-ordination of Humanitarian Affairs. Available online at www.irinnews.org [accessed 19 October 2007].

Iso-Aloha, S. (1980). *The Social-Psychology of Leisure and Recreation*. Dubuque, Iowa: Brown.

Jafari, J. (1981). Editor's page. *Annals of Tourism Research*, 8, 7.

Jafari, J. (1990). Editor's page. *Annals of Tourism Research*, 16, 3.

Jenkins, J. (1991). Tourism development strategies. In L. J. Lickorish (ed.), *Developing Tourism Destinations.* Harlow: Longman, pp. 61–77.

Jenkins, J. (1993). Tourism policy in rural New South Wales: policy and research. *Geojournal*, 29, 281–90.

Jenkins, P. (1997). *Tourism Policy and Planning: Case Studies from the Caribbean*. New York: Cognizant Communications Corporation.

Johanssen, Y. and Diamantis, D. (2004). Ecotourism in Thailand and Kenya: a private sector perspective. In D. Diamantis (ed.), *Ecotourism.* London: Thomson, pp. 298–312.

Jurowski, C. (1996). Tourism means more than money to the host community. *Parks and Recreation*, 31, 110–18.

Knudson, D. M., Cable, T. T. and Beck, L. (1995). *Interpretation of Natural and Cultural Resources*. State College, Pennsylvania: State College Venture Publishing.

Kotler, P., Haider, D. and Rein, I. (1993). *Marketing Places: Attracting Investment, Industry and Tourism to Cities, States and Nations*. New York: Free Press.

Kozak, M. and Rimington, M. (2000). Tourists satisfaction with Mallorca, Spain as an off-season holiday destination. *Journal of Travel Research,* 38 (3), 260–9.

Krippendorf, J. (1987). *The Holiday Makers*. London: Heinemann.

Kuo, I. and Mason, P. (2013). Managing megalithic monuments. In B. Garrod and A. Fyall (eds), *Contemporary Cases in Heritage*. Oxford, Goodfellow Publishers, pp. 130–74.

Lang, R. (1985). Planning for integrated development. Paper presented at Conference on Integrated Development Beyond the City, 14–16 June, Rural Tourism and Small Town Research and Studies Programme, Mount Allison University, Sackville, New Brunswick, Canada.

Lasswell, H. (1936). *Who Gets What, When and How?* New York: McGraw Hill.

Lavery, P. (1987). *Travel and Tourism*. Kings Norton, Cambridge, UK: Elm Publications.

Laws, E. (1993). *Tourist Destination Management: Issues, Analysis and Policies*. London: Routledge.

Leberman, S. I. and Mason, P. (2002). Planning for recreation and tourism at the local level. *Tourism Geographies*, 4, 3–21.

Leiper, N. (1990). *The Tourism System*. Palmerston North: New Zealand Massey University Department of Management Systems.

Leiper, N. (1999). Ten myths about tourism. *Conference Proceedings 1999 CAUTHE National Research Conference*. Adelaide, pp. 1–11.

Lickorish, L. J. (1991). Roles of government and private sector. In L. J. Lickorish (ed.), *Developing Tourism Destinations*. Harlow: Longman, pp. 121–46.

Lickorish, L. (1994). *An Introduction to Tourism*. London: Sage.

Lominé, L. and Edmunds, J. (2007). *Key Concepts in Tourism*. London: Palgrave Macmillan.

Mabey, D. (1994). Youth leadership: commitment for what. In S. York and D. Jordan (eds), *Bold Ideas: Creative Approaches to the Challenge of Youth Programming.* University of Iowa, Iowa City, Iowa: Institute for Youth Leaders.

MacAdam, P. (1999). Geographical information systems and their application within tourism. *Journal of Sustainable Tourism*, 7 (1), 62–74.

McArthur, S. (1996). Interpretation in Australia: is it running on borrowed time? *Australian Parks and Recreation*, Winter, pp. 33–6.

McCabe, V., Poole, B., Weeks, P. and Leiper, N. (2000). *The Business and Management of Conventions*. Melbourne: John Wiley and Sons.

MacCannell, D. (1995). *The Tourist Papers*. London: Routledge.

McCool, S. and Martin, S. (1994). Community attitudes towards tourism development. *Journal of Travel Research*, 32, 29–34.

McKercher, B. (1993). Some fundamental truths about tourism: understanding tourism's social, and environmental impacts. *Journal of Sustainable Tourism*, 1, 6–16.

Maher, P. (2011). Antarctic human dimensions: ambassadors for the experience. In P. Maher, E. Stewart and M. Luck (eds), *Polar Tourism: Human, Environmental and Governance Dimensions.* New York: Cognizant Communications, pp. 121–41.

Malloy, D. and Fennell, D. (1998). Ecotourism and ethics: moral development and organizational cultures. *Journal of Travel Research*, 36, 47–56.

Mannell, R. and Kleiber, D. (1997). *A Social Psychology of Leisure*. State College, Pennsylvania: State College Venture Publishing.

Maslow, A. (1943). A theory of human motivation. *Psychological Review*, 50, 7–23.

Maslow, A. (1954). *Motivation and Personality*. New York: Harper.

Mason, P. (1990). *Tourism: Environment and Development Perspectives*. Godalming, UK: World Wide Fund for Nature.

Mason, P. (1991). Internal Report on the Annapurna Conservation Area Project. Prepared for WWF UK, Godalming (unpublished).

Mason, P. (1992). The environmentally-friendly traveller. In M. Shales (ed.), *The Travellers Handbook*. London: Wexas, pp. 32–6.

Mason, P. (1994). A visitor code for the Arctic? *Tourism Management*, 14 (2), 93–8.

Mason, P. (1995). *Tourism: Environment and Development Perspectives*. Godalming, UK: World Wide Fund for Nature.

Mason, P. (1999). *Wellington Zoo: Visitor Survey and Keeper Evaluation. An Interim Report to the Zoo Management Committee*. Palmerston North, New Zealand: Department of Management Systems, Massey University.

Mason, P. (2000). Zoo tourism: the need for more research. *Journal of Sustainable Tourism*, 8 (4), 333–9.

Mason, P. (2005). Visitor management in protected areas: from hard to soft approaches? *Current Issues in Tourism*, 9 (3), 181–94.

Mason, P. (2007a). No better than a band aid for a bullet wound? The effectiveness of tourism codes of conduct. In R. Black and A. Black (eds), *Quality Assurance and Accreditation in Ecotourism*. Wallingford, UK: CABI, pp. 45–64.

Mason, P. (2007b). The roles of the modern zoo: conflicting or complementary? *Tourism Review International* 11 (3), 251–63.

Mason, P. (2013a). Zoning, land use planning and tourism. In A. Holden and D. Fennell (eds), *The Routledge Handbook of Tourism and the Environment*. London: Routledge, pp. 266–85.

Mason, P. (2013b). The Future of the British Seaside Resort, Presentation given at Scarborough Business School, Hull University, 10 March, 2013.

Mason, P. and Mowforth, M. (1995). *Codes of Conduct in Tourism*, Research Paper No. 1, Department of Geographical Sciences, University of Plymouth.

Mason, P. and Mowforth, M. (1996). Codes of conduct in tourism. *Progress in Tourism and Hospitality Research*, 2, 151–67.

Mason, P. and Leberman, S. I. (1998). *Mountain Biking in the Palmerston North Area: Participants, Preferences and Management Issues*. Report to the Recreation and Community Development Unit of the Palmerston North City Council, June. Department of Management Systems, Massey University, New Zealand.

Mason, P. and Legg, S. (1999). Antarctic tourism: activities, impacts, management issues and a proposed research agenda. *Pacific Tourism Review*, 3, 71–84.

Mason, P. and Cheyne, J. (2000). Resident attitudes to tourism development. *Annals of Tourism Research*, 27 (2), 391–412.

Mason, P. and Leberman, S. (2000). Local planning for recreation and tourism: mountain biking in the Manawatu region of New Zealand. *Journal of Sustainable Tourism*, 8, 84–97.

Mason, P. and Christie, M. (2003). Training tour guides to be critically reflective practitioners. *Tourism Recreation Research*, 28 (1), 22–3.

Mason, P. and Kuo, I.-L. (2008). Visitor attitudes to Stonehenge: international icon or national disgrace. *Journal of Heritage Tourism*, 2 (3), 168–83.

Mason, P., Johnston, M. and Twynam, D. (2000a). The World Wide Fund for Nature Arctic Tourism Project. *Journal of Sustainable Tourism*, 8 (4), 305–23.

Mason, P., Leberman, S. and Barnett, S. (2000b). Walkway users: an urban based case study from New Zealand. *Conference Proceedings: Tourism 2000: Time for Celebration?* (M. Robinson, P. Long and B. Bramwell, eds), pp. 207–20.

Matthieson, A. and Wall, G. (1982). *Tourism: Economic, Social and Environmental Impacts*. London: Longman.

Medlik, S. (1993). *Dictionary of Travel Tourism and Hospitality*. Oxford: Butterworth-Heinemann.

Middleton, V. (1994). *Marketing in Travel and Tourism*. London: Routledge.

Middleton, V. T. R. and Hawkins, R. (1998). *Sustainable Tourism: A Marketing Perspective*. London: Butterworth-Heinemann.

Moore, R. L. (1994). *Conflicts on Multiple-use Trails: Synthesis of the Literature and State of the Practice*. Raleigh, NC: North Carolina University. FHWA-PD-94–031.

Morgan, N., Pritchard, A. and Pride, R. (2010). *Destination Branding*, Oxford: Butterworth-Heinemann.

Moscardo, G. (1996). Mindful visitors: heritage and tourism. *Annals of Tourism Research*, 23, 376–97.

Moscardo, G. (1999). *Making Visitors Mindful*. Champaign, IL: Sagamore.

Moscardo, G. and Pearce, P. (1986). Visitor centres and environmental interpretation. *Journal of Environmental Psychology*, 6, 89–108.

MOTCCA (2013). Ministry of Tourism, Culture and Civil Aviation Nepal. *Nepal Tourism News*, Autumn 2013.

Moutinho, L. (2000). *Strategic Tourism Management*. Wallingford: CAB International.

Mowforth, M. (1992). *Ecotourism Terminology and Definitions*. Occasional Paper No. 1, University of Plymouth.

Mowforth, M. and Munt, I. (1998). *Tourism and Sustainability*. London: Routledge.

Muller, H. (1994). The thorny path to sustainable tourism development. *Journal of Sustainable Tourism*, 2 (3), 131–6.

Murphy, P. (1985). *Tourism: A Community Approach*. London: Methuen.

Murphy, P., Pritchard, N. and Smith, B. (2000). The destination product and its impact on traveller perceptions. *Tourism Management*, 21 (1), 43–52.

New Zealand Tourism Board (1992). *Residents Perception and Acceptance of Tourism in Selected New Zealand Communities*. Wellington: Ministry of Tourism.

New Zealand Tourism Board (1996). *Tourism in New Zealand: Facts and Figures*. Wellington: Ministry of Tourism.

New Zealand Tourism Board (2004). *Tourism in New Zealand: Facts and Figures*. Wellington: Ministry of Tourism.

New Zealand Tourist Board (2007). *Tourism in New Zealand: Facts and Figures*. Wellington: Ministry of Tourism.

Nyaupane, G. and Thapa, B. (2004). Evaluation of ecotourism: a comparative assessment in the Annapurna Conservation Area Project. *Journal of Ecotourism*, 3 (1), 2–45.

O'Grady, R. (1980). *Third World Stopover*. Geneva: Risk Books, World Council of Churches.

Olafsdottir, R. and Rannstrom, M. (2009). A GIS approach to ecological sensitivity for tourism development in fragile environments: a case study of SE Iceland. *Scandinavian Journal of Hospitality and Tourism*, 9 (1), 22–38.

Orams, M. (1994). Creating effective interpretation for managing interaction between tourists and wildlife. *The Australian Journal of Environmental Education*, 10, 21–34.

Orams, M. (1995). Using interpretation to manage nature-based tourism. *Journal of Sustainable Tourism*, 4, 81–94.

Page, S. J. and O'Connell, J. (2009). *Tourism: A Modern Synthesis*, 3rd edn. Andover, UK: South Western Cengage Learning.

Page, S. J. and Thorn, K. J. (1997). Towards sustainable tourism planning in New Zealand: public sector planning responses. *Journal of Sustainable Tourism*, 5, 59–77.

Pantin, D. and Francis, J. (2005). *Community-based Sustainable Tourism*, University of the West Indies, Appendix 3, of the Final Technical Report of project R8325.

Parker, S. (2000). Collaboration on tourism policy making: environmental and commercial sustainability on Bonaire, NA. In B. Bramwell and B. Lane (eds), *Tourism Collaboration and Partnerships: Policy Practice and Sustainability.* Clevedon, UK: Channel View Publications, pp. 78–97.

Pearce, D. (1995). Tourism in the Pacific Region. *Progress in Tourism and Hospitality Research*, 1, 1–9.

Pearce, D. G. (1989). *Tourist Development*. London: Longman.

Pearce, P. (1988). *The Ulysses Factor: Evaluating Visitors in Tourist Settings*. New York: Springer Verlag.

Pearce, P. (1993). Fundamentals of tourist motivations. In D. Pearce and R. Butler (eds), *Tourism Research: Critiques and Challenges.* London: Routledge, pp. 113–34.

Pearce, P., Moscardo, G. and Ross, G. (1996). *Tourism Community Relationships*. Oxford: Pergamon.

Pearce, P., Moscardo, G., Miller, A. and Ross, G. (1998). *Tourism: Bridges Across Continents*. Sydney: McGraw-Hill.

Pedersen, A. (1998). The Arctic Tourism Project. In *Arctic Bulletin*, 5 (Spring) 11–15, Oslo, WWF Arctic Programme.

Plog, S. (1973). Why destination areas rise and fall in popularity. *Cornell Hotel and Restaurant Administration Quarterly*, 12, 13–16.

Pond, K. L. (1993). *The Professional Guide*. New York: Van Nostrand Reinhold.

Poon, A. (1993). *Tourism, Technology and Competitive Strategies*. Wallingford: CAB International.

Prentice, R. C. (1995). *Tourism as Experience. Tourists as Consumers. Insight and Enlightenment.* Edinburgh: Inaugural Lecture Queen Margaret College.

Pretes, M. (1995). Post-modern tourism: the Santa Claus industry. *Annals of Tourism Research*, 22 (1), 1–15.

Pretty, J. (1995). The many interpretations of participation. *Tourism in Focus*, 16, 4–5.

Prideaux, B. (2000). The resort development spectrum: a new approach to modelling tourism development. *Tourism Management*, 21 (3), 225–40.

Prosser, R. (1994). Social change and the growth of tourism. In E. Cater and G. Lowman (eds), *Ecotourism: A Sustainable Option?* Chichester: John Wiley and Sons, pp. 19–37.

Prosser, R. (1998). Tourism. In *Encyclopaedia of Ethics*. Vol. 4, Chicago, IL: Houghton Mifflin, pp. 373–401.

Ramthun, R. (1995). Factors in user group conflict between hikers and mountain bikers. *Leisure Sciences*, 17, 159–70.

Raybould, M., Digance, J. and McCullough, C. (1999). Fire and festival: authenticity and visitor motivation at an Australian folk festival. *Pacific Tourism Review*, 3, 201–12.

Richter, L. (1989). *The Politics of Tourism Asia*. Honolulu: University of Hawaii Press.

Ridenour, J. (1995). Foreword. In D. M. Knudson, T. T. Cable and L. Beck (eds), *Interpretation of Natural and Cultural Resources.* State College, Pennsylvania: State College Venture Publishing, pp. xii–xiv.

Ritchie, J. R. B. and Crouch, G. (2003). *The Competive Destination: A Sustainable Tourism Perspective*. Wallingford: CABI.

Ritchie, J. and Goeldner, C. (1994). *Travel, Tourism and Hospitality Research: A Handbook for Managers and Researchers*. New York: John Wiley and Sons.

Ritchie, J. and Zins, M. (1978). Culture as a determinant of the attractiveness of a tourist region. *Annals of Tourism Research*, 5, 252–67.

Ryan, C. (1991). *Recreational Tourism*. London: Routledge.

Ryan, C. (1997). *The Tourist Experience*. London: Cassell.

Ryan, C. (1998). Visitor management in Kakadu National Park. In M. Shackley (ed.), *Visitor Management at World Heritage Sites.* London: Butterworth-Heinemann, pp. 178–92.

Ryan, C. and Saward, J. (2003). The zoo as ecotourism attraction. *Journal of Sustainable Tourism*, 12 (3), 245–66.

Saarinen, J. (2006). Traditions in sustainability in tourism studies. *Annals of Tourism Research*, 33 (4), 1121–40.

Santa Claus Village. (2014). History. Available online at www.santaclausvillage.info/history [accessed 2 October 2014].

Scarborough Borough Council. (2011). *Scarborough Tourism Strategy 2011–2014.* Scarborough Council, Scarborough, Yorkshire.

Seakhoa-King, A. (2007). Conceptualising Quality in a Tourism Destination, Unpublished PhD Thesis, Bedfordshire University, Luton.

Seaton, A. and Bennett, M. (1996). *Marketing Tourism Products.* London: International Thomson Business Press.

Shackley, M. (1998). *Visitor Management at World Heritage Sites.* London: Butterworth-Heinemann.

Simeon, R. (1976). Studying public policy. *Canadian Journal of Political Science*, 9, 558–80.

Smith, S. (1994). The tourism product. *Annals of Tourism Research*, 21 (3), 582–95.

Smith, M. and Duffy, R. (2003). *The Ethics of Tourism Development.* London: Routledge.

Spink, J. (1994). *Leisure and the Environment.* Oxford: Butterworth-Heinemann.

Stewart, E. J., Hayward, B. M., Devlin, P. J. and Kirby, V. G. (1998). The place of interpretation: a new approach to the evaluation of interpretation. *Tourism Management*, 19, 257–66.

Stonehouse, B. (1990). A traveller's code for Antarctic visitors. *Polar Record*, 26, 56–8.

Stonehouse, B. (1996). Briefing papers for Conference WWF Arctic Tourism Guidelines, held at the Scott Polar Institute, University of Cambridge, August.

Swarbrooke, J. (1999). *Sustainable Tourism Management.* Wallingford: CABI Publications.

Taylor, P. (1975). *Principles of Ethics: An Introduction.* Encino, CA: Dickenson.

Theobold, A. (1994). *Global Tourism.* Wallingford, UK: CABI Publications.

Theroux, P. (2013). *Last Train to Zona Verde.* London: Hamish Hamilton.

TIANZ (2007). Tourism Industry Association of New Zealand. Available online at www.tianz. org.nz/main/key-tourism-statistics/ [accessed 19 October 2007].

TIANZ (2014). Tourism Industry Association of New Zealand. Available online at www.TIANZ. com [accessed 30 September 2014].

Tilden, F. (1957). *Interpreting Our Heritage.* Chapel Hill, NC: University of North Carolina Press.

Tomlejnovic, R. and Faulkner, B. (2000). Tourism and world peace: a conundrum for the twenty-first century. In B. Faulkner, G. Moscardo and E. Laws (eds), *Tourism in the Twenty-First Century.* London: Continuum.

TourismNewZealand. (2013). Available online at www.tourismnewzealand.com [accessed 10 November 2014].

Tribe, J. (2000). The philosophic practitioner. *Annals of Tourism Research*, 27 (3), 437–51.

Uhlik, K. S. (1995). Partnerships: step by step: a practical model of partnership formation. *Journal of Park and Recreation Administration*, 143, 13–24.

Ujma, D. (2002). Channel Relationships in Tourism: A Comparative Study of the UK and Poland, Unpublished PhD thesis, Luton, University of Luton, UK.

UNEP (1995). *Environmental Codes of Conduct Technical Report* 29. Paris, United Nations Environment Programme.

UNEP/WTO (2005). *Making Tourism More Sustainable: A Guide for Policy Makers.* Paris: United Nations Environment Programme/World Tourism Organization.

Urry, J. (1990). *The Tourist Gaze.* London: Sage.

Valentine, P. (1992). Nature-based tourism. In B. Weiler and C. M. Hall (eds), *Special Interest Tourism.* London: Bellhaven, pp. 105–28.

Veal, A. J. (1994). *Leisure Policy and Planning.* Harlow, UK: Longman/ILAM.

VisitFinland (2014). Available online at www.VisitFinland.com [accessed 2 October 2014].

Wall, G. (1997). Rethinking impacts of tourism. In C. Cooper, B. Archer and S. Wanhill (eds), *Tourism Development.* Chichester: John Wiley and Sons, pp. 1–10.

Wallace, G. and Pierce, S. (1996). An evaluation of ecotourism in Amazonas, Brazil. *Annals of Tourism Research*, 23, 843–7.

Watkins, R., Cocklin, C. and Laituru, M. (1997). The use of geographic information systems for resource evaluation: a New Zealand example. *Journal of Environmental Planning and Management*, 40, 37–57.

Watson, A. E. (1995). An analysis of recent progress in recreation conflict research and perceptions of future challenges and opportunities. *Leisure Sciences*, 17, 235–8.

WCED (1987). *World Commission on Environment and Development, The Brundtland Report.* London: Pan/WCED.

Wearing, D. and Neil, J. (1999). *Ecotourism: Potential, Pitfalls and Possibilities.* London: Butterworth-Heinemann.

Weaver, D. (2000). A broad context of destination development scenarios. *Tourism Management,* 21 (3), 217–34.

Weaver, D. (2001). *The Encyclopedia of Ecotourism.* Wallingford, UK: CABI.

Weaver, D. (2006). *Sustainable Tourism.* Oxford: Butterworth-Heinemann.

Weiping, L. (2010). Exploring Images of Indonesia as Perceived by Indonesian Tourism Industry Members and UK Residents 'Pre-The Bali Bombings' and 'Post-The Bali Bombings', Unpublished PhD thesis, Bedfordshire University, Luton.

Wheeler, B. (1993). Sustaining the ego? *Journal of Sustainable Tourism*, 1, 121–9.

Wildavsky, A. (1987). *Speaking Truth to Power: The Art and Craft of Public Policy Analysis*, 2nd edn. New Brunswick: Transaction.

Wilkinson, P. (1997). *Tourism Planning on Islands.* New York: Cognizant Communications.

Williams, S. (1998). *Tourism Geography.* London: Routledge.

Williams, S. (2014). *Tourism Geography*, 3rd edn. London: Routledge.

Williams, D., Patterson, M., Roggenbuck, J. and Watson, A. (1992). Beyond the commodity metaphor: examining symbolic attachment to place. *Leisure Sciences*, 14, 29–46.

Wood, D. and Gray, B. (1991). Towards a comprehensive theory of collaboration. *Journal of Applied Behavioural Sciences*, 27 (2), 139–62.

Wood, K. and House, S. (1991). *The Good Tourist.* London: Mandarin.

WTO (1991). *Yearbook of Statistics.* Madrid: World Tourism Organization.

WTO (2005). *Yearbook of Tourism Statistics*, 55th edn. Madrid: World Tourism Organization.

WTO (2007). *UNWTO World Tourism Barometer*, Vol. 5 No. 2, June, World Tourism Organization.

WTO (2014). *UNWTO Tourism Highlights, 2014.* Madrid: World Tourism Organization.

WTTC (2007). *Namibia's Tourism Satellite Account.* Oxford: World Travel and Tourism Council.

WTTRC (1995). *Database on Codes of Conduct for the Travel and Tourism Industry.* Oxford: World Travel and Tourism Council.

Zhong, L., Deng, J. and Xiang, B. (2007). Tourism development and the tourism area life-cycle model: a case study of Zhangjiajie National Forest Park, China. *Tourism Management*, 28 (1), 112–27.

Ziffer, K. (1989). *Ecotourism: The Uneasy Alliance*, Working Paper No. 1. Washington, DC, Conservation International.

INDEX